Intelligent Crowdsourced Testing

Qing Wang • Zhenyu Chen • Junjie Wang •
Yang Feng

Intelligent Crowdsourced Testing

 Springer

Qing Wang
Institute of Software
Chinese Academy of Sciences
Beijing, China

Junjie Wang
Institute of Software
Chinese Academy of Sciences
Beijing, China

Zhenyu Chen
Software Institute
Nanjing University
Nanjing, Jiangsu, China

Yang Feng
Software Institute
Nanjing University
Nanjing, Jiangsu, China

ISBN 978-981-16-9642-8   ISBN 978-981-16-9643-5   (eBook)
https://doi.org/10.1007/978-981-16-9643-5

This Springer imprint is published by the registered company Springer Nature Singapore Pte Ltd.
The registered company address is: 152 Beach Road, #21-01/04 Gateway East, Singapore 189721,
Singapore

Foreword

At every minute of every day there are probably hundreds of millions of computers that are idle. It is staggering to contemplate the enormity of the amount of computing capacity sitting idle and unused the totality of all of these devices. And it is intriguing to consider what might be accomplished if even a modest fraction of that capacity could be put to good use. Indeed, others have not only contemplated such usage but some have also tapped into it. In one such project, that computing power is used to analyze electromagnetic spectrum for possible emissions from extraterrestrial civilizations. Another project attempts to use that computing power to evaluate approaches to predicting the structure of the proteins expressed by a gene, given only the DNA sequence of that gene.

In this fascinating book, the authors suggest how all of that unused computing power could be put to use by software engineers, using it to perform otherwise unachievably thorough testing of software through crowdsourced testing. The prospect of using the combined computational capacity of millions of idle computers all around the world to carry out unprecedentedly thorough testing, thereby improving the quality of the world's software, is exciting and intriguing. It is the subject of this book.

While the upside potential of crowdsourced testing is enormous, the difficulties in doing this are also enormous. They range from deciding how much capacity is available on which computers to how to apportion testing tasks to each available computer, to deciding how to integrate all of the testing results that have been returned, to knowing what to do when intentionally overlapping testing tasks have returned inconsistent results. This book addresses all of these problems, and more. In doing so, it makes for fascinating reading and contemplation, and also lays out a challenging and invigorating research agenda.

I congratulate the authors for this important and intrepid undertaking. Their vision is broad and exciting, and their research roadmap is challenging and stimulating. This book seems destined to become a seminal work in an area of boundless importance and promise.

Orleans, MA, USA   Leon J. Osterweil
15 October 2021

Preface

Software is everywhere today. It leads our every step. It is part of everything we do. Software makes our everyday work easier and simplifies our daily lives. We use software to work, study, and communicate with friends. It allows us to shop, make payments, travel, and do a lot more.

Yet when one programs, one makes mistakes. Every 1000 lines of code easily contain up to 16 errors, and a company's software has millions of lines, so that is a lot of errors. Once the software errors reveal themselves, they have consequences that range from "annoying" to "very severe." There has been a long list of software errors that have caused big disruptions. Airport systems can't function for a day, banking systems of entire countries shut down, and spacecrafts explode, among other mishaps.

There is no way to prove that a piece of software is 100% bug free. Nevertheless, there are things we can do to improve software quality. Among which, software testing is the most important strategy. Software testing is a method to check whether the actual software product matches expected requirements and to ensure that software product is defect free. If there are any bugs or errors in the software, it can be identified early and can be solved before delivery of the software product. Properly tested software product ensures reliability, security, and high performance, which further results in time saving, cost effectiveness, and customer satisfaction.

Software testing involves execution of software/system components using manual or automated tools to evaluate one or more properties of interest. Traditionally, it was conducted by dedicated quality assurance teams with formally trained testers. Although these quality assurance teams are reliable, the high cost and delayed responses made them hard to scale and non-flexible for rapid update needs for the software industry today. Automated testing could be one solution, but the inability to create realistic user behavior test cases makes them hard to rely on given the variations in software products.

Crowdsourced testing is an emerging practice that enables testing with more flexibility and scalability than quality assurance teams. Crowdsourced testing, also known as crowdtesting, is a fresh approach to quality assurance. It combines human skills with technology to eliminate some of the problems involved in conventional testing. Instead of carrying out testing within an organization, crowdsourcing uses a dispersed, temporary workforce of multiple individual testers. This on-demand community of testers is able to test the software more quickly and effectively than an in-house team. Crowdsourced testing offers companies an opportunity to have their products tested by real users on real devices across the globe, ensuring a customer-centric emphasis.

Thanks to the advantages of crowdsourced testing, it has been adopted by a growing number of organizations, including, but not limited to, Google, Facebook, Walmart, PayPal, and Uber. In particular, Google has deployed crowdsourced testing on its 14 major software product lines. Crowdsourced testing schema has also spawned a number of crowdsourced testing platforms. For example, Applause, which is the pioneer of global crowdsourced testing schema and the largest crowd-sourced testing platform, provides usability, compatibility, security, functionality, accessibility, and other types of testing services. Synack, which is the world's largest secure crowdsourced testing platform, provides crowdsourced testing services to the U.S. Department of Defense, one-third US banks, and three-thirds credit card companies. The crowdsourced testing market is expected to register a compound annual growth rate of 10.7% over the forecast period 2021 to 2026.

Despite this increasing prevalence, crowdsourced testing is a new testing schema with unmatured operational strategies and underdeveloped supporting technologies.

Meanwhile, intelligent techniques have seen successful in addressing various software engineering problems, for example, code generation, code recommendation, and bug fix and repair. Especially, artificial intelligence can be leveraged to enhance software quality assurance efficiently, for example, testing automation tools, guiding human testers in improving test coverage.

Benefiting from the rapid development of artificial intelligence, this book employs intelligent algorithms to facilitate various activities in crowdsourced testing. It provides supporting technologies in terms of the crowdsourced testing task, the crowd workers, and the testing results, which can increase the bug detection efficiency, reduce the manual effort, and potentially attract more crowd workers to promote the prosperity of a platform.

The aims of this book are to present the state-of-the-art technologies of using artificial intelligence algorithms to improve the crowdsourced testing activities, to provide actionable guidelines for industry practitioners, to inspire the researchers, and to encourage further research in this important and challenging area. This book is written for both software testing related researchers and industry practitioners. Researchers who want to obtain the knowledge of crowdsourced testing can find how we utilize artificial intelligence algorithms to improve various crowdsourced testing activities, and get inspiration in their own field. Industry practitioners of crowdsourced testing can use the introduced technologies of this book to upgrade their testing practice and improve testing efficiency. Besides, industry practitioners of other forms of software testing can also borrow the ideas presented in this book to facilitate similar tasks in their own scenarios.

We thank the researchers and students in the Laboratory for Internet Software Technologies, Institute of Software Chinese Academy of Science, and those in the Laboratory of Intelligent Software Engineering, Nanjing University, for their dedication to the area of crowdsourced testing. We also thank the staff at MoocTest, China Software Testing Contest, and IEEE International Contest on Software Testing for their contribution on the experimental dataset.

We wish you interesting and enjoyable reading. We hope that you will benefit from this book and that you will be able to make use of the values of crowdsourced testing for accelerating and promoting the quality assurance activities.

Beijing, China   Qing Wang
Nanjing, China   Zhenyu Chen
Beijing, China   Junjie Wang
Nanjing, China   Yang Feng
October 2021

About the Authors

Qing Wang is a researcher at the Institute of Software Chinese Academy of Sciences (ISCAS). She is also the deputy chief engineer of ISCAS and director of the Laboratory for Internet Software Technologies at ISCAS. She currently serves as a director of the Board of Directors of the International Software and Systems Processes Association (ISSPA), a member of the International Software Engineering Research Network (ISERN), a member of the editorial boards of *Information and Software Technology Journal* (IST) and the *Journal of Software Evolution and Process* (JSEP), and a CMMI Lead Appraiser. She has served as the general chair of ESEM in 2015, and the program chair of ICSP from 2007 to 2009. Her research lies in the area of software process, software quality assurance, requirement engineering, knowledge engineering, big data, and artificial intelligence for software engineering. Qing has 20 years of experience in software process and quality assurance technologies. Her recent research related to software process and quality management has won the second prize of National Progress in Science and Technology of China and second prize of Progress in Science and Technology of Beijing. She has edited/co-edited 5 books and published more than 100 papers in international high-level conferences and journals.

Zhenyu Chen is the founder of Mooctest (mooctest.net), and he is currently a professor at the Software Institute, Nanjing University. He received his bachelor's and doctoral degrees in Mathematics from Nanjing University. Zhenyu worked as a postdoctoral researcher in the School of Computer Science and Engineering at Southeast University, China. His research interests focus on software analysis and testing. He has more than 100 publications in journals and proceedings, including TOSEM, TSE, JSS, SQJ, IJSEKE, ISSTA, ICST, and QSIC. He has served as the associate editor of *IEEE Transactions on Reliability*; PC co-chair of QRS 2016, QSIC 2013, AST2013, and IWPD2012; and program committee member of many international conferences. He also founded NJSD (Nanjing Global Software Development Conference). Zhenyu has won research funding from several competitive sources such as NSFC. He owns more than 40 patents (22 granted), and some of his patents have been transferred into well-known software companies such as Baidu, Alibaba, and Huawei.

Junjie Wang is an associate researcher at the Institute of Software, Chinese Academy of Sciences (ISCAS). She received her PhD degree from ISCAS in 2015. Junjie was a visiting scholar at North Carolina State University from Sep. 2017 to Sep. 2018 and worked with Prof. Tim Menzies. Her research interests include crowdsourced testing, mining software repositories, and intelligent software engineering. She has more than 20 high-quality publications and has received the ACM SIGSOFT Distinguished Paper Award at ICSE in 2019 and 2020, respectively, as well as IEEE Best Paper Award at QRS in 2019.

Yang Feng received his bachelor's and master's degrees in software engineering from Nanjing University in 2011 and 2013, respectively. He obtained his doctoral degree from the University of California, Irvine. He has published more than 30 refereed papers and regularly serves as PC member and reviewer for international conferences and journals. His current research interests lie in software testing, crowdsourced software engineering, and program analysis.

Contents

Part I
Preliminary of Crowdsourced Testing

Chapter 1
Introduction

1.1 Why We Need Crowdsourced Testing

The Internet is a decisive technology of the information Age, as the electrical engine was the vector of technological transformation of the Industrial Age. This global network of computer networks, largely based nowadays on platforms of wireless communication, provides ubiquitous capacity of multimodal, interactive communication in chosen time, transcending space. At the heart of these communication networks, the Internet ensures the production, distribution, and use of digitized information in all formats. The speed and scope of the transformation of our communication environment by Internet and wireless communication has triggered all kind of innovations around the world, among which crowdsourcing is the one that cannot be ignored.

Even though the practice of crowdsourcing can be track back to the late of 1990s, Jeff Howe firstly presents the systematic study on this topic in 2006 [30]. He described this new paradigm as "the practice of obtaining needed services, ideas, or content by soliciting contributions from a large group of people and especially from the online community rather than from traditional employees or suppliers". By turning to a large group of people for ideas and solutions, crowdsourcing can generate a lot of benefits over internal ideation processes. Not only can businesses get access to great ideas, but they can also drive marketing buzz and engage their customers. People involved in crowdsourcing sometimes work as paid freelancers, while others perform small tasks voluntarily. For example, traffic apps like Waze encourage drivers to report accidents and other roadway incidents to provide real-time, updated information to app users. The benefits of crowdsourcing include: unexpected solutions to tough problems, greater diversity of thinking, reduced management burden, more marketing buzz, faster problem solving, and customer-centric data, etc.

Quality, in terms of validity and verifiability, determines the success of a software project. Many current software products are used by thousands or even millions of

© The Author(s), under exclusive license to Springer Nature Singapore Pte Ltd. 2022
Q. Wang et al., *Intelligent Crowdsourced Testing*,
https://doi.org/10.1007/978-981-16-9643-5_1

people, helping them do their jobs effectively and efficiently or, alternately, causing them untold frustration and the costs of lost work or lost business. Testing is defined as "the process of executing a program with the intent of finding errors". Hence, it is a destructive process of trying to find errors whose presence is assumed in a program. Its main goal is to establish a certain confidence that a program does what it is supposed to do. However, software testing cannot guarantee the complete absence of errors; instead, software testing attempts to be as complete as possible by identifying the largest possible number of errors. The best software is that which has been tested by thousands of users under thousands of different conditions. This is where the concept of crowdsourcing can help.

Crowdsourced testing, i.e., utilizing crowdsourcing paradigm for software testing, is the process of having a large group of individuals review one's mobile apps, websites, mobile applications, software, products, or services to identify any defects or areas that can be improved before launching as part of the user acceptance testing stage. This form of testing, which is done remotely, differs from traditional in-house user testing by having the opportunity to branch out worldwide to receive feedback from multiple groups of people varying in age, sex, cultural backgrounds, etc. To receive feedback from testers, virtual machines or device emulators connected to a crowdsourced testing platform can be utilized, or, in some cases, testers may use their own devices to test any software, apps, etc. and submit their feedback. Once all the information is compiled and reviewed, developers can use the testers' feedback to improve the applications or products they are working on.

1.2 Benefits of Crowdsourced Testing

Crowdsourced testing involves many individuals, often with better quality assurance and a reduced cost. Other major advantages that ensure an application is ready for launch include:

Speed—The importance of developers getting timely and relevant bug information is crucial. With such a large, global number of people involved in the testing, crowdsourced testing leads to fast execution and better results.

Efficiency—Crowd teams help some clients in time-varying bursts to manage peak workloads. This peak-demand testing strategy leads to the most efficient utilization of testing resources. Companies benefit from these burstable instances because they receive a high volume of quality assurance resources for a short period of time only when necessary, meaning they can manage day-to-day testing with fewer resources when necessary.

Cost-effective—To reduce labor costs and dramatically improve efficiencies, today's software development teams tap into on-demand crowdsourced quality assurance services. It allows you to conduct testing without adding a permanent employee and the salary, pension, and other costly benefits incurred. Costs are dramatically reduced by applying the time-varying resource provisioning of managed crowdtesting.

Testing coverage—Crowdsourcing testing allows companies to attain the best test coverage as testing is performed on an extensive range of devices and platforms. This aids in unearthing bugs that might have been tedious to discover with conventional test mechanisms. The volume obtained via crowdsourcing testing assists in expediting the software product release cycle.

Geolocation—With testers located across the globe, it is much simpler for testing functions that depend on geolocation in crowdsourced testing. Testing in particular markets can also disclose any issues a website or application may have due to distinct cellular network or Internet speeds.

Usability testing capability—Through the power of crowdsourced testing, companies are able to determine quickly where their mobile application needs to be revised, updated, or fixed in order to avoid losing out on potential users. Crowdsourced testing delivers real users, on real devices, in their target markets.

While the pros of speed and flexibility of crowdtesting are remarkable, some issues can arise if one has not created a concrete test plan or rely on unsupervised testers from a marketplace. In addition, because payment usually depends on the number of bugs found and not their severity, testers may seek out and identify many small, less-important bugs rather than devote a lot of time and effort to finding one or two large, debilitating bugs

1.3 Current Practice of Crowdsourced Testing

Crowdsourced testing is an emerging paradigm that can improve the cost-effectiveness of software testing and accelerate its process. First, the project manager provides a test task for crowdsourced testing, including the software under test and test requirements. Then, the crowdsourced testing task is usually in the format of open call and incentives provision, so a large number of crowd workers can sign in to perform the task based on its test requirements, and are required to submit crowdsourced test reports.

Currently, crowdsourced testing has been adopted into the practice of a growing number of software organizations, including, but not limited to, Google, Facebook, Amazon, Microsoft, Alibaba, PayPal, Uber, Mcdonald's. Specifically, Google has deployed crowdsourced testing on its 14 major software product lines.

Meanwhile, crowdsourced testing schema has also spawned many startups that in turn propose plenty of methods, techniques, tools and platforms accelerating the development of crowdsourced testing. Applause (also known as uTest), which is one of the pioneers of global crowdsourced testing schema and the largest crowdsourced testing platform, provides usability, compatibility, security, functionality, accessibility and other types of testing services for Microsoft, Facebook, Disney, Wal-Mart, General Electric, Delta Air Services and thousands of other enterprises. Synack, which the world's largest secure crowdsourced testing platform, provides crowdsourced testing services to the U.S. Department of Defense, one-third of U.S.

banks, etc. Testing platform has more than a thousand different models of mobile phones, tablets, smart TVs and OTT terminals, and has provided crowdsourced testing services for more than 2.9 million applications. Almost all of the world top Internet companies, such as Facebook, Tencent, Alibaba, have organized their own crowdsourced testing team and built up crowdsourcing platforms. They not only employ crowdsourced testing for improving their products but also provide testing services and testing solutions for various end users.

According to Applause, the world's most popular crowdsourced testing platform, crowdsourced testing can increase testing capacity by 200%, increase the number of product releases per year by 150%, reduce the critical defect fixes needed by 50%, accelerate the planned revenue by 30%, increase the customer retention rate by 10% and conversion rate by 10%. In detail, through the rapid testing and feedback, quality assurance teams can better keep up with the increasing pace of development, which can potentially lead to the success of the product launch. The authentic feedback from real users in real-world settings helps a company improve app performance and deliver better customer experiences, which increases the customer satisfactory and their retention rates. And the remote, distributed teams help a company scale the test capability without the burden of additional overhead costs.

Due to the advantages of crowdsourced testing, the crowdsourced testing market is projected to register a Compound Annual Growth Rate of 10.7% over the prediction period 2021–2026. The main driving factors for the market comprise the increasing requirement of companies to enhance the user experience for competing in the current global market, increasing digital transformation, and building brand alertness, therefore aiding companies to adopt techniques to release their mobile apps or websites to the public fast.

1.4   Challenges of Crowdsourced Testing and Solutions

Despite of the aforementioned advantages, with the continuous development of crowd-sourced testing, the number of testing tasks, crowdsourced workers and test reports has increased dramatically, and the current crowdsourced testing still faces many challenges.

1. **Testing task recommendation and management.** Trade-offs such as "how much testing is enough" are critical yet challenging project decisions in software engineering. Insufficient testing can lead to unsatisfying software quality, while excessive testing can result in potential schedule delays and low cost-effectiveness. This is especially true for crowdsouced testing given the complexity of mobile applications and unpredictability of distributed crowdsourced testing processes. Experience-based decisions may result in ineffective crowd-sourced testing processes, e.g., there is an average of 32% wasteful spending in current crowdsourced testing practices. Therefore, how to automate task closing

decisions and perform trade-off analysis is a critical research domain to improve the efficiency of crowdsourcing testing.

2. **Characterization and task selection strategies of crowd worker.** Crowdsourced testing tasks are entrusted to the online crowd workers. Typically, a crowdsourced test task aims to detect as many bugs as possible within a limited budget. However not all crowd workers are equally skilled at finding bugs; Inappropriate workers may miss bugs, or report duplicate bugs, while hiring them requires nontrivial budget. Therefore, how to recommend a group of appropriate crowd workers for a testing task so that fewer workers can detect more software bugs has become an important challenge for the development of crowdsourced testing.

3. **Test result analysis and management.** Crowd workers typically perform testing tasks and report their experiences through test reports. In the crowdsourced testing, the workers perform the tasks and then submit their test reports, which are simple and informal descriptions of the behavior of the software system. These test reports are composed of natural-language descriptions, sometimes accompanied with screenshots, and an assessment as to whether the worker believes that the software behaved correctly or behaved incorrectly. In a crowdsourced setting, the test reports are less structured and the number of test reports can be prohibitive. So, it is often impossible to manually inspect all test reports in a limited time.

In this book, we summarize our previous researches in the crowdsourced testing domain. For testing task recommendation and management, many researchers aim at exploring automated decision support to raise completion awareness crowdsourced testing processes, and manage crowdsourced testing practices more effectively. Particularly, in this book, we leverage dynamical bug arrival data associated with crowdsourced testing reports, and investigate whether it is possible to determine that, at certain point of time, a task has obtained satisfactory bug detection level. For characterization and task selection strategies of crowd worker, finding appropriate workers for particular software engineering tasks has long been recognized as being important and invaluable. With the emergence of crowdsourcing, there are several researches focusing on developer recommendation for crowdsourced software development. The aforementioned studies either recommend one worker or assume the recommended set of workers are independent with each other. However, in crowdsourced testing, a set of workers need to be recommended to accomplish a test task together. Furthermore, the recommended set of workers are dependent on each other because their performance can together influence the final test outcomes. In this book, we introduce some different approaches to recommend a set of crowd workers for crowdsourced testing tasks. For test result analysis and management, the aforementioned features of mobile crowdsourced test reports, i.e., high duplicate ratio, short text descriptions and rich screenshots, motivate us to propose some techniques to leveraging both the text and image information from duplicate reports to enhance developers' understanding of bugs, such as test report classification, duplicate detection, prioritization, summarization and quality assessment.

Chapter 2
Preliminaries

2.1 Crowdsourced Testing

2.1.1 General Procedure of Crowdsourced Testing

Figure 2.1 presents the overall procedure of crowdsourced testing. The project manager provides a test task for crowdsourced testing, including the software under test and test requirements. The crowdsourced testing task is usually in the format of *open call*, so a large number of crowd workers can sign in to perform the task based on its test requirements, and are required to submit crowdsourced test reports. The project manager then inspects these submitted test reports, confirm whether it is a bug, debug and fix it. Note that not every test report involves a bug, and different reports might describe the same bug (i.e., duplicate reports).

In order to attract workers, crowdsourced testing tasks are often financially compensated. The commonly-used payout schema includes paid by participation, paid by bug, and paid by first bug. Under *paid by participation* schema, workers are equally paid when they submit reports in a test task. It is mainly used for the newly-launched platform because it can encourage crowd worker's participation. Under *paid by bug* schema, only those crowd workers who detect bugs are paid (no matter whether it is a duplicate bug). Under *paid by first bug* schema, the crowd workers who detect the first bug are paid (the following duplicates would not be paid).

© The Author(s), under exclusive license to Springer Nature Singapore Pte Ltd. 2022
Q. Wang et al., *Intelligent Crowdsourced Testing*,
https://doi.org/10.1007/978-981-16-9643-5_2

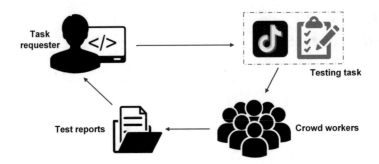

Fig. 2.1 The procedure of crowdsourced testing

2.1.2 Important Concepts of Crowdsourced Testing

We introduce three important concepts in crowdsourced testing: *Test task*, *Test report*, and *Crowd worker*.

A **test task** is the input to a crowdsourced testing platform provided by a task publisher. It contains task ID, task name, test requirements (mostly written in natural language), and the software under test (not considered in this work). Table 2.1 shows an example of a test task.

A **test report** is the test outcome submitted by a crowd worker after the test task is completed. It contains report ID, worker ID (i.e., who submit the report), task ID (i.e., which task is conducted), description of how the test was performed and what happened during the test, the screenshot of the bug. It can also include the bug label and duplicate label which are usually assigned by the project manager. Table 2.1 shows an example of a test report. Specifically, the labels are assigned by the project manager to indicate whether the report contains a "bug" (i.e., bug label), and whether the report is a "duplicate" of other reports (i.e., duplicate label). Note that, in the following sections, we refer to "bug report" (also short for "bug") as the report contains bugs, while refer to "test report" (also short for "report") as any report submitted in the test task (including bug reports and reports without bugs).

A **crowd worker** is a registered worker in the crowdsourced testing platform, and is described by worker ID, her/his context attributes (e.g., device model). The platform also records the worker's historical test reports. A test task can be conducted by hundreds of crowd workers.

Table 2.1 An example of crowdsourced test task, test report, and crowd worker

Test task	
Task ID	T000012
Name	IQIYI testing
Requirement 1	Browse the videos through list mode IQIYI, rank the videos using different conditions, check whether the rank is reasonable
Requirement 2	Cache the video, check whether the caching list is right
Test report	
Report ID	R1002948308
Task ID	T000012
Worker ID	W5124983210
Description	I list the videos according to the popularity. It should be ranked according to the number of views. However, there were many confused rankings, for example, the video "Shibuya century legend" with 130 million views was ranked in front of the video "I went to school" with 230 million views
Screenshot	
Bug label	Bug
Duplicate label	R1002948315, R1002948324
Crowd worker	
Worker Id	W5124983210
Context	Phone type: *Samsung SN9009*
	Operating system: *Android 4.4.2*
	ROM information: *KOT49H.N9009*
	Network environment: *WIFI*
Historical Reports	R1002948308, R1037948352

2.2   Basic Introduction to Artificial Intelligence Technology

2.2.1   Supervised Learning

In supervised learning, models are trained using labelled dataset, where the model learns about each type of data. Once the training process is completed, the model is tested on the basis of test data (a subset of the training set), and then it predicts the output.

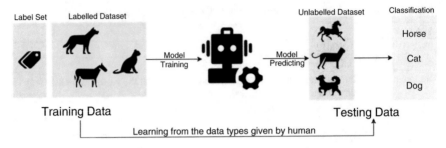

Fig. 2.2 An example of supervised learning

The working of supervised learning can be easily understood by the below example and diagram (Fig. 2.2):

Suppose we have a dataset of different types of shapes which includes square, rectangle, triangle, and polygon. Now the first step is that we need to train the model for each shape.

- If the given shape has four sides, and all the sides are equal, then it will be labelled as a square.
- If the given shape has three sides, then it will be labelled as a triangle.
- If the given shape has six equal sides then it will be labelled as hexagon.

Now, after training, we test our model using the test set, and the task of the model is to identify the shape.

The machine is already trained on all types of shapes, and when it finds a new shape, it classifies the shape on the bases of a number of sides, and predicts the output.

2.2.1.1 Probabilistic Supervised Learning

Most supervised learning algorithms are based on estimating a probability distribution $p(y|x)$. We can do this simply by using maximum likelihood estimation to find the best parameter vector θ for a parametric family of distributions $p(y|x; \theta)$. We have that linear regression corresponds to the family:

$$p(y|x; \theta) = \mathcal{N}(y; \theta^\top x, I). \tag{2.1}$$

We can generalize linear regression to the classification scenario by defining a different family of probability distributions. If we have two classes, class 0 and class 1, then we need only specify the probability of one of these classes. The probability of class 1 determines the probability of class 0, because these two values must add up to 1.

The normal distribution over real-valued numbers that we used for linear regression is parametrized in terms of a mean. Any value we supply for this mean is valid. A distribution over a binary variable is slightly more complicated, because its mean must always be between 0 and 1. One way to solve this problem is to use the logistic sigmoid function to squash the output of the linear function into the interval (0, 1) and interpret that value as a probability:

$$p(y = 1|x; \theta) = \sigma(y; \theta^\top x). \tag{2.2}$$

This approach is known as logistic regression (a somewhat strange name since we use the model for classification rather than regression).

In the case of linear regression, we were able to find the optimal weights by solving the normal equations. Logistic regression is somewhat more difficult. There is no closed-form solution for its optimal weights. Instead, we must search for them by maximizing the log-likelihood. We can do this by minimizing the negative log-likelihood using gradient descent.

This same strategy can be applied to essentially any supervised learning problem,by writing down a parametric family of conditional probability distributions over the right kind of input and output variables.

2.2.1.2 *k*-Nearest-Neighbor Classification

The *k*-nearest-neighbor (kNN) approach to classification is a relatively simple approach to classification that is completely nonparametric. Given a point x_0 that we wish to classify into one of the *k* groups, we find the *k* observed data points that are nearest to x_0. The classification rule is to assign x_0 to the population that has the most observed data points out of the *k*-nearest neighbors. Points for which there is no majority are either classified to one of the majority populations at random, or left unclassified.

The kNN method for approximating a discrete-valued function $f : \Re \to C$ is described as follows:

- Training procedure: For each training instance $\langle x, f(x) \rangle$, add the instance to the training set. $f(x)$ is of the form $f : \Re^n \to C$, where C is a finite set $\{c_1, c_2, \ldots, c_{|C|}\}$.
- Classification procedure: Given a new instance x to be classified, let $x_1, x_2, \ldots, x_k$ denote the *k* instances in the training set that are nearest (most similar) to x.

$$f(x) \leftarrow \arg\max_{c \in C} \Sigma_{i=1}^{k} \delta(c, f(x_i)), \tag{2.3}$$

where $\delta(a, b) = 1$ if $a = b$ and $\delta(a, b) = 0$ otherwise.

2.2.1.3 Support-Vector Machine

Support Vector Machine (SVM) is based on the principle of structural risk minimization. They are used for pattern classification and nonlinear regression. For linearly separable data, SVM finds a hyperplane which separates the data with the largest margin. For linearly inseparable data, it maps the data x in the input space I into a high dimension space $H - x \in \mathbb{R}^I \mapsto \Phi(x) \in \mathbb{R}^H$ with kernel function $\Phi(x)$—to find the separating hyperplane.

SVM was originally developed for two-class classification problems. Subsequently, SVMs were developed for multiclass problems. Each SVM separates a single class from all the remaining classes (one-vs-rest approach). Each SVM is trained to distinguish all instances of a single class from the instances of all other classes. During testing, the class label y of a class pattern x is determined by:

$$y = \begin{cases} n \text{ if } d_n(x) + t_l > 0 \\ 0 \text{ if } d_n(x) + t_l \le 0 \end{cases} \tag{2.4}$$

where $d_n(x) = \max\{d_i(x)\}_{i=1}^{N_l}$, $d_i(x)$ is the distance from x to the SVM hyperplane corresponding to class i, and tl is the classification threshold.

2.2.1.4 Decision Tree

A decision tree consists of split nodes N^{split} and leaf nodes N^{leaf}. Each split node N^{split} performs a split decision and routes a data sample x to the left child node $cl(s)$ or to the right child node $cr(s)$. When using axis-aligned split decisions the split rule is based on a single split feature $f(s)$ and a threshold value $\theta(s)$:

$$x \in cl(s) \Leftrightarrow x_{f(s)} < \theta(s), \tag{2.5}$$

$$x \in cr(s) \Leftrightarrow x_{f(s)} \ge \theta(s). \tag{2.6}$$

The data sample x is routed to the left child node if the value of feature $f(s)$ of x is smaller than a threshold $\theta(s)$ and to the right child node otherwise. All leaf nodes $l \in N^{leaf}$ store votes for the classes $y^l = (y_1^l, \ldots, y_C^l)$, where C is the number of classes.

Decision trees are grown using training data. Starting at the root node, the data is recursively split into subsets. In each step the best split is determined based on a criterion. Commonly used criteria are Gini index and entropy:

$$\text{Gini index: } G(E) = 1 - \Sigma_{j=1}^{C} p_j^2, \tag{2.7}$$

$$\text{Entropy: } H(E) = -\Sigma_{j=1}^{C} p_j \log p_j. \tag{2.8}$$

The algorithm for constructing a decision tree works as follows:

1. Randomly sample n training samples with replacement from the training dataset.
2. Create a root node and assign the sampled data to it.
3. Repeat the following steps for each node until all nodes consists of a single sample or samples of the same class:

   a. Randomly select m variables out of M possible variables.
   b. Pick the best split feature and threshold according to a criterion, for example Gini index or entropy.
   c. Split the node into two child nodes and pass the corresponding subsets.

2.2.2   Unsupervised Learning

Unsupervised learning is a machine learning technique in which models are not supervised using training dataset. Instead, models itself find the hidden patterns and insights from the given data. It can be compared to learning which takes place in the human brain while learning new things. It can be defined as:

Unsupervised learning is a type of machine learning in which models are trained using unlabeled dataset and are allowed to act on that data without any supervision.

Unsupervised learning cannot be directly applied to a regression or classification problem because unlike supervised learning, we have the input data but no corresponding output data. The goal of unsupervised learning is to find the underlying structure of dataset, group that data according to similarities, and represent that dataset in a compressed format (Fig. 2.3).

Clustering is a method of grouping the objects into clusters such that objects with most similarities remains into a group and has less or no similarities with the objects of another group. Cluster analysis finds the commonalities between the data objects and categorizes them as per the presence and absence of those commonalities.

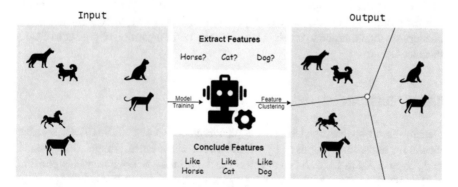

Fig. 2.3 An example of unsupervised learning

2.2.2.1   K-Means Clustering

The k-means clustering algorithm divides the training set into k different clusters of examples that are near each other. We can thus think of the algorithm as providing a k-dimensional one-hot code vector h representing an input x. If x belongs to cluster i, then $h_i = 1$, and all other entries of the representation h are zero.

The k-means algorithm works by initializing k different centroids $\{\mu^{(1)}, \ldots, \mu^{(k)}\}$ to different values, then alternating between two different steps until convergence. In one step, each training example is assigned to cluster i, where i is the index of the nearest centroid $\mu^{(i)}$. In the other step, each centroid $\mu^{(i)}$ is updated to the mean of all training examples $x^{(j)}$ assigned to cluster i.

2.2.2.2   Hierarchical Clustering

Connectivity-based clustering, also known as hierarchical clustering, is based on the core idea of objects being more related to nearby objects than to objects farther away. These algorithms connect "objects" to form "clusters" based on their distance. A cluster can be described largely by the maximum distance needed to connect parts of the cluster. At different distances, different clusters will form, which can be represented using a dendrogram, which explains where the common name "hierarchical clustering" comes from: these algorithms do not provide a single partitioning of the data set, but instead provide an extensive hierarchy of clusters that merge with each other at certain distances. In a dendrogram, the y-axis marks the distance at which the clusters merge, while the objects are placed along the x-axis such that the clusters don't mix.

Once distances are defined between every pair of points, the clustering algorithm proceeds by iteratively identifying subclusters. The procedure can be top down or bottom up. In the top down process, at the beginning, all points are assumed to be in a single cluster. As the algorithm proceeds, the single cluster is split into two or more parts. However, the divisive clustering has to examine exponential number of subsets to determine where to split. This problem is mitigated by bottom up approach. In this formulation, in the beginning, all points are assigned to individual clusters. The clusters are then merged to result in next level by defining notion of cluster to cluster distances.

2.2.2.3   DBSCAN

Density-based spatial clustering of applications with noise (DBSCAN) is a data clustering algorithm proposed by Martin Ester, Hans-Peter Kriegel, Jörg Sander and Xiaowei Xu in 1996. It is a density-based clustering non-parametric algorithm: given a set of points in some space, it groups together points that are closely packed together (points with many nearby neighbors), marking as outliers points that lie alone in low-density regions (whose nearest neighbors are too far away).

Consider a set of points in some space to be clustered. Let ϵ be a parameter specifying the radius of a neighborhood with respect to some point. For the purpose of DBSCAN clustering, the points are classified as core points, (density-) reachable points and outliers, as follows:

- A point p is a **core point** if at least minPts points are within distance ϵ of it (including p).
- A point q is **directly reachable** from p if point q is within distance ϵ from core point p. Points are only said to be directly reachable from core points.
- A point q is **reachable** from p if there is a path $p_1, \ldots, p_n$ with $p_1 = p$ and $p_n = q$, where each p_{i+1} is directly reachable from p_i. Note that this implies that the initial point and all points on the path must be core points, with the possible exception of q.
- All points not reachable from any other point are **outliers** or **noise points**.

Now if p is a core point, then it forms a cluster together with all points (core or non-core) that are reachable from it. Each cluster contains at least one core point; non-core points can be part of a cluster, but they form its "edge", since they cannot be used to reach more points.

The DBSCAN algorithm can be abstracted into the following steps:

1. Find the points in the ϵ (eps) neighborhood of every point, and identify the core points with more than minPts neighbors.
2. Find the connected components of core points on the neighbor graph, ignoring all non-core points.
3. Assign each non-core point to a nearby cluster if the cluster is an ϵ (eps) neighbor, otherwise assign it to noise.

2.2.3   Semi-Supervised Learning

Semi-supervised learning is an approach to machine learning that combines a small amount of labeled data with a large amount of unlabeled data during training. Semi-supervised learning falls between unsupervised learning (with no labeled training data) and supervised learning (with only labeled training data). It is initially motivated by its practical value in learning faster, better, and cheaper. In many real world applications, it is relatively easy to acquire a large amount of unlabeled data $\{x\}$. For example, documents can be crawled from the Web, images can be obtained from surveillance cameras, and speech can be collected from broadcast. However, their corresponding labels $\{y\}$ for the prediction task, such as sentiment orientation, intrusion detection, and phonetic transcript, often requires slow human annotation and expensive laboratory experiments. This labeling bottleneck results in a scarce of labeled data and a surplus of unlabeled data. Therefore, being able to utilize the surplus unlabeled data is desirable (Fig. 2.4).

Unlabeled data, when used in conjunction with a small amount of labeled data, can produce considerable improvement in learning accuracy. The acquisition of

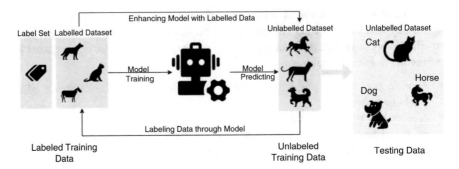

Fig. 2.4 Framework of semi-supervised learning

labeled data for a learning problem often requires a skilled human agent (e.g. to transcribe an audio segment) or a physical experiment (e.g. determining the 3D structure of a protein or determining whether there is oil at a particular location). The cost associated with the labeling process thus may render large, fully labeled training sets infeasible, whereas acquisition of unlabeled data is relatively inexpensive. In such situations, semi-supervised learning can be of great practical value. Semi-supervised learning is also of theoretical interest in machine learning and as a model for human learning.

In order to make any use of unlabeled data, some relationship to the underlying distribution of data must exist. Semi-supervised learning algorithms make use of at least one of the following assumptions:

1. **Continuity assumption**: *Points that are close to each other are more likely to share a label.* This is also generally assumed in supervised learning and yields a preference for geometrically simple decision boundaries. In the case of semi-supervised learning, the smoothness assumption additionally yields a preference for decision boundaries in low-density regions, so few points are close to each other but in different classes.
2. **Cluster assumption**: *The data tend to form discrete clusters, and points in the same cluster are more likely to share a label* (although data that shares a label may spread across multiple clusters). This is a special case of the smoothness assumption and gives rise to feature learning with clustering algorithms.
3. **Manifold assumption**: *The data lie approximately on a manifold of much lower dimension than the input space.* In this case learning the manifold using both the labeled and unlabeled data can avoid the curse of dimensionality. Then learning can proceed using distances and densities defined on the manifold.

2.2.3.1   Generative Models

Generative approaches to statistical learning first seek to estimate $p(x|y)$, the distribution of data points belonging to each class. The probability $p(y|x)$ that a given point x has label y is then proportional to $p(x|y)p(y)$ by Bayes' rule. Semi-supervised learning with generative models can be viewed either as an extension of supervised learning (classification plus information about $p(x)$) or as an extension of unsupervised learning (clustering plus some labels).

Generative models assume that the distributions take some particular form $p(x|y, \theta)$ parameterized by the vector θ. If these assumptions are incorrect, the unlabeled data may actually decrease the accuracy of the solution relative to what would have been obtained from labeled data alone. However, if the assumptions are correct, then the unlabeled data necessarily improves performance.

The unlabeled data are distributed according to a mixture of individual-class distributions. In order to learn the mixture distribution from the unlabeled data, it must be identifiable, that is, different parameters must yield different summed distributions. Gaussian mixture distributions are identifiable and commonly used for generative models.

The parameterized joint distribution can be written as $p(x, y|\theta) = p(y|\theta)p(x|y, \theta)$ by using the chain rule. Each parameter vector θ is associated with a decision function $f_\theta(x) = \underset{y}{\arg\max} \, p(y|x, \theta)$. The parameter is then chosen based on fit to both the labeled and unlabeled data, weighted by λ:

$$\underset{\Theta}{\arg\max} \left(\log p \left(\{x_i, y_i\}_{i=1}^{l} \mid \theta \right) + \lambda \log p \left(\{x_i\}_{i=l+1}^{l+u} \mid \theta \right) \right) \tag{2.9}$$

2.2.3.2   Low-Density Separation

Another major class of methods attempts to place boundaries in regions with few data points (labeled or unlabeled). One of the most commonly used algorithms is the transductive support vector machine, or TSVM (which, despite its name, may be used for inductive learning as well). Whereas support vector machines for supervised learning seek a decision boundary with maximal margin over the labeled data, the goal of TSVM is a labeling of the unlabeled data such that the decision boundary has maximal margin over all of the data. In addition to the standard hinge loss $(1 - yf(x))_+$ for labeled data, a loss function $(1 - |f(x)|)_+$ is introduced over the unlabeled data by letting $y = \text{sign} \, f(x)$. TSVM then selects $f^*(x) = h^*(x) + b$ from a reproducing kernel Hilbert space $\mathcal{H}$ by minimizing the regularized empirical risk:

$$f^* = \underset{f}{\arg\min} (\sum_{i=1}^{l} (1 - y_i f(x_i))_+ +$$

$$\lambda_1 \|h\|_{\mathcal{H}}^2 + \lambda_2 \sum_{i=l+1}^{l+u} (1 - |f(x_i)|)_+) \tag{2.10}$$

An exact solution is intractable due to the non-convex term $(1 - |f(x)|)_+$, so research focuses on useful approximations. Other approaches that implement low-density separation include Gaussian process models, information regularization, and entropy minimization (of which TSVM is a special case).

2.2.3.3   Laplacian Regularization

Laplacian regularization has been historically approached through graph-Laplacian. Graph-based methods for semi-supervised learning use a graph representation of the data, with a node for each labeled and unlabeled example. The graph may be constructed using domain knowledge or similarity of examples; two common methods are to connect each data point to its k-nearest neighbors or to examples within some distance ϵ. The weight W_{ij} of an edge between x_i and x_j is then set to $e^{\frac{-\|x_i - x_j\|^2}{\epsilon}}$.

Within the framework of manifold regularization, the graph serves as a proxy for the manifold. A term is added to the standard Tikhonov regularization problem to enforce smoothness of the solution relative to the manifold (in the intrinsic space of the problem) as well as relative to the ambient input space. The minimization problem becomes:

$$\underset{f \in \mathcal{H}}{\text{argmin}}(\frac{1}{l} \sum_{i=1}^{l} V\left(f\left(x_i\right), y_i\right) + \lambda_A \|f\|^2_{\mathcal{H}} +$$
$$\lambda_I \int_{\mathcal{M}} \|\nabla_{\mathcal{M}} f(x)\|^2 dp(x)) \tag{2.11}$$

where $\mathcal{H}$ is a reproducing kernel Hilbert space and $\mathcal{M}$ is the manifold on which the data lie. The regularization parameters λ_A and λ_I control smoothness in the ambient and intrinsic spaces respectively. The graph is used to approximate the intrinsic regularization term. Defining the graph Laplacian $L = D - W$ where $D_{ii} = \sum_{j=1}^{l+u} W_{ij}$ and $\mathbf{f}$ the vector $[f(x_1) \ldots f(x_{l+u})]$, we have:

$$\mathbf{f}^T L \mathbf{f} = \sum_{i,j=1}^{l+u} W_{ij} \left(f_i - f_j\right)^2 \approx \int_{\mathcal{M}} \|\nabla_{\mathcal{M}} f(x)\|^2 dp(x) \tag{2.12}$$

2.2.3.4   Heuristic Approaches

Some methods for semi-supervised learning are not intrinsically geared to learning from both unlabeled and labeled data, but instead make use of unlabeled data within a supervised learning framework. For instance, the labeled and unlabeled examples $x_1, \ldots, x_{l+u}$ may inform a choice of representation, distance metric, or kernel for the data in an unsupervised first step. Then supervised learning proceeds from only the labeled examples. In this vein, some methods learn a low-dimensional representation using the supervised data and then apply either low-density separation or graph-based methods to the learned representation. Iteratively refining the representation and then performing semi-supervised learning on said representation may further improve performance.

2.2.3.5   Self-Training

Self-training is a wrapper method for semi-supervised learning First a supervised learning algorithm is trained based on the labeled data only. This classifier is then applied to the unlabeled data to generate more labeled examples as input for the supervised learning algorithm. Generally only the labels the classifier is most confident in are added at each step.

Co-training is an extension of self-training in which multiple classifiers are trained on different (ideally disjoint) sets of features and generate labeled examples for one another.

Co-training is a semi-supervised learning technique that requires two views of the data. It assumes that each example is described using two different sets of features that provide complementary information about the instance. Ideally, the two views are conditionally independent (i.e., the two feature sets of each instance are conditionally independent given the class) and each view is sufficient (i.e., the class of an instance can be accurately predicted from each view alone). Co-training first learns a separate classifier for each view using any labeled examples. The most confident predictions of each classifier on the unlabeled data are then used to iteratively construct additional labeled training data.

- Given:
  - a set L of labeled training examples
  - a set U of unlabeled examples
- Create a pool U' of examples by choosing u examples at random from U
- Loop for k iterations:
  - Use L to train a classifier h_1 that considers only the x_1 portion of x
  - Use L to train a classifier h_2 that considers only the x_2 portion of x
  - Allow h_1 to label p positive and n negative examples from U'
  - Allow h_2 to label p positive and n negative examples from U'
  - Add these self-labeled examples to L
  - Randomly choose $2p + 2n$ examples from U to replenish U'

2.2.4   Conclusion

In conclusion, machine learning aims to extract data features $f = \{f_1, f_2, \ldots, f_n\}$ from massive data X. Features are given by human or extracted by machines. For supervised learning, the data is labelled manually firstly, and then machine try to learn the features f given by label. For unsupervised learning, machine tends to find the hidden patterns and insights from the given data automatically. In other words, the features f are determines without manual influence.

However, on the one hand, people prefer model to learn the features that people want it to learn. On the other hand, manually labeling features requires expensive cost. Therefore, semi-supervised learning is proposed. It aims to use a small amount of labeled data to affect the process of model learning, so that the features f are determined by human. For more unlabeled data, the model needs to determine the features f of the data first, and then the model could be trained to learn the required features.

2.3   Typical Applications of Artificial Intelligence Technology

Artificial intelligence techniques have become one of the primary drivers for the automation of software engineering. This section introduces the common applications of AI techniques that are often employed in the practice of crowdsourced software engineering.

2.3.1   Natural Language Processing

Natural language processing (NLP) is the intersection of computer science, artificial intelligence and linguistics. The goal is to allow computers to process, understand and use human language to perform tasks such as language translation and question answering.

Many natural language processing techniques have been adopted in assisting crowdsourced testing tasks. For example, researchers utilized the knowledge graph to generate crowdsourced requirements[25]. Meanwhile, those techniques can also be used to improve the efficiency and effectiveness of other tasks such as testing cases generation[49], test reports classification[48, 98] and prioritization[22, 116], test reports comprehension[27].

Besides, machine translation is a technology that uses computers to translate between different languages. By borrowing machine translation's concepts and strategies, researchers explored some works such as extracting the features code to generate natural language summaries for source code fragement[4, 63].

Question answering system is one of the most popular applications of natural language processing. Researchers have built crowdsourced knowledge-based question answering systems[73, 85, 108] by integrating information from GitHub and StackOverflow. Furthermore, the bug fixing information from the QA sites can also be leveraged as crowd experience to assist program debugging, which is named crowdsourced debugging[11, 59].

The commonly used libraries[1] for natural language processing include NLTK, Spacy, TextBlob, CoreNLP, Gensim, scikit-learn.

2.3.2 Image Understanding

Image understanding is defined as, in *Encyclopedia of Artificial Intelligence*[84], "integrating explicit models of a visual problem domain with one or more methods for extracting features from images and one or more methods for matching features with models using a control structure." Based on feature extraction and matching, higher-level image content learning and inference can be achieved. Image understanding has been applied in many aspects, such as image indexing, image classification, object detection, scene recognition, image description.

For crowdsourced software engineering, one of the most common applications is prioritizing software testing artifacts (such as test reports[22, 48, 116]) that contain images by proper feature extraction and distance calculation. Meanwhile, in crowdsourced mobile testing, researchers utilize image semantic segmentation to detect application screenshot layouts and widgets, then generate testing tasks[118], testing cases[117] or testing reports[60] based on those layouts and widgets. Furthermore, image description is automatically generating natural language descriptions for images by analyzing and understanding its content. It has been adopted to assist crowdsourced testing[49] recently. The GitHub bug reports contain a wealth of crowdsourced knowledge which is important for software maintenance. Image understanding techniques have been applied to bug report comprehension[27] and duplicate report detection[15].

The commonly used libraries for image understanding include general machine learning libraries[2] such as TensorFlow, CUDA, Keras, CAFFE and computer vision specific libraries[3] such as OpenCV, Scikit-Image, Matplotlib, SimpleCV.

---

[1] NLTK: https://www.nltk.org, Spacy: https://spacy.io, TextBlob: https://textblob.readthedocs.io/en/dev, CoreNLP: https://stanfordnlp.github.io/CoreNLP, Gensim: https://github.com/RaRe-Technologies/gensim, scikit-learn: https://scikit-learn.org.

[2] TensorFlow: https://www.tensorflow.org, CUDA: https://developer.nvidia.com/cuda-toolkit, Keras: https://keras.io, CAFFE: https://caffe.berkeleyvision.org.

[3] OpenCV: https://opencv.org, Scikit-Image: https://scikit-image.org, Matplotlib: https://matplotlib.org, SimpleCV: http://simplecv.org.

Chapter 3
Book Structure

3.1 How the Book is Structured

Despite the successful application of crowdsourced testing as we introduced in previous chapters, there are still challenges faced to fully take advantage of this new testing paradigm. For example, previous chapters mentioned there are large number of duplicate reports submitted by diversified crowd workers who conduct the testing in parallel. It is extremely valuable to automatically detect those duplicate reports and aggregate them together for a summarized view, which can facilitate the crowdsourced testing managers in their following bug resolving activities. Another example is that the previous industrial case study has also revealed that some crowd workers can detect bugs in a crowdsourced testing task, while others may fail to detect bugs in the same task. If there is automatic support for recommending a set of crowd workers to a specific crowdsourced testing task, more bugs can be detected, and the bug detection activity would be more efficient.

In current practice, there is little technical support during task delivery, task execution, and results inspection. This requires the project managers devote much time in finding the right crowd workers for a task, or summarizing the found faults from the large number of submitted reports, etc. We assume if equipped with supporting technologies for various activities during crowdsourced testing process, the whole crowdsourced testing can be more cost-effective.

Crowdsourced testing task, crowd workers and testing results are the three main entities in a crowdsourced testing platform. During crowdsourced testing, a crowdsourced testing task is distributed on the platform, and crowd workers can sign in the task and conduct testing. The crowd workers would generate crowdsourced testing results, e.g., testing reports, and submit to the platform. In this way, a large number of testing reports are received for the crowdsourced testing task. They are then inspected and verified to find the detected bugs.

Q. Wang et al., *Intelligent Crowdsourced Testing*,
https://doi.org/10.1007/978-981-16-9643-5_3

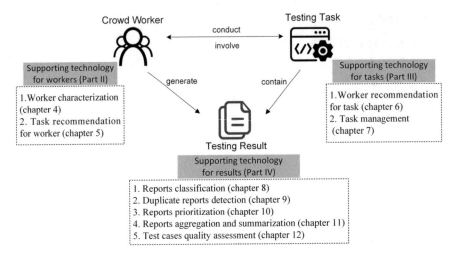

Fig. 3.1 Book structure

Taken in this sense, this book aims at providing supporting technologies during crowdsourced testing process, respectively from the perspectives of crowd workers, testing tasks, and testing results, as shown in Fig. 3.1.

Part II presents the supporting technologies for crowd workers, with a worker characterization model in Chap. 4 and the task recommendation for crowd workers in Chap. 5. In the worker characterization model, a crowd worker is characterized with the activeness, preference, expertise, and device, automatically extracted from the historical repositories of a crowdsourced testing platform. Then armed with the worker characterization model, the proposed task recommendation approach can recommend suitable testing tasks for a crowd worker, so as to maximize their winning chances in taking a task and potentially minimize the wasteful effort.

Part III introduces the supporting technologies for testing tasks, in which we first introduce the crowd worker recommendation for tasks in Chap. 6, followed by the crowdsourced testing task management in Chap. 7. The proposed crowd worker recommendation approaches are based on the worker characterization model introduced in part II, and can recommend a set of capable crowd workers for a specific testing task. The crowdsourced testing task management approaches focus on the automated decision support to manage the crowdsourced testing practices more effectively.

Part IV relates with the supporting technologies for testing results, organized into reports classification, duplicate detection, reports prioritization, reports summarization, and quality assessment of test cases. First, the reports classification and duplication detection approaches will be presented respectively in Chaps. 8 and 9, which help classify the testing reports with bugs and duplicate reports involving same bug. Then we introduce the reports prioritization approaches in Chap. 10 to facilitate the inspection of received testing reports so that the bugs can be revealed earlier. Following that, the reports summarization approach introduced in Chap. 11 can detect and aggregate the duplicate reports, and identify the most informative report in each duplicate report cluster. Furthermore, we will present the quality assessment of crowdsourced testing cases to help the task requester in deciding the quality of the submitted reports.

Finally, in Part V, we wrap the book with conclusions and future perspectives about this new testing schema. We will discuss the fairness and popularity bias in the recommendation of crowdsourced testing, as well as the guidance when conducting testing tasks. Since the crowdsourced testing platform can accumulate rich data, we bring forward the data-enable crowdsourced testing and screenshot learning, which aim at taking advantage of these data for more effective testing management and decision support.

Part II
Supporting Technology for Crowdsourced Testing Workers

Chapter 4
Characterization of Crowd Worker

This chapter presents how we characterize the crowd workers so as to conduct the task recommendation and worker recommendation to facilitate the crowdsourced testing practice. We propose a data-driven crowd worker characterization which characterizes the crowd workers automatically mining from the historical crowdsourced testing repositories. We first conduct explorations about the crowd worker's characteristics from mining the historical repositories to motive the characterization in Sect. 4.1, then present the characterization with *activeness*, *preference*, *expertise*, and *device* in Sect. 4.2.

4.1 Exploration of Crowd Worker's Characteristics

This subsection presents explorations about the characteristics of crowd workers on a crowdsourced testing dataset, which can influence their test participation and bug detection performance.

Activeness Figure 4.1 shows the distribution of crowd workers' activity intensity. The x-axis is the random-selected 20 crowd workers among the top-50 workers ranked by the number of submitted reports, and the y-axis is 20 equal-sized time interval which is obtained by dividing the whole time space. We color-code the blocks, using a darker color to denote a worker submitting more reports during the specific time interval. We can see that the crowd workers' activities are greatly diversified and not all crowd workers are equally active in the crowdsourced testing platform at specific time. Intuitively, the inactive crowd workers would be less likely to conduct the task, let alone detect bugs.

Preference Figure 4.2 shows the distribution of crowd workers' activity at a finer granularity. The x-axis is the same as Fig. 4.1, and the y-axis is the random-selected 20 terms (which capture the content under testing) from the top-50 most popular

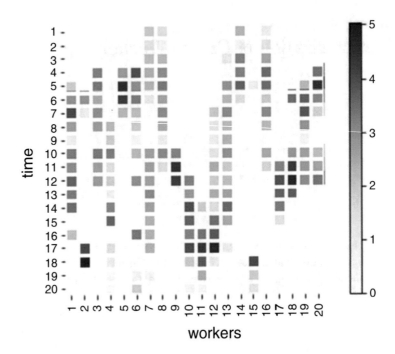

Fig. 4.1 Crowd worker's activeness

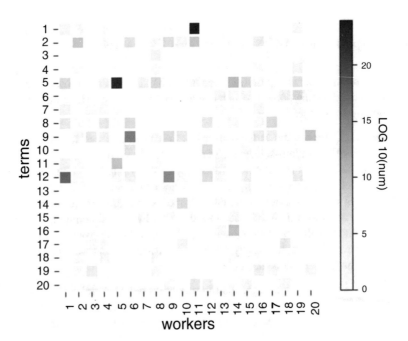

Fig. 4.2 Crowd worker's preference

descriptive terms. The block in the heat map demonstrates the number of reports which are submitted by the specific worker and contain the specific term. We color-code the blocks, using a darker color to denote a worker submitting reports with corresponding terms more frequently, i.e., worker's preference in different aspects. The differences across columns in the heat map further reveal the diversified preference across workers. Considering there are usually dozens of crowdsourced testing tasks open in the platform, even if a crowd worker is active, he/she cannot take all tasks. Intuitively, if a crowd worker has a preference on the specific aspects of a task, he/she would show greater willingness in taking the task and further detecting bugs.

Expertise Similarly, we explore the heat map with the terms from the crowd workers' *bug reports* (rather than *reports*), we observe a similar trend. This indicates the crowd workers' diversified expertise over different crowdsourced testing tasks. We also conduct correlation analysis between the number of bug reports (i.e., denoting expertise) and number of reports (i.e., denoting preference) for each pair of the 20 crowd workers on the top-50 most popular terms, the median coefficients is 0.26 indicating these two types of characteristics are not tightly correlated with each other. *Preference* focuses more on whether a crowd worker would take a specific task, and *expertise* focuses more on whether a crowd worker can detect bugs in the task.

The above exploration results reveal that workers have greatly diversified activeness, preferences, and expertise, which significantly affect their availability on the platform, choices of tasks, and quality of their submissions. Hence, we characterize the crowd workers from these three aspects through automatically mining the software repositories.

4.2 Crowd Worker's Characterization

Based on the observations from Sect. 4.1, *activeness, preference, and expertise of crowd workers* are utilized for characterizing the crowd workers of a general crowdsourced testing platform. In addition, we include *device of crowd workers* as a separate dimension, since several studies reported its diversifying role in crowdsourced testing environment. Before providing the details of workers' characterization, we first present how we conduct the data preprocessing to facilitate the workers' characterization.

4.2.1 Data Preprocessing

There are two types of textual documents in our crowdsourced testing data: one is test reports and the other is test requirements. Each document goes through standard word segmentation, stopwords removal, with synonym replacement being applied to reduce noise. As an output, each document is represented using a vector of terms.

Descriptive Term Filtering After the above steps, we find that some terms may appear in a large number of documents, while some other terms may appear in only very few documents. Both of them are less predictive and contribute less in workers' characterization. Therefore, we construct a *descriptive terms list* to facilitate the effective modeling. We first preprocess all the documents and obtain the terms of each document. We rank the terms according to the number of documents in which a term appears (i.e., document frequency, also known as *df*), and filter out 5% terms with the highest document frequency and 5% terms with the lowest document frequency (i.e., less predictive terms). Note that, since the documents in crowdsourced testing are often short, the term frequency (also known as *tf*), which is another commonly-used metric in information retrieval, is not discriminative, so we only use document frequency to rank the terms. In this way, the final *descriptive terms list* is formed and used to represent each document in the vector space of the descriptive terms.

4.2.2   Activeness

Activeness measures the degree of availability of crowd workers to represent relative uncertainty associated with inactive crowd workers. Activeness of a crowd worker w is characterized using the following four attributes:

LastBug: Duration (in hours) between now and the time when worker w's last *bug* is submitted.

LastReport: Duration (in hours) between now and the time when worker w's last *report* is submitted.

NumBugs-X: Number of bugs submitted by worker w in past X time, e.g., past 2 weeks.

NumReports-X: Number of reports submitted by worker w in past X time, e.g., past 8 h.

Based on the concepts in Chap. 2, we can derive the above attributes of worker w from the historical reports submitted by him/her.

4.2.3   Preference

Preference measures to what degree a potential crowd worker might be interested in a candidate task. The higher the preference, the greater the worker's willingness/potential in taking the task/detecting bugs. Preference of a crowd worker w is characterized using the following attribute:

ProbPref: the preference of worker w regarding each descriptive term. In other words, it is the probability of recommending the worker w when aiming at generating a report with specific term t_j. It is measured based on bayes rules as follows:

$$ProbPref(w, t_j) = P(w|t_j) = \frac{tf(w, t_j)}{\sum_{w_k} tf(w_k, t_j)} \cdot \frac{\sum_{w_k} df(w_k)}{df(w)} \tag{4.1}$$

where $tf(w, t_j)$ is the number of occurrences of t_j in historical reports of worker w, $df(w)$ is the total number of reports submitted by worker w, and k is an iterator over all available crowd workers at the platform.

As mentioned in Sect. 4.2.1, after data preprocessing, each report is expressed with a set of descriptive terms. This attribute can be derived from the crowd worker's historical submitted reports.

4.2.4 Expertise

Expertise measures a crowd worker's capability in detecting bugs. When a crowd worker brings in matching expertise required for the given task, he/she would have greater possibility in detecting bugs. Expertise of a crowd worker w is characterized using the following attribute:

ProbExp: the expertise of worker w regarding each descriptive term. It is measured similarly as *ProbPref* as follows:

$$ProbExp(w, t_j) = P(w|t_j) = \frac{tf(w, t_j)}{\sum_{w_k} tf(w_k, t_j)} \cdot \frac{\sum_{w_k} df(w_k)}{df(w)} \tag{4.2}$$

where $tf(w, t_j)$ is the number of occurrences of t_j in historical *bug reports* of worker w, $df(w)$ is the total number of *bug reports* submitted by worker w, and k is an iterator over all available crowd workers at the platform.

The difference between *ProbProf* and *ProbExp* is that the former is measured based on worker's submitted *reports*, while the latter is based on worker's submitted *bug reports*, following the motivating studies in Sect. 4.1. The reason why we characterize expertise in terms of each term is because it enables the more precise matching with the inadequate-tested terms, and the identification of more diverse workers for finding unique bugs in a much-finer granularity.

4.2.5 Device

Device measures the device-related attributes of the crowd worker which is critical in testing an application and in revealing device-related bugs [103]. Device of a crowd worker w is characterized using all his/her device-related attributes including: ***Phone type*** used to run the testing task, ***Operating system*** of the device model, ***ROM type*** of the phone, ***Network environment*** under which a task is run. These are necessary to reproduce the bugs for the software under test, shared among various crowdsourced testing platforms. Also our worker characterization is scalable to a reduced set or enhanced set of attributes.

Chapter 5
Task Recommendation for Crowd Worker

5.1 Introduction

A wealth of previous literature has shown the inequalities gap between task requesters' and workers' decision support provided in crowdsourcing platforms [35, 55, 56]. On the one hand, many platforms allow requesters to assess worker performance data and support the gauging of qualification criterion in order to control the quality of crowd submissions. On the other hand, workers are usually provided with very limited support throughout the task selection and completion processes [35, 55]. In particular, most workers must manually browse through a long list of open tasks before they determine which ones to sign up. Manual task selection not only is time consuming, but also tends to be sub optimal due to subjective, ad hoc worker behaviors.

Several researchers and practitioners have explored approaches to provide workers with better opportunities to obtain information when choosing tasks, e.g., TurkOpticon [34], TurkBench [26], CrowdWorkers[8], TurkScanner [80], etc. Despite the usefulness of these tools in simple crowdsourcing jobs, task selection in crowdsourced testing is still challenging. One of the dominant differences is that, not every registered crowd workers can detect bugs considering crowdsourced testing as a more professional and specialized activity. Generally speaking, in cases of workers failing to detect unique bugs, they do not receive any payment. For example, if a crowd worker selects a task driven purely by his/her arbitrary opinion or ad-hoc choice, it is likely that the worker ends up with being unable to discover any bugs due to skill-/expectation- mismatch. This means that their hours' or days' effort spending on downloading the app, reading the instructions, and exploring its functionalities, all gets wasted. Therefore, if without appropriate decision support, a large amount of crowd work could be wasted due to sub optimal task selection behaviors.

This chapter first conducts a pilot study to shed light on the necessity and feasibility of task recommendation. Results reveal that, among a crowd worker's

Q. Wang et al., *Intelligent Crowdsourced Testing*,
https://doi.org/10.1007/978-981-16-9643-5_5

signed tasks, only in an average of 26% tasks he/she can successfully detect unique bugs and win the award; this number drops to 7% regarding to the set of all public open tasks. The portion of wasted work is an alarming signal, and also suggests the practical need of better decision support from the crowd worker's point of views. We advocate a more effective alternative to manual task selection would be to provide personalized task recommendation considering the diverse distribution of worker preference and expertise, with objectives to increase their winning chances and to potentially reduce the frequency of unpaid crowd work.

To that end, with the crowd worker's characterization in Chap. 4, this chapter proposes a personalized task recommendation approach PTRec to aid dynamic worker decision in selecting crowdsourced testing tasks. It extracts a set of features automatically, and employs machine learning algorithm to generate dynamic and personalized task recommendation which best matches worker's expertise and interest. The features capture the progress status of tasks, the availability of crowd workers, the matching degree between the task and crowd workers, as well as the task's competitive advantages among other open tasks. Section 5.2 will present the details of this approach.

5.2 Learning-Based Personalized Task Recommendation

5.2.1 *Motivation*

In order to better understand and address the issue of unpaid crowd work, we first examine the crowd workers' participation data using 636 historical tasks from real-world crowdsourced testing projects. Figure 5.1 illustrates the box-plot comparison across three metrics, i.e., the number of daily open tasks, the number of registered

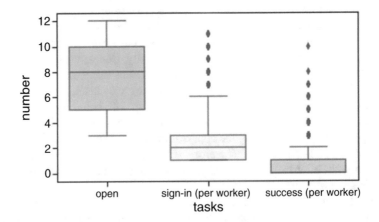

Fig. 5.1 Crowd worker's participation status

tasks per worker, and the number of winning tasks per worker, measured in data across a duration of 245 days. A maximum of 12 and a median of 8 tasks are open to the crowd workers in the crowdsourced testing platform.

When browsing the list of open tasks, crowd workers usually narrow down to a median of 2 tasks to sign in, and eventually win in a median of zero tasks (an average of 0.58). This indicates the average success rate is 26% among a worker's signed tasks, and 7% among all open tasks. This also implies that, on average, a large portion (i.e. 74%) of crowd workers' effort is wasted. Additionally, unpaid work associated with inappropriate task choice could discourage the crowd workers from future participation, which will harm the healthy growth of crowdsourcing community.

This motivates the study reported in this chapter, in seeking for a more effective alternative to manual task selection, by providing automatic task recommendation to maximize their winning chances and minimize wasteful effort.

5.2.2 Approach

Based on the worker characterization, the personalized task recommendation approach PTRec first extracts 60 features automatically, and employs random-forest learner to generate dynamic task recommendation which best matches worker's expertise and interest. Figure 5.2 shows the overview of the proposed PTRec.

PTRec trains the random forest learner with historical repositories of crowd-sourced testing platform, then conducts task recommendation for specific worker with the trained model. Suppose a query worker and a set of open tasks, it iterates over the open tasks as a candidate task and predicts the probability of the worker in detecting bugs in the candidate task. The utilized features for learning consider the matching degree between the query worker and a candidate task in current open tasks, as well as the wining potential of the candidate task over other open tasks.

The task recommendation is in the form of a ranked list of open tasks based on the predicted probability. PTRec also provides a personalized task recommendation visualization dashboard to facilitate the task selection and visualization of task matching status.

5.2.2.1 Feature Extraction

At the recommendation time *recTime*, for the query worker w, the following data are obtained for feature extraction: (1) *candidate task*: the specific open task under examination; (2) *competing tasks*: the set of open tasks except query task; (3) *historical tasks*: the set of closed tasks; (4) *historical reports*: the set of submitted reports of the query worker.

To build an effective machine learner, we extract 60 features based on workers' characterization and crowdsourced testing tasks as summarized in Table 5.1. These

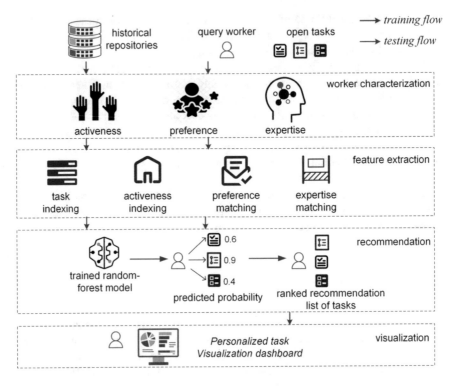

Fig. 5.2 Overview of PTRec

features are not only extracted based on the candidate task, but also consider other open tasks to derive the competing status among these tasks.

Features #1–#6 (i.e., *task indexing*) capture the progress status of tasks to derive the winning potential of candidate task among other open tasks. Features #7–#18 (i.e., *activeness indexing*) capture the activeness of the query worker. Previous work demonstrated the developer's recent activity has greater indicative effect on his/her future behavior than the activity happened long before, so we extract the activeness-related features with varying time intervals. Features #19–#39 capture the matching degree between a crowd worker's *preference* and the candidate task, as well as the competing matching status of the candidate task among open tasks. Features #40–#60 capture the matching degree between the a crowd worker's *expertise* and the candidate task, also including the competing advantages over other open tasks.

The first group of 6 features (*task indexing*) can be calculated directly. The second group of 12 features (*activeness indexing*) can be fetched using the activeness attributes defined in Chap. 4. The third and fourth group of features are obtained in a similar way by examining the similarities. For brevity, we only present the details to produce the fourth group of features, i.e. #40–#60.

Previous work has proven extracting features from different perspectives can help improve the learning performance, so we extract the similarity-related features from

Table 5.1 Feature extraction for query worker w towards the candidate task t

Category	Feature			
	In terms of candidate task t		In terms of open tasks	
Task indexing	1	Duration (in hours) between *recTime* and the time t begins	2–3	Number of open tasks whose begin time is earlier/later than t
	4	Number of reports received in t	5–6	Number of open tasks whose received reports are more/less than t
Activeness Indexing	7–18	LastBug, LastReport; NumBugs-8 hours, NumBugs-24 hours, NumBugs-1 week, NumBugs-2 week, NumBugs-all (i.e., in the past); NumReports-8 hours, NumReports-24 hours, NumReports-1 week, NumReports-2 week, NumReports-all (i.e., in the past)		
Preference matching	19	Partial-ordered cosine similarity (*POCosSim*) between $w's$ preference and t	20–21	Number of open tasks whose *POCosSim* with $w's$ preference is larger/smaller than the *POCosSim* between $w's$ preference and t
	22	Partial-ordered euclidean similarity (*POEucSim*) between $w's$ preference and t	23–24	Number of open tasks whose *POEucSim* with $w's$ preference is larger/smaller than the *POEucSim* between $w's$ preference and t
	25–29	Partial-ordered jaccard similarity with the cutoff threshold θ (*POJacSim@θ*) between $w's$ preference and t, θ is 0.0, 0.1, 0.2, 0.3, 0.4	30–39	Number of open tasks whose *POJacSim@θ* with $w's$ preference is larger/smaller than the *POJacSim@θ* between $w's$ preference and t

(continued)

Table 5.1 (continued)

Category	Feature			
	In terms of candidate task t		In terms of open tasks	
Expertise matching	40	$POCosSim$ between $w's$ expertise and t	41–42	Number of open tasks whose $POCosSim$ with $w's$ expertise is larger/smaller than the $POCosSim$ between $w's$ expertise and t
	43	$POEucSim$ between $w's$ expertise and t	44–45	Number of open tasks whose $POEucSim$ with $w's$ expertise is larger/smaller than the $POEucSim$ between $w's$ expertise and t
	46–50	$POJacSim@\theta$ between $w's$ expertise and t, θ is 0.0, 0.1, 0.2, 0.3, 0.4	51–60	Number of open tasks whose $POJacSim@\theta$ with $w's$ expertise is larger/smaller than the $POJacSim@\theta$ between $w's$ expertise and t

different viewpoints. Cosine similarity, euclidean similarity, and jaccard similarity are the three commonly-used similarity measurements and have proven to be efficient in previous researches, therefore we utilize all these three similarities for feature extraction. To facilitate the extraction of features, we build the task terms vector for each task, by calculating the inverse document frequency of each term $idf(t_i)$ in the task's requirements descriptions. In addition, a crowd worker might have extra expertise beyond the task's requirements, to alleviate the potential bias introduced by the unrelated expertise, we define the partial-ordered similarity to constrain the similarity matching only on the descriptive terms within the task terms vector.

Partial-ordered cosine similarity (POCosSim) is calculated as the cosine similarity between a task and a worker's expertise, with the similarity matching constraint only on terms appeared in task terms vector.

$$POCosSim = \frac{\sum x_i * y_i}{\sqrt{\sum x_i^2}\sqrt{\sum y_i^2}} \tag{5.1}$$

where x_i is the value of term t_i in the task terms vector, y_i is $ProbExp(w, t_i)$, and t_i is the ith descriptive term in task terms vector.

Partial-ordered euclidean similarity (POEucSim) is calculated as the euclidean similarity between a task and a worker's expertise, with a minor modification on the distance calculation.

$$POEucSim = \begin{cases} \sqrt{\sum (x_i - y_i)^2}, & if \quad x_i >= y_i \\ 0, & if \quad x_i < y_i, \end{cases} \tag{5.2}$$

where x_i and y_i is the same as in *POCosSim*.

Partial-ordered jaccard similarity with the cutoff threshold of θ (POJacSim@θ) is calculated as the modified jaccard similarity between a task and a worker's expertise based on the set of terms whose probabilistic values are larger than θ.

$$POJacSim = \frac{A \cap B}{A} \tag{5.3}$$

where A is a set of descriptive terms whose corresponding value in task terms vector is larger than θ, and B is a set of descriptive terms whose $ProbExp(w, t_i)$ is larger than θ.

5.2.2.2 Task Recommendation

Training Data Preparation For a *recTime* in the training dataset, we first obtain the set of open tasks, and iterate over the open tasks as a candidate task with other tasks as competing tasks. We obtain the characterization of all registered crowd workers in terms of *recTime*, and extract the features in Table 5.1 for each crowd worker towards the candidate task. We treat the workers who detect bugs after *recTime* in the candidate task as positive instances. Since there are large number of crowd workers who didn't submit a bug in a specific task (i.e., potential negative instances) and unbalanced data could significantly affect the model performance, to make our dataset balanced, we randomly sample an equal number of crowd workers (who didn't submit bugs in the query task) with the positive instances as negative instances. The instances close to the boundary between the positive and negative regions can easily bring noise to the machine learner, therefore, to facilitate the generation of more effective learning model, we choose crowd workers who are different from the positive instances, i.e., to select those majority instances which are away from the boundary.

Model Training With the positive and negative instances, we build Random Forest machine learner to learn the bug detection performance of crowd workers. The random forest is an ensemble approach to boost the prediction stability and performance.

Task Recommendation Generation At the *recTime*, for a query worker and a set of open tasks, we iterate over all open tasks as a candidate task. We first obtain the query workers' characterization, extract the features in Table 5.1, and apply the trained random forest model to predict the bug detection probability of the worker towards the candidate task. The ranked list of open tasks is presented to the query worker based on the predicted probability.

5.2.2.3   Personalized Task Visualization Dashboard

Based on the recommendation results as well as the workers' characterization, we design a personalized task recommendation dashboard to facilitate the task selection and visualization of task matching status. As shown in Fig. 5.3, the dashboard contains three areas. The top area displays the worker's win vs. sign-in ratio (i.e., number of tasks in which a worker received payment among all registered tasks) and the average ratio of all registered workers. It also lists the name and keywords of recent five tasks the worker has won. The middle area shows the characterization of crowd workers derived from the worker's past activities. The bottom area displays the list of ongoing tasks with the predicted recommendation probability, the expertise matching status, and the preference matching status, etc. It also provides information about task progress, i.e., elapsed time, number of registered testers, number of submitted reports. The bottom part supports sorting with all the aforementioned attributes, and the preview of tasks information, and the one-click sign-in of the task. With this dashboard, crowd workers can obtain a summarized view about their personalized experience in terms of all ongoing tasks, and browse the tasks list with various metrics to facilitate their task choosing.

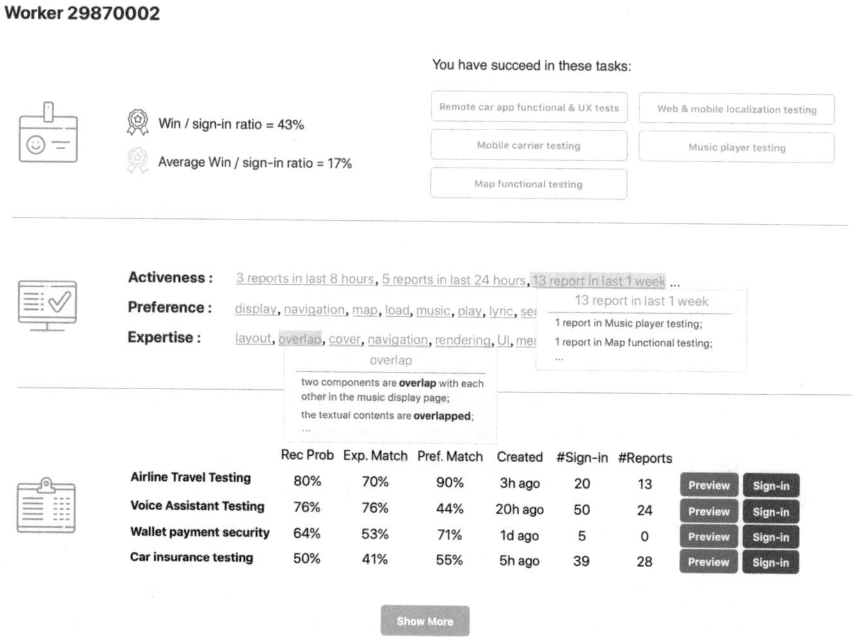

Worker 29870002

You have succeed in these tasks:

Win / sign-in ratio = 43%

Average Win / sign-in ratio = 17%

Remote car app functional & UX tests	Web & mobile localization testing
Mobile carrier testing	Music player testing
Map functional testing	

Activeness : 3 reports in last 8 hours, 5 reports in last 24 hours, 13 report in last 1 week ...

13 report in last 1 week
1 report in Music player testing;
1 report in Map functional testing;
...

Preference : display, navigation, map, load, music, play, lyric, see

Expertise : layout, overlap, cover, navigation, rendering, UI, me

overlap

two components are **overlap** with each other in the music display page;
the textual contents are **overlapped**;
...

	Rec Prob	Exp. Match	Pref. Match	Created	#Sign-in	#Reports		
Airline Travel Testing	80%	70%	90%	3h ago	20	13	Preview	Sign-in
Voice Assistant Testing	76%	76%	44%	20h ago	50	24	Preview	Sign-in
Wallet payment security	64%	53%	71%	1d ago	5	0	Preview	Sign-in
Car insurance testing	50%	41%	55%	5h ago	39	28	Preview	Sign-in

Show More

Fig. 5.3 Overview of personalized task recommendation dashboard

5.2.3   *Experiment*

5.2.3.1   Experiment Design

(1) Experimental Dataset

The experimental dataset is collected from a popular crowdsourced testing platform. In total, there are 636 mobile application testing tasks from various domains, involving 2404 crowdworkers and 80,200 submitted reports. For each testing task, we collected its task-related information, all the submitted test reports and related information, e.g., submitter, device, etc. The minimum, average, and maximum number of reports (*and unique bugs*) per task are 20 (*3*), 126 (*24*), and 876 (*98*) respectively.

(2) Experimental Setup

To simulate the usage of PTRec in practice, we employ a commonly-used longitudinal data setup. We sort the 245 days during when we collected the data in chronological order, and obtain the set of open tasks in each day. We then employ the former *N-1* days as the training dataset to train PTRec and use the tasks in the *Nth* day as the testing dataset to evaluate the performance of task recommendation. We experiment *N* from 100 to 245 to ensure a relatively stable performance because a too small training dataset could not reach an effective model. For each day in the testing dataset, we choose 4 representative *recTime*, i.e., 0:00, 6:00, 12:00, 18:00, for task recommendation to better demonstrate the effectiveness of our approach.

(3) **Evaluation Metrics**

Given a *recTime*, we measure the performance of task recommendation based on whether it can recommend the "right" tasks to the crowd worker in which he/she can detect bugs. We employ the widely-used precision and recall in terms of each crowd worker to evaluate the recommendation performance.

Precision is the proportion of tasks that are correctly recommended (i.e., in which a crowd worker detected bugs) among all recommended tasks to the crowd worker. *Recall* is the proportion of tasks that are correctly recommended among all tasks that needed to be recommended (i.e., all tasks in which the crowd worker have detected bugs).

Besides, as our task recommendation aims at saving the effort of crowd workers in the unsuccessful attempt of testing. We define another metrics *savedEffort* to intuitively measure how much effort can be saved in terms of each crowd worker in a specific *recTime*. Suppose the crowd worker needs to examine all open tasks which is the case in real-world practice, and the save effort is derived considering this total effort. We first obtain the difference between number of open tasks and number of recommended tasks for a crowd worker, and treat it as amount of saved effort. *savedEffort* is computed as the percentage of this difference among number of open tasks.

(4) **Ground Truth and Baselines**

The ***Ground Truth*** of task recommendation, i.e., *tasks needed to be recommended to a crowd worker*, in terms of *recTime* is obtained based on the historical bug detection records in the crowdsourced testing platform. If a crowd worker detected bugs after *recTime* in a specific task, we treat the task as ground truth. Based on this treatment, we can obtain the set of tasks needed to be recommended for each crowd worker, and the value of three evaluation metrics can be derived. For the crowd worker which has zero tasks needed to be recommended, we delete it when summarizing the evaluation results.

To further explore the performance of PTRec, we compare it with three baselines.

Naive: this baseline is designed to simulate the common scenario of crowd-sourced testing, i.e., crowd workers randomly choosing tasks. Specifically, in *recTime*, it randomly recommends open tasks to the crowd worker. The analysis of our experimental dataset has revealed that a crowd worker would detect bugs in 20% tasks among open tasks, we keep the recommendation ratio as 20%.

InterestDriven: this baseline is designed by simulating another typical scenario of crowd workers' testing habit, i.e., choose tasks according to his/her interest. We use the domain of the testing applications to represent the crowd worker's interest. *InterestDriven* records the domains of testing task in which a crowd worker has detected bugs, and chooses the tasks belonging to the recorded domains. If there are no tasks satisfied, use the recommendation produced by *Naive* baseline.

DCW-DS [111]: this baseline is the state-of-the-art method for task recommendation in crowdsourced software development scenario. It extracts the features

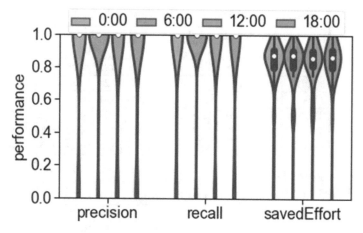

Fig. 5.4 Performance of PTRec (RQ1)

about the dynamic competition status and static attributes, and designs an analytics-based dynamic recomendation systems for crowd workers to make decision on their matching tasks with high winning probability.

5.2.3.2   Results and Analysis

RQ1: How Effective Is PTRec for Task Recommendation?
Figure 5.4 demonstrates the distribution and probability density of the task recommendation performance under four *recTime* with violin plot, which is a combination of box lot and density plot. The thick black bar in the centre represents the interquartile range, and the white dot in the middle is the median value.

We can see that the proposed PTRec can achieve an average precision of 82% and average recall of 84% at *recTime* 0:00, indicating a high recommendation performance. In 79% cases the recommendation can achieve full precision, and in 83% cases the recommendation can achieve full recall. This indicates, the crowd workers can find new bugs (and win the award) in the recommended tasks in an average of 82% cases. In addition, PTRec can save an average of 81% effort that workers have to spend on manually exploring the whole list of open tasks.

For other different *recTime* settings, the performance of PTRec does not exert significant difference. The average precision and recall ranges from 80%–83%, and 82%–86% respectively, while the average saved effort is from 80%–83%. This implies, whenever a crowd worker wants to query "which tasks should i perform", the proposed PTRec can provide a relatively accurate recommendation. For brevity, in the following discussion, we use the performance obtained under *recTime* 0:00.

Table 5.2 presents more elaborated performance, in terms of the average and standard deviation of the recommendation, grouped by number of open tasks.

Table 5.2 Performance in terms of different number of open tasks (RQ1)

		Number of open tasks									
		3	4	5	6	7	8	9	10	11	12
Precision	AVG	0.76	0.73	0.79	0.79	0.85	0.90	0.95	0.90	0.90	0.91
	STDEV	0.41	0.41	0.37	0.40	0.33	0.28	0.20	0.24	0.29	0.27
Recall	AVG	0.77	0.77	0.84	0.78	0.85	0.91	0.95	0.95	0.89	0.93
	STDEV	0.41	0.40	0.35	0.40	0.33	0.28	0.20	0.20	0.29	0.24
SavedEffort	AVG	0.76	0.73	0.79	0.86	0.85	0.89	0.89	0.89	0.92	0.91
	STDEV	0.15	0.26	0.16	0.09	0.09	0.04	0.03	0.04	0.02	0.05

Table 5.3 Performance in terms of different features (RQ2)

	Precision		Recall		SavedEffort	
	AVG	STDEV	AVG	STDEV	AVG	STDEV
PTRec	*0.82*	*0.36*	*0.84*	*0.35*	*0.81*	*0.16*
noTsk	0.80	0.37	0.82	0.36	0.82	0.16
noAct	0.70	0.43	0.72	0.43	0.84	0.16
noPref	0.78	0.39	0.80	0.38	0.82	0.16
noExp	0.75	0.41	0.77	0.40	0.83	0.16

Results show that under diverse task supply levels, i.e., workers' potential choices ranging from 3 to 12 open tasks, PTRec can generally achieve high performance. Particularly, as there are more open tasks (e.g., 8 or more), PTRec can achieve higher precision and recall, as well as lower standard deviation. Since there would be a greater demand for task recommendation when there are more tasks, the better performance in these scenarios further indicates the effectiveness of the proposed PTRec.

We further analyze the cases of wrong recommendation and summarize the reasons as follows. Firstly, there are newcomers who cannot be characterized by our worker characterization model, thus no task can be recommended to them. This is commonly known as the cold-start problem in recommendation. Secondly, there are some successful workers in a task who do not follow the mechanism we designed in this work. For example, we found some workers possess quite irrelevant expertise with the task under testing (i.e., have very low probability to be recommended by our approach), yet successfully detect bugs (i.e., should be recommended). This is a drawback of all history-based recommendation techniques as our PTRec, and because of these outliers, hardly any history-based recommendation can achieve 100% accuracy.

RQ2: Is Each Category of Features Employed in PTRec Necessary?
Table 5.3 shows the comparison results between PTRec and its four variants. Specifically, *noAct*, *noPref*, and *noExp* are different variants of PTRec without the features related with activeness, preference, and expertise respectively. *noTsk* denotes the variant of PTRec without task related features as shown in Table 5.1. We use bold values to indicate the best performance per metric.

It is clear that when dropping any subset of features, the corresponding variant (i.e. the last four rows in the table) suffers performance decline in both *precision* and *recall*. This indicates the necessity and importance of the inclusion of the features. Without activeness-related features, the performance of recommended tasks undergoes the most significant performance decline, indicating the relative largest contribution of these features in task recommendation. A possible explanation is that this category of features captures the time-related information and models the volatility of the platform, which the model heavily depends on in order to effectively learn time-sensitive behavior of workers. Expertise-related features exert a slightly larger influence on the recommendation performance than preference-related features, although they are modeled similarly. This might because the crowd worker's bug detection records are more informative in predicting their future bug detection performance, compared with the general participation activities. The task-related feature plays the smallest influence on the recommendation performance, which further indicates the contribution of worker-related features and importance of precise characterization of workers.

RQ3: Can PTRec Outperform Existing Techniques for Task Recommendation?
Table 5.4 demonstrates the performance of PTRec comparing with three baselines. We use bold values to indicate best performance per metric. Generally speaking, PTRec significantly outperforms all baseline approaches. The average precision and recall of *Naive* is only 29% and 23%, indicating randomly choosing tasks could be quite ineffective. The average precision of *InterestDriven* is 55%, although the average recall is 84%. The precision achieved by PTRec is 49% higher than it of *InterestDriven*, indicating solely referring to past involved domains would be not enough, and finer-grained information should be explored as the proposed PTRec.

The average precision and recall of *DCW-DS* is 67% and 70% respectively. In comparison, the average precision achieved by our proposed PTRec is 22% higher than *DCW-DS*, and the average recall is 20% higher. The advantage of our proposed PTRec over *DCW-DS* is because PTRec utilizes the contextualized information during the crowdsourced testing process, and models the finer-grained expertise matching regarding each descriptive term. This further indicates the usefulness and necessity of precise characterization of crowd workers.

Table 5.4 Performance comparison with baselines (RQ3)

	Precision		Recall		SavedEffort	
	AVG	STDEV	AVG	STDEV	AVG	STDEV
PTRec	*0.82*	*0.36*	*0.84*	*0.35*	*0.81*	*0.16*
Naive	0.29	0.44	0.23	0.39	0.94	0.09
InterestDriven	0.55	0.39	0.84	0.34	0.44	0.39
DCW-DS	0.67	0.45	0.70	0.45	0.84	0.17

5.2.4   Discussion

5.2.4.1   Generalization of PTRec

PTRec is proposed to serve as the automatic assistant for workers when choosing tasks in crowdsourced testing environment. With PTRec, one can display the recommendation on the personalized recommendation dashboard, or push the personalized task recommendation results to registered crowd workers through email periodically, or employ chatbot for message notification, etc. All of them can facilitate the task selection of crowd workers.

In other types of crowdsourcing, there were also approaches or tools proposed to provide workers with more information for task selection. Their main focus was helping workers find higher paying tasks. However, our point is to reduce workers' time on task exploration and unsuccessful testing, which is another attempt for increasing their hourly payment. Besides, tasks matching worker's past experience would improve their productivity which can also increase their hourly wages. In this way, finer-grained characterization of workers and personalized task recommendation as our approach is needed.

Our proposed PTRec is based on automatically characterizing the crowd workers using natural language processing and machine learning techniques, which are independent of different crowdsourcing types. We believe that the proposed approach is generally applicable to support other types of crowdsourcing, e.g., find a more proper software development task, or a question to answer in Q&A service, since more sophisticated skillsets reflecting these specialty crowdsourcing types maybe implicitly represented by corresponding descriptive terms learned from historical records. Therefore, the feature extraction and machine learner components will not be affected and can be reused.

5.2.4.2   Objectivity vs. Fairness

The personalized task recommendation of this study lies in the characterization of workers learned from historical data of the crowdsourced testing platform. This facilitates the generation of an objective list of task recommendation which is not influenced by community bias or value commitments. However, like other history-based recommendation, the proposed approach also suffers from the cold-start problem [109], i.e., unable to provide recommendation for newcomers who do not own any history yet. Therefore, the objectivity in recommendation may, on the other hand, lead to loss of fairness to newcomers which is critical for a thriving crowdsourcing market [14], or overloaded expert workers who potentially become bottleneck. With our experimental data, the most overloaded worker (i.e., recommended with the maximum number of tasks) in each experimental day would receive more than 5 tasks in 51% days, with an maximum of 9 tasks. It seems that overloading experienced worker is not a major issue in our experiments. However, the significance of this issue may vary with respect to different crowdsourcing platform and different machine learning algorithms, and additional attention is necessary to avoid such issues of history-based decision making support.

To mitigate the drawback of history-based recommendation, one can use a calibrated characterization for newcomers, e.g., incorporate such static attributes of the workers as occupation, interest for modeling. By summarizing hot technical aspects from recent open tasks, a decision tree type of preference/expertise questionnaire can be formulated and is presented to the new comers, so that a default worker characterization can be configured for the new comers and used for recommendation systems like PTRec. Another attempt could be modeling and learning the multitasking capability of crowd workers to better overcome the load balancing problem. One can also acquire the most frequent number of tasks an expert worker is taking daily, and set this number as a threshold when balancing the recommendation.

Part III
Supporting Technology for Crowdsourced Testing Tasks

Chapter 6
Crowd Worker Recommendation for Testing Task

6.1 Introduction

One challenging problem with crowdsouced testing is optimizing crowd workers' participation. Crowd resources, while cheap, are not free. Hence, when scaling up crowdsouced testing, it is necessary to maximize the information gain from every member of the crowds. Also, not all crowd workers are equally skilled at finding bugs. Inappropriate workers may miss bugs, or report duplicated bugs, while hiring them requires nontrivial budgets. Furthermore, because of the *unknownness, largeness* and *undefinedness* of the crowd workers [29], we should not involve all the workers in a crowdsourced testing task. Therefore, it is of great value to recommend a set of appropriate crowd workers for a test task so that more software bugs can be detected with fewer workers.

Finding appropriate workers for particular software engineering tasks has long been recognized as being important and invaluable. There are many lines of related studies about worker recommendation, such as bug triage [37, 90], mentor recommendation [9], and expert recommendation [52]. With the emergence of crowdsourcing, there are several researches focusing on developers recommendation for crowdsourced software development [54, 111]. The aforementioned studies either recommend one worker or assume the recommended set of workers are independent with each other. However, in crowdsourced testing, a set of workers need to be recommended to accomplish a test task together. Furthermore, the recommended set of workers are dependent on each other because their performance can together influence the final test outcomes.

This chapter presents two crowd worker recommendation approaches. The first approach, multi-objective crowd worker recommendation (MOCOM), aims at recommends a minimum set of crowd workers who could help detect the maximum number of bugs for a crowdsourced testing task. The recommendation results is obtained through maximizing the bug detection probability of workers, the relevance with the test task, the diversity of workers, and minimizing the test cost.

MOCOM works well at the beginning of a new task, yet has limited applicability when considering the highly dynamic and volatile crowdsourced testing processes. This is because it does not consider constantly changing context information of ongoing testing processes. We then investigate how to fill in this gap and explore the necessity and feasibility of dynamically in-process worker recommendation.

From a pilot study, we find the prevalence of long-sized *non-yielding windows*, i.e., consecutive testing reports containing no new bugs during crowdsourced testing process. This indicates the ineffectiveness of current crowdsourced testing practice because these non-yielding windows would (1) cause wasteful spending of task requesters; (2) potentially delay the progress of crowdsourced testing. It also implies the potential opportunity for accelerating testing process by recommending appropriate crowd workers in a dynamic manner, so that the non-yielding windows could be shortened. Therefore, we further propose the second approach, context-aware in-process crowd worker recommendation (iRec), to dynamically recommend a diverse set of capable crowd workers based on various contextual information at a specific point of crowdsourced testing process, aiming at shortening the non-yielding window and improving bug detection efficiency.

Sections 6.2 and 6.3 will respectively present the details of these two approaches.

6.2   Multi-Objective Crowd Worker Recommendation

6.2.1   Motivation

Currently, in most crowdsourced testing platforms, before participating in crowd-sourced testing, workers need to search proper test tasks to perform from a large number of published test tasks. This mode is ineffective for bug detection because of the following two reasons: first, workers may choose test tasks they are not good at, which cannot guarantee the quality of testing; second, a test task may be conducted by many workers with similar experience or expertise which would result in many duplicated bugs and waste of resources.

We suggest a recommendation mode to bridge the gap between crowd workers and test tasks. Our goal is to recommend a set of appropriate workers for a test task. The task publisher can invite these workers on purpose, or attract them with more rewards. In this way, more bugs can be detected with fewer crowd workers and less cost.

To understand current real-world crowdsourced testing practice, we conduct a pilot study with the dataset in Sect. 6.2.3, and observations are shown in Fig. 6.1.

(1) Although a large number of crowd workers can participate in a test task, not every worker could successfully detect bugs in the task. Figure 6.1a shows the number of crowd workers participated in each test task, and the number of crowd workers detected bugs in the task. The percentage of workers who have detected bugs among all the involved workers is only 52.6%.

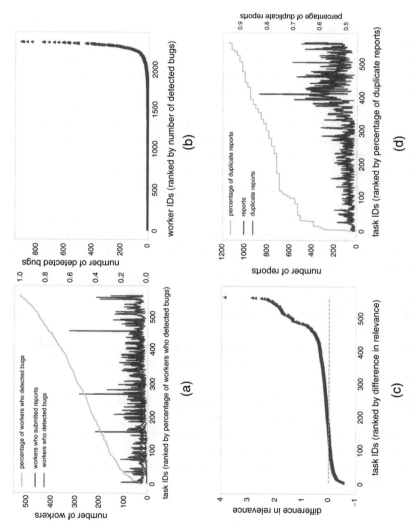

Fig. 6.1 Observations related with crowd worker participation and performance. (**a**) Observation 1. (**b**) Observation 2. (**c**) Observation 3. (**d**) Observation 4

Motivated by this observation, it would be of great value to recommend an appropriate set of candidate workers to perform a test task in order to detect more bugs with fewer workers and less cost. This is especially important when the number of candidate workers is large, which is typical in the context of crowdsourced testing.

(2) Different crowd workers might have different bug detection capability. Figure 6.1b shows the number of bugs detected by each crowd worker. We can see that most workers only detected very few bugs, while there is a small portion of workers who have detected much more bugs than others.

This observation motivates us to look for capable workers, who demonstrate greater capability in history and would be more likely to detect bugs in future.

(3) Crowd workers would be more likely to detect bugs when conducting tasks they are familiar with. Figure 6.1c shows the relationship between workers' familiarity with the test task and their bug detection performance. Given a test task, we first calculate the familiarity between each worker and the test task (i.e., cosine similarity between worker's historical reports and task's requirements). We then average two similarity values, one for the workers who have detected bugs (sim_p), and the other for the workers who have not detected bugs (sim_n). Following that, we obtain the difference for the two similarity values for each task, i.e., (sim_p—sim_n)/sim_n. A positive value denotes the familiarity for the workers who have detected bugs is greater than those who have not detected bugs in the task, while a negative value denotes the opposite phenomenon. From Fig. 6.1c, we can see that most projects demonstrate positive values, indicating workers have higher possibility to detect bugs in the test tasks they are familiar with.

This observation motivates us to select workers with expertise relevant to a given test task.

(4) For each test task, a number of duplicate reports may be reported by different crowd workers, as shown in Fig. 6.1d. An average of 80% reports are duplicates of other reports.

This observation motivates us to decrease the duplicate reports by looking for diverse crowd workers so as to further reduce the waste of cost.

In summary, the above observations motivate the need of recommending a subset of crowd workers for a given test task. They also motivate us to consider workers' capability, their relevance with the test task, as well as the diversity of the selected set of workers.

6.2.2   Approach

Motivated by the findings in previous section, we model the worker recommendation problem as a multi-objective optimization problem. We propose a Multi-Objective Crowd wOrker recoMmendation approach (MOCOM), which can maximize the bug detection probability of workers, the relevance with the test task, the diversity of workers, and minimize the test cost.

In this section, we first present the modeling of crowd workers, followed by the measurement of the four objectives. Then we present the multi-objective optimization framework for crowd worker recommendation.

6.2.2.1 Modeling of Crowd Worker

In this work, we model a crowd worker from three dimensions, i.e., device, capability, and domain knowledge. The following subsections illustrate the details of these three dimensions. Note that, we introduce the characterization of crowd workers in Chap. 4, this section explores a different modeling of crowd workers to show the feasibility of worker characterization by mining the historical repositories.

Device represents the hardware (e.g., device model), software (e.g., the operating system of the device), and environment (e.g., network environment) owned by a crowd worker. The reason we consider device as one characteristic of a crowd worker is that crowd workers often run the testing task under their specific devices-related information, which can influence the testing outcomes [53, 107]. We use the four related attributes, i.e., device model, operating system, ROM type, and network environment, to model the device of a crowd worker.

Capability represents the ability of a crowd worker abstracted from her/his historical testing outcomes. A crowd worker's past performance can reflect her/his capability to a great extent, and has great indicative effect on her/his future bug detection performance. Hence, we consider the capability as an essential dimension to characterize a crowd worker.

We use the following attributes to characterize a crowd worker's capability, i.e.,

- *(1) Number of projects which the worker participated in*
- *(2) Number of **test** reports submitted by the worker*
- *(3) Number of **bug** reports submitted by the worker*
- *(4) Percentage of **bug** reports submitted by the worker*
  It is computed as the number of bug reports submitted by the worker divided by the number of test reports submitted by the worker.
- *(5) Degree of duplicate bug reports of the worker*
  It is computed as the *duplicate index* of a worker divided by the number of bug reports submitted by the worker. In it,

$$duplicate\ index = \sum_{r} \frac{1}{number\ of\ r's\ duplicates} \qquad (6.1)$$

where *r* is the bug report submitted by a worker, and *number of r's duplicates* is the number of duplicates of report r in the test task. For example, worker *W5124983210* in Table 2.1 submitted two bug reports *R1002948308* and *R1037948352*, where *R1002948308* has 2 duplicates, and *R1037948352* has 6 duplicates. Then percentage of duplicate bugs of worker $W5124983210$ is $(1/2 + 1/6) / 2$. The reason why we do not directly use the number of duplicates divided by the number of bug reports is that we want to not only represent the number of duplicates but also distinguish the degree of duplicates (i.e., using duplicate index).

Domain knowledge represents the domain experience a crowd worker obtained through performing testing tasks. The application under test usually come from various domains, and they call for the crowd workers with specific domain knowledge to better explore their functionality. We also observed that crowd workers are more likely to detect bugs when conducting tasks they are familiar with. This is why we regard domain knowledge as another important criterion to characterize a crowd worker.

We use the "descriptive terms" extracted from a crowd worker's historical submitted reports (as described in Chap. 4) to represent her/his domain knowledge and represent it as a vector.

In Table 6.1, we summarize all the attributes mentioned above. We also present an example of each attribute based on the crowd worker $W5124983210$ (in Table 2.1). We will use these attributes to characterize the crowd workers and measure the objectives.

6.2.2.2 Measurement of Four Objectives

Since the purpose of crowd worker recommendation is to help find more bugs with fewer crowd workers, the design of MOCOM considers four objectives.

First, we should recommend the crowd workers with ***maximized bug detection probability***, since they can potentially improve the bug detection performance. Second, we should look for the crowd workers with ***maximized relevant*** expertise

Table 6.1 Characterization of crowd worker

Device	
Phone type	Samsung SN9009
Operating system	Android 4.4.2
ROM information	KOT49H.N9009
Network environment	WIFI
Capability	
Number of projects participated	15
Number of reports submitted	19
Number of bugs detected	7
Percentage of bugs detected	36.8%
Percentage of duplicate bugs	41.5%
Domain Knowledge	
Descriptive terms extracted from historical reports	< video, list, popularity, rank, view, ...>

with the test task because they have more background knowledge and can increase the bug detection likelihood. This is also because the crowdsourcing task can be complexity and user-driven, hence we should consider the workers' relevance with the task so as to improve the bug detection performance. Third, we should select a set of crowd workers with *diverse* characteristics, because different workers might explore different areas of the application under testing which would help detect more bugs and reduce duplicate reports. Last but not least, we should consider the *test cost* which is an essential consideration in crowdsourcing field. We then illustrate the details of these four objectives.

Objective 1: Maximize Bug Detection Probability of Crowd Workers

We build a machine learning model to learn the bug detection probability for each worker. The primary focus of building the model is to determine which features can be utilized for learning the bug detection probability.

Motivated by the findings in Sect. 6.2.1, we assume a crowd worker's capability is tightly related with the bug detection probability. So we treat all the crowd worker's capability-related attributes as the features in the machine learning model.

Apart from that, previous work demonstrated the open source developer's recent activity has greater indicative effect on his future behavior than the activity happened long before [121, 122]. Therefore, we further take the time-related factors into consideration, and better model the crowd worker's past experience. Take one of the capability attribute *number of reports submitted* as an example, we also extract the *number of reports submitted in the past 2 weeks, number of reports submitted in the past 1 months*, and *number of reports submitted in the past 2 months*. The reason why we use these three time intervals is that our dataset shows more than 75% crowd worker's past activities occur in the past 2 months.

In this way, the original one attribute (i.e., *number of reports submitted*) can yield four features in the machine learning model, and the original five capability attributes in Table 6.1 generate 20 features in our learning model (demonstrated in Table 6.2).

Table 6.2 Features for machine learning model

Number of projects in the past	Number of projects in past *2 weeks*
Number of projects in past *1 month*	Number of projects in past *2 month*
Number of reports in the past	Number of reports in past *2 weeks*
Number of reports in past *1 month*	Number of reports in past *2 month*
Number of bugs in the past	Number of bugs in past *2 weeks*
Number of bugs in past *1 month*	Number of bugs in past *2 month*
Percentage of bugs in the past	Percentage of bugs in past *2 weeks*
Percentage of bugs in past *1 month*	Percentage of bugs in past *2 month*
Percentage of duplicates in the past	Percentage of dup. in past *2 weeks*
Percentage of dup. in past *1 month*	Percentage of dup. in past *2 month*
Time interval between last submission and task publish time (in days)	

Furthermore, we employ another time-related feature in our machine learning model. It is the time interval between the crowd worker's last submission on this platform and the test task's publishing time, measured in number of days. Intuitively, the longer this time interval is, the less likely the crowd worker would take part in this task.

In summary, we list all the aforementioned 21 features which are used in our machine learning model in Table 6.2. We employ Logistic Regression as our machine learning model, which is widely reported as effective in many different classification tasks in software engineering. Based on the logistic regression model trained on the training dataset, given a task in the testing dataset, we can obtain its bug detection probability of all candidate workers. Specifically, for a set of candidate crowd workers (i.e., one solution in Sect. 6.2.2.3), we add up their bug detection probability on the given test task and consider the summation as the bug detection probability of the test task.

Objective 2: Maximize Relevance of Crowd Workers with Test Task
For relevance objective, we need to measure the relevance between the candidate crowd workers and a test task.

We use the similarity between a worker's domain knowledge and a test task to denote the relevance. It is computed based on the cosine similarity between the descriptive terms of the crowd worker's domain knowledge and the descriptive terms of the test task's requirements. A larger similarity value denotes the worker's domain knowledge is more tightly relevant with the test task. The reason why we use cosine similarity is that past researches have demonstrated its effectiveness in high-dimensional textual data, which is exactly our case.

Given a specific test task, to obtain the relevance for a set of candidate crowd workers (i.e., one solution in Sect. 6.2.2.3), we first combine the domain knowledge of all selected workers as a unified vector, then compute the cosine similarity between the unified vector and a test task's requirements.

Objective 3: Maximize Diversity of Crowd Workers
For the diversity objective, we need to measure the diversity of a set of selected crowd workers. Objective 2 (i.e., maximize relevance) aims at finding workers who are familiar with a test task. Apart from that, the nature of software testing calls for diverse workers who can help explore various parts of the app and reduce duplicate reports. Hence objective 3 (i.e., maximize diversity) aims at finding workers with diverse background. Note that, although these two objectives seem conflicting with each other, the multi-objective optimization framework utilized in this work can help reach a balance between relevance maximization and diversity maximization.

To explore the diversity, we use count-based method to measure it, and count how many different attribute values appeared in the selected set of crowd workers (i.e., one solution in Sect. 6.2.2.3).

Remember that the crowd workers are characterized by three dimensions: device, capability, and domain knowledge. For capability dimension, it is unreasonable to consider the diversity because we require all the selected workers are capable, rather than some of them are capable while others are not. Accordingly, we compute the diversity based on other two dimensions, i.e., crowd workers' device and domain knowledge. Specifically, for device, we count how many different phone types, operating systems, ROM types, and network environments contained in the set of workers. For domain knowledge, we count how many different terms appeared in the domain knowledge of the workers.

Note that, device only has four attributes, while the domain knowledge has thousands of attributes (i.e., the number of unique descriptive terms). In order to eliminate the influence of different number of attributes on the diversity measurement, we compute the diversity respectively for device and domain knowledge, then obtain the final diversity values using a weight parameter. We have experimented with different weights, it turns out a weight of 0.5 (i.e., device and domain knowledge are equally treated) can obtain relative good and stable performance. So we use this weight in the evaluation.

Objective 4: Minimize Test Cost
The cost is an unavoidable objective when recommending workers for the crowdsourced tasks. The most important cost in crowdsourced testing is the reward for workers. We suppose all the workers who participate in a test task are equally paid, which is a common practice in real-world crowdsourced testing platforms. In this way, the cost for a set of selected workers (i.e., one solution in Sect. 6.2.2.3) is measured as its size.

6.2.2.3 Multi-Objective Optimization Framework

We have mentioned in Sect. 6.2.2.2 that MOCOM needs to optimize four objectives. Obviously, it is difficult to get optimal results for all objectives at the same time. For example, to maximize bug detection probability, we might need to hire more crowd works, thus, sacrifice the fourth objective, i.e., minimize test cost. Our proposed MOCOM seeks a *Pareto front* (or set of solutions). Solutions outside Pareto front cannot dominate (better than, under all objectives) any solutions within the front.

MOCOM uses *NSGA-II* algorithm (i.e., Non-dominated Sorting Genetic Algorithm-II) to optimize the aforementioned four objectives. NSGA-II is a widely used multi-objective optimizer in and out of Software Engineering area. According to [28], more than 65% optimization techniques in software analysis are based on Genetic Algorithm (for problems with single objective), or NSGA-II (for problems with multiple objectives). For more details of NSGA-II algorithm, please see [19].

In our crowd worker recommendation scenario, a Pareto front represents the optimal trade-off between the four objectives determined by NSGA-II. The tester can then inspect a Pareto front to find the best compromise between having a crowd worker selection that balances bug detection probability, relevance, diversity, and test cost or alternatively having a crowd worker selection that maximizes one/two/three objective/s penalizing the remain one/s.

MOCOM has the following four steps:

(1) Solution Encoding Like other recommendation problems [99], we encode each worker as a binary variable. If the worker is selected, the value is one; otherwise, the value is zero. The solution is represented as a vector of binary variables, whose length equals to the number of candidate crowd workers. The solution space for the crowd worker recommendation problem is the set of all possible combinations whether each crowd worker is selected or not.

(2) Initialization The starting population is initialized randomly, i.e., randomly selecting K (K is the size of initial population, set as 200 as other studies) solutions among all possible solutions (i.e., the solution space).

(3) Genetic Operators For the evolution of binary encoding for the solutions, we exploit standard operators, i.e., single point crossover, bitflip mutation, to produce the next generation [99]. We use binary tournament as the selection operator, in which two solutions are randomly chosen and the fitter of the two will survive in the next population.

(4) Fitness Functions Since our goal is to optimize the four considered objectives, each candidate solution is evaluated by our objective functions described in Sect. 6.2.2.2. For bug detection probability, relevance, and diversity, the larger these values are, the faster the convergence of a solution is. The test cost benefits from the smaller values.

6.2.3 Experiment

This section first introduces how we design the experiment, followed by the results and analysis.

6.2.3.1 Experimental Design

(1) Experiment Setup

We use the dataset in Chap. 5 for evaluation. To simulate the usage of MOCOM in practice, we employ a commonly-used longitudinal data setup. That is, all the 636 experimental test tasks were sorted in the chronological order, and then divided into 20 non-overlapped and equally sized folds with each fold having 30 test tasks (the last fold has 36 tasks). We then employ the former N-1 folds as the training dataset to train MOCOM and use the test tasks in the Nth fold as the testing dataset to evaluate the performance of worker recommendation. We experiment N from 11 to 20 to ensure a relative stable performance because a too small training dataset could not reach an effective model. Note that, what varies in the different experiments is the size of training set which goes from 10 to 19 folds, while the testing set always contains one fold of test tasks.

The role of the training dataset is extracting the capability and domain knowledge of the crowd workers based on their historical submitted reports, and building the machine learning model for predicting bug detection probability. For each test task in the testing dataset, we run MOCOM and baseline methods to recommend a set of crowd workers, and evaluate their performance. In total, we have 306 test tasks (i.e., $9 * 30 + 36$) to evaluate MOCOM.

We configured NSGA-II with the setting of *initial population* = 200, *maximum fitness evaluation (i.e., number of runs)* = 20,000 as recommended by previous work.

(2) Evaluation Metrics

Given a test task, we measure the performance of a worker recommendation approach based on whether it can find the "appropriate" workers who can detect bugs. Following previous studies, we use the commonly-used bug detection rate for the evaluation.

Bug Detection Rate at k (BDR@k) is the percentage of bugs detected by the recommended k crowd workers in a test task out of all bugs historically detected in the specific task. Formally, given a set of recommended k workers (i.e., W) and a test task (i.e., T), the *BDR@k* is defined as follows:

$$BDR@k = \frac{\#bugs \ detected \ by \ workers \ in \ W}{\#all \ bugs \ of \ T} \quad (6.2)$$

Note that, "bugs" here are referred as no duplicate bugs. We inspect the Pareto front produced by our approach, and find the recommended worker set under different k values. Since a smaller subset is usually preferred in crowd worker recommendation due to the limited budget, we obtain *BDR@k* when k is 3, 5, 10, 20, 50, and 100.

To compare the *BDR@k* values of the different worker recommendation approaches, we additionally use two metrics.

Firstly, we employ $\%\Delta$ which is the percent difference between the *BDR@k* of two approaches.

$$\%\Delta(\mu_1, \mu_2) = \frac{\mu_2 - \mu_1}{\mu_1} \quad (6.3)$$

where μ_1 and μ_2 are the *BDR@k* values of two worker recommendation approaches.

Secondly, we use the Mann-Whitney U statistical test to determine if the difference between the *BDR@k* is statistically significant. The Mann-Whitney U test has the advantage that the sample populations need not be normally distributed (non-parametric). If the p-value of the test is below 0.05, then the difference is considered statistically significant.

(3) Ground Truth and Baselines

The Ground Truth of bug detection performance is obtained based on the historical crowd workers who participated in test tasks. In detail, we first rank the crowd workers based on their submitted reports in chronological order, then obtain the $BDR@k$ based on this order. For example, $BDR@3$ is based on all bugs detected by the first three crowd workers who participated in test tasks. The maximum value of $BDR@k$ of ground truth is 1.00 because we suppose all the bugs have been detected when a test task is closed.

To further explore the performance of MOCOM, we compare MOCOM with five commonly-used and state-of-the-art baselines.

ExReDiv [16]: This is a weight-based crowd worker recommendation approach. It linearly combines experience strategy (i.e., select experienced workers), relevance strategy (i.e., select workers with expertise relevant to the test task), and diversity strategy (i.e., select diverse workers).

MOOSE [17]: This is a multi-objective crowd worker recommendation, which can maximize the coverage of test requirement, maximize the test experience of the selected crowd workers, and minimize the cost.

Cocoon [107]: This crowd worker recommendation approach is based on maximizing the testing quality under the test context coverage constraint. In it, the testing quality of each worker is measured based on the number of bugs reported in history.

STRING [47]: This approach is designed for black-box test case selection. It uses string distances on the text of test cases for comparing and prioritizing test cases. In detail, this approach first converts each test case into a string of text, and greedily selects one test case which is farthest from the set of already-selected test cases. In our crowd worker selection scenario, we treat a crowd worker as a test case and consider her/his historical submitted reports as the content of test case.

TOPIC [92]: This is another popular black-box test case selection approach. It represents the test cases using the linguistic data of test cases (i.e., their identifier names, comments, and string literals), and applies topic modeling to the linguistic data to model the functionality of each test case. Then it gives high priority to the test cases which test different functionality of the system under test. In our crowd worker selection scenario, we also treat a crowd worker as a test case and consider her/his historical submitted reports as the linguistic content. Although *STRING* and *TOPIC* are designed for test case selection and consider different aspects from other three worker recommendation baselines, we want to investigate whether test case selection approaches can also do the crowd worker recommendation problem.

6.2.3.2   Results and Analysis

RQ1: How Effective Is MOCOM in Crowd Worker Recommendation?

To answer this research question, we first present some general views of our approach for worker recommendation, measured in bug detection rate. To further

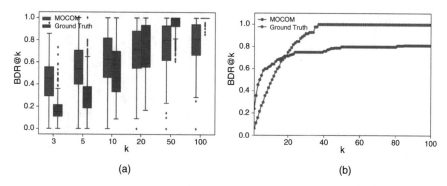

Fig. 6.2 Performance of MOCOM (RQ1). (**a**) Bug detection rate for projects. (**b**) Median bug detection rate curve

demonstrate the advantages of MOCOM, we then compare its performance with five commonly-used and state-of-the-art baseline methods.

Figure 6.2a demonstrates $BDR@k$ under six representative k values. We can see the median $BDR@k$ is 0.46 when k is 3, the median $BDR@k$ is 0.62 when k is 10, and the median $BDR@k$ is 0.70 when k is 20. To put it another way, with 3 recommended workers, the median for the percentage of detected bugs is 46%. In addition, a median of 62% of all bugs can be detected with 10 recommended workers, and a median of 70% of all bugs can be detected with 20 recommended workers. This indicates the effectiveness of our approach.

Figure 6.2b shows $BDR@k$ curve when k increases from 1 to 100. We can easily observe that $BDR@k$ of MOCOM increases rapidly and reaches 75% when a median of 24 crowd workers are employed. This means with the crowd workers recommended by our proposed MOCOM, only a median of 24 workers are needed to detect 75% of all potential bugs.

In Fig. 6.2a, b, we also present the $BDR@k$ of *ground truth*. We can observe that when k is below 20, the bug detection rate ($BDR@k$) achieved by our proposed MOCOM is much higher than the $BDR@k$ of groundtruth. This implies our proposed approach can detect more bugs with few crowd workers, which is the main concern and contribution of this work. We also notice that $BDR@k$ of MOCOM is lower than $BDR@k$ of groundtruth when k is larger than 20.

Figure 6.3 presents the $BDR@k$ values of our propose MOCOM and the five baselines. We can easily observe that our proposed MOCOM is much more effective, considering the bug detection performance ($BDR@k$) of these recommended workers. This is particularly true when the k is smaller than 50.

Table 6.3 demonstrates the results of %Δ between our proposed MOCOM and the five baselines. $BDR@5$ of MOCOM has 50% to 607% improvement compared with the baselines, while $BDR@20$ of MOCOM undergoes 19% to 80% improvement compared with the baselines.

We additionally conduct Mann-Whitney U Test for $BDR@k$ between our proposed MOCOM and the five baseline approaches. Results show that for k is 3,

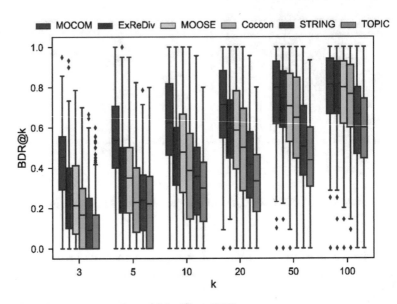

Fig. 6.3 Performance comparison with baselines (RQ1)

Table 6.3 Results of %Δ for median BDR@k of baselines(RQ1)

	$k = 3$	$k = 5$	$k = 10$	$k = 20$	$k = 50$	$k = 100$
MOCOM vs. ExReDiv	69%	50%	33%	19%	6%	0%
MOCOM vs. MOOSE	111%	53%	31%	21%	13%	1%
MOCOM vs. Cocoon	171%	135%	61%	42%	23%	6%
MOCOM vs. STRING	397%	123%	75%	71%	58%	21%
MOCOM vs. TOPIC	INF	607%	56%	80%	71%	36%

Table 6.4 Results of Mann-Whitney U Test (RQ1)

	$k = 3$	$k = 5$	$k = 10$	$k = 20$	$k = 50$	$k = 100$
MOCOM vs. ExReDiv	0.000**	0.000**	0.000**	0.000**	0.035**	0.630
MOCOM vs. MOOSE	0.000**	0.000**	0.000**	0.000**	0.000**	0.188
MOCOM vs. Cocoon	0.000**	0.000**	0.000**	0.000**	0.000**	0.008**
MOCOM vs. STRING	0.000**	0.000**	0.000**	0.000**	0.000**	0.000**
MOCOM vs. TOPIC	0.000**	0.000**	0.000**	0.000**	0.000**	0.000**

5, 10, 20, and 50, the *p-value* between our proposed MOCOM and each of the
five baselines are all below 0.05 (details are in Table 6.4). This signifies that the
bug detection performance of the crowd workers recommended by our approach is
significantly better than existing approaches, which further indicates the advantages
of our approach over the five commonly-used and state-of-the-art baseline methods.

Furthermore, unsurprisingly, the two baseline methods which are originally
designed for test case selection (i.e., *STRING* and *TOPIC*) perform bad for
crowd worker recommendation. And the three baseline methods which are pro-

posed specifically for crowd worker recommendation (i.e., *ExReDiv*, *MOOSE*, and *Cocoon*) perform better. This indicates, once again, the need of designing approach for crowd worker recommendation exclusively, because the characteristics of crowd workers are different from other objects (e.g., test case) in software testing.

Among the three baselines for crowd worker recommendation (i.e., *ExReDiv*, *MOOSE*, and *Cocoon*), we can observe that *ExReDiv* is a little better than the other two. This might occur *ExReDiv* also considers the crowd worker's relevance with the test task, and the diversity among the selected crowd workers, although not as comprehensive as our proposed MOCOM. Moreover, experimental results show that relevance and diversity are important factors which should be considered in crowd worker recommendation, which is shown below.

RQ2: How Effective Is the Machine Learning Model in Predicting the Bug Detection Probability?

We build a machine learning model to better obtain the bug detection probability, which serves as one objective in MOCOM. This research question aims at investigating the effectiveness of our machine learning model on predicting the bug detection probability considering the predicted probability with the actual bug detection results. We use the three most commonly-used metrics (i.e., Precision, Recall, and F-Measure to measure the effectiveness of prediction. We treat the worker with a predicted probability greater than 0.5 as a bug finder, otherwise as not a bug finder. In the historical submitted reports, we can obtain who have detected bugs, and who have not. Hence, the three metrics are computed based on the worker's predicted bug detection results and the actual bug detection results.

Figure 6.4 presents the effectiveness for predicting the bug detection probability. We can easily see that our machine learning model can achieve high precision,

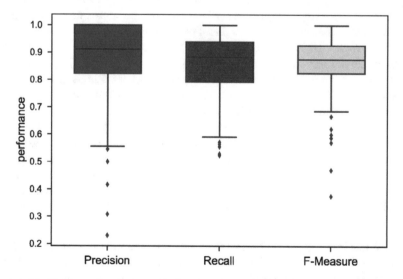

Fig. 6.4 Machine learner performance for bug detection probability (RQ2)

Table 6.5 Feature importance rank (RQ2)

Rank	Feature	Rank	Feature
1	Number of bugs in past 2 *weeks*	12	Number of projects in past *1 month*
2	Number of bugs in past *1 month*	13	Number of projects in the past
3	Percentage of bugs in past 2 *weeks*	14	Number of reports in past 2 *month*
4	Number of bugs in past 2 *month*	15	Number of projects in past 2 *month*
5	Number of projects in past 2 *weeks*	16	Number of reports in past *1 month*
6	Number of reports in past 2 *weeks*	17	Percentage of dup. in past *1 month*
7	Percentage of bugs in past *1 month*	18	Number of reports in the past
8	Number of bugs in the past	19	Percentage of bugs in the past
9	Percentage of dup. in past 2 *weeks*	20	Percentage of dup. in past 2 *month*
10	Time interval between last submission and task publish time	21	Percentage of dup. in the past
11	Percentage of bugs in past 2 *month*		

recall, and f-measure. Specifically, the median precision is about 0.91, the median recall is about 0.89, and the median f-measure is 0.89. Furthermore, in 75% of the experimental projects, our machine learning model can achieve the precision of 0.82, the recall of 0.79, and the f-measure of 0.82. This implies that our machine learning model can predict the crowd worker's bug detection probability with high accuracy. Therefore, we can use the predicted bug detection probability as one objective in our multi-objective crowd worker recommendation approach.

We further explore the relative importance of different features in our machine learning model. We first obtain the Information Gain for each feature in every project, then treat it as its rank and compute the average rank across all the experimental projects for each feature. Table 6.5 presents the rank of the features.

Generally speaking, the features which capture the more recent activities of crowd workers are ranked much higher. For example, the feature *number of bugs in past 2 weeks (1st rank)* is ranked higher than *number of bugs in the past (8th rank)*, while the former is about the workers' activity in the past 2 weeks and the latter is about the workers' activity in the whole past. This indicates the need of considering the time-related factors when modeling crowd worker's capability in predicting bug detection probability.

In addition, the features which relate with bug detection activity are ranked higher than these about general activities. For example, the feature *number of bugs in past 2 weeks (1st rank)* and *percentage of bugs in the past 2 weeks (3rd rank)* are ranked higher than *number of projects in past 2 weeks (5th rank)* and *number of reports in past 2 weeks (6th rank)*. This implies, compared with general activities in the crowdsourced testing platform, the past bug detection activity can better model the crowd worker's capability and bug detection probability.

RQ3: What Is the Contribution of Each Objective to the Overall Approach?

Four objectives are utilized for facilitating crowd worker recommendation. This research question explores the performance of MOCOM when removing each of the

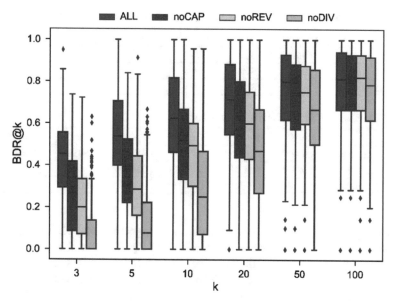

Fig. 6.5 Performance of MOCOM under different objectives (RQ3)

other three objectives in order to investigate the contribution of each objective. For the crowd worker recommendation problem, the objective of cost is indispensable, which cannot be removed. Hence, we remove each of the other three objectives, run MOCOM with the remaining objectives, and evaluate the bug detection rate ($BDR@k$).

Figure 6.5 presents the $BDR@k$ under different settings, where *ALL* denotes using all the four objectives (i.e., our proposed MOCOM), *noCAP* denotes the recommendation without the objective *maximizing bug detection probability of workers*, *noREV* denotes the recommendation without the objective *maximizing relevance with the test task*, and *noDIV* denotes the recommendation without the objective *maximizing diversity of workers*.

We can easily observe that without any of the three objectives, the bug detection performance ($BDR@k$) would decline dramatically. This is particularly true when k is smaller than 50. This indicates all the objectives are necessary for recommending an appropriate set of crowd workers.

Specifically, Table 6.6 demonstrates the results of $\%\Delta$ for MOCOM with different objectives. $BDR@5$ of our approach with all four objectives has 36% to 282% improvement compared with the recommendation with three objectives, while $BDR@20$ of our approach with all four objectives undergoes 11% to 53% improvement compared with the recommendation with three objectives.

We additionally conduct Mann-Whitney U Test for $BDR@k$ between the recommendation under all objectives (i.e., *ALL*) and the recommendation under partial objectives (i.e., *noCap*, *noREV*, and *noDIV*). Results show that when k is equal

Table 6.6 Results of %Δ for BDR@k of different objectives (RQ3)

	$k = 3$	$k = 5$	$k = 10$	$k = 20$	$k = 50$	$k = 100$
ALL vs. noCap	69%	36%	20%	11%	6%	1%
ALL vs. noREV	126%	88%	26%	19%	6%	−1%
ALL vs. noDIV	INF	282%	119%	53%	23%	8%

Table 6.7 Results of Mann-Whitney U Test (RQ3)

	$k = 3$	$k = 5$	$k = 10$	$k = 20$	$k = 50$	$k = 100$
ALL vs. noCap	0.000**	0.000**	0.000**	0.000**	0.038**	0.556
ALL vs. noREV	0.000**	0.000**	0.000**	0.000**	0.011**	0.415
ALL vs. noDIV	0.000**	0.000**	0.000**	0.000**	0.000**	0.066

to 3, 5, 10, 20, and 50, the *p-value* between all objectives and partial objectives are all below 0.05 (details are in Table 6.7). This signifies that the bug detection performance between using all objectives and partial objectives is significantly different, which further indicates all the objectives are necessary, and they together contribute to the worker recommendation performance.

Furthermore, the bug detection performance would undergo the most dramatic decline without the diversity objective (i.e., *noDIV*). This might occur without considering diversity, the selected workers tend to possess similar background and would report duplicate bugs so as to influence their bug detection rate. This proves, once again, the importance of diversity in software testing.

Note that, one can easily generate a mistaken perception that bug detection probability is the most "bug-related" feature in our approach. Thus one may feel confused that *noCAP* (i.e., recommendation without the bug probability objective) can still results in a "still quite good" model. However, the bug detection probability in our model denotes the general ability of bug detection, rather than the specialized ability of detecting bugs for a specific task in testing dataset. This is because the features, utilized to build the machine learning model for capability prediction, all involve the general past activities of the crowd workers. This is why we include the second objective "relevance of crowd workers with test task" to help select the workers who are more capable for a specific task. The results of *noCAP* is better than *noREV* indicates that the general capability of bug detection contributes less to worker recommendation, while the specialized background with the task contributes more to worker recommendation.

6.2.4   Discussion

6.2.4.1   Further Exploration of Results

In Sect. 6.2.3.2, we show that when k is below 20, the bug detection rate (*BDR@k*) achieved by MOCOM is much larger than that of ground truth, which implies the effectiveness of our approach. However, we also notice that *BDR@k* of MOCOM is smaller than *BDR@k* of ground truth when k is larger than 20. In addition, the median *BDR@k* of ground truth can achieve 1.00, while the median *BDR@k* of MOCOM can only reach 0.80 even 100 workers are employed (Fig. 6.2b). The possible reasons for this phenomenon are as follows.

Firstly, as our evaluation is conducted on the historical reports, we assume that the historical submitted bugs are the total number of bugs. This is why *BDR@k* of ground truth can achieve 1.00.

Secondly, we find that there are newcomers in some projects who do not have historical data. For these workers, we cannot model their capability and domain knowledge. Under this situation, our approach would not recommend them to perform test tasks. This is the cold-start problem in recommendation, which has not been well solved. In our experimental dataset, there are 128 test tasks whose *BDR@100* values are less than 0.80. Among these 128 test tasks, 43 (33.5%) tasks have newcomers, who would not be recommended by our approach. However they have detected 5% of total bugs in the ground truth.

To mitigate the impact of newcomers, we plan to incorporate the static attributes of crowd workers (e.g., occupation, interest) to help model the crowds. In addition, we suggest the project manager employ our recommended workers to find the 80% bugs with most of the budgets. Meanwhile, the same test task can also be delivered to the newcomers or other crowds with the leaving tiny proportion of budgets. With this varying pricing mechanism, our work recommendation approach can play a better role, and the crowdsourced task can be tested in a more cost-effective way.

Thirdly, there are some bug-finders who did not follow the mechanism we designed in this work. For example, we found several bug-finders did not submit any reports in the past 6 months, or their past experience are not tightly related with the task's test requirements. In this case, our approach has very low probability of recommending them to perform the test task. These outliers are common in recommendation problems, and because of this, almost all the recommendation problems can not achieve 100% recall. We will explore other influential factors to better improve the recommendation results.

6.2.4.2 Usefulness in Terms of Payout Schema

This section discusses whether our proposed MOCOM still works with other types of payout schema.

Paid by Participation Our proposed approach is based on this payout schema in which workers are equally paid when they submit reports in a test task. It is a commonly-used payout schema especially for the newly-launched platform because it can encourage crowd worker's participation. Evaluation results show that MOCOM detects more bugs with fewer crowd workers (i.e., less cost) thus improves the cost-effectiveness of current crowdsourced testing practice.

Paid by Bug In this schema, only those crowd workers who detect bugs are paid (no matter whether it is a duplicate bug). It is also a commonly-used payout schema. Because the reduced cost is measured by the number of workers in our current evaluation, for this payout schema, the reduced cost might not remain the same as current evaluation results. However, our evaluation results have also showed that with the recommended crowd workers, the number of duplicate reports is reduced. Since the duplicate reports also need to be paid, the reduction in duplicates can help save cost, as well as decrease the effort to manage these duplicates. Hence, in this schema, with our proposed approach, the costs-effectiveness of crowdsourced testing can also be improved.

Paid by First Bug In this schema, the crowd workers who detect the first bug are paid (the following duplicates would not be paid). It is another popular payout schema, in which any worker recommendation approach would not save cost because the total cost is the number of bugs contained in the software system. However, as our approach can detect more bugs with fewer crowd workers, for this payout schema, it means that, with our recommended crowd workers, bugs can be reported earlier than current crowdsourced testing practice. This is important since a large quantity of software are developed under agile model which calls for rapid iteration. In addition, the reduction in duplicate reports by our approach can also help decrease the effort to manage the duplicates.

6.3   Context-Aware In-Process Crowd Worker Recommendation

6.3.1   Motivation

Most open call formats of crowdsourced testing frequently lead to ad hoc worker behaviors and ineffective outcomes. In some cases, workers may choose tasks they are not good at and end up with finding none bugs. In other cases, many workers with similar experience may submit duplicate bug reports and cause wasteful spending of the task requester. More specifically, an average of 80% duplicate reports are observed in our dataset.

To better understand this issue, we examine the bug arrival curve for the historical crowdsourced testing projects. We notice that there are frequently *non-yielding windows*, i.e., the flat segments, of the increasing bug arrival curve. Such flat windows correspond to a collection of test reports failing to reveal new bugs, i.e., either no bugs or only duplicate bugs. We refer to the length of a non-yielding window as the number of consecutive test reports.

Figure 6.6a illustrates the bug arrival curve of an example task with highlighted non-yielding windows (length >10, only for illustration purpose). The non-yielding windows can (1) cause wasteful spending on these non-yielding reports; (2) potentially delay the progress of crowdsourced testing.

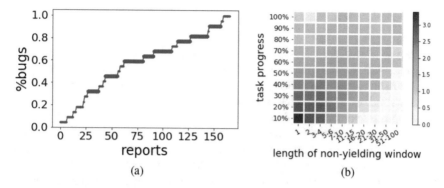

Fig. 6.6 Observations on non-yielding windows. (**a**) Bug arrival curve. (**b**) Distribution of non-yielding windows

We further investigate this phenomenon with the dataset in Sect. 6.3.3 and present a summarized view in Fig. 6.6b. The x-axis shows the length of the non-yielding window, while the y-axis shows the relative position of the non-yielding window expressed using the task's progress. We can observe that the long-sized non-yielding window is quite common during crowdsourced testing process. There are 84.5% (538/636) tasks with at least one 10-sized non-yielding window, 67.8% (431/636) tasks with at least one 15-sized window. Furthermore, these long-sized non-yielding windows mainly take place in the second half of crowdsourced testing processes. For example, 90.7% (488/538) 10-sized non-yielding windows happened at the latter half of the process.

We further explore the cost waste of these non-yielding windows. Specifically, an average of 39% cost[1] is wasted on these 10- or longer-sized non-yielding windows of all experimental tasks, and an average of 32% cost is wasted on these 15- or longer-sized non-yielding windows. In addition, an average of 33 h[2] are spent on these 10- or longer-sized non-yielding windows of all experimental tasks.

The prevalence of long-sized non-yielding windows indicates that current workers possibly have similar bug detection capability with previous workers on the same task. This also suggests the unsuitability of existing one-time worker recommendation approaches, and indicates the need for in-process crowd worker recommendation. We hope to explore if we can learn from the dynamic, underlying contextual information in order to mitigate such situation.

---

[1] Following previous work, we treat the number of reports as the amount of cost.

[2] We measure the duration of each non-yielding window using the time difference between the last and first report's submission time associated with that window.

6.3.2 Approach

Figure 6.7 shows the overview of the proposed iRec. It can be automatically triggered when the size of non-yielding window exceeding a certain threshold value (i.e., *recThres*) is observed during crowdsourced testing process. For brevity, we use the term *recPoint* to denote the point of time under recommendation, as illustrated at the top-right corner of the figure.

iRec has three main components. First, it models the time-sensitive testing contextual information in two perspectives, i.e., the process context and the resource context, respectively, with respect to the *recPoint* during the crowdsourced testing process. The process context characterizes the process-oriented information related to the crowdsourced testing progress of the current task, while resource context reflects the availability and capability factors concerning the competing crowd worker resources in the crowdsourced testing platform. Second, a learning-based ranking component extracts 26 features from both process context and resource context, and learns the success knowledge of the most appropriate crowd workers, i.e., the workers with the greatest potential to detect bugs abstracted from historical tasks. Third, a diversity-based re-ranking component adjusts the ranked list of

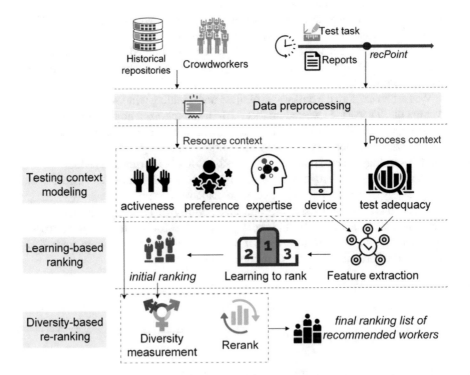

Fig. 6.7 Overview of iRec

recommended workers by optimizing the worker diversity in order to potentially reduce duplicate bugs.

6.3.2.1 Testing Context Modeling

To extract the time-sensitive contextual information at *recPoint*, the following data are obtained for further processing: (1) *test task*: the specific task currently under testing and recommendation; (2) *test reports*: the set of already received reports for this specific task up till the *recPoint*; (3) all registered *crowd workers* (with historical reports a crowd worker submitted, including reports in this specific task); (4) historical test tasks. All the reports and tasks' requirements are preprocessed and represented with a vector of descriptive terms.

The testing context model is constructed in two perspectives, i.e., process context and resource context, to capture the in-process progress-oriented information and crowd workers' characteristics respectively.

(1) Process Context

To model the process context of a crowdsourced testing task, we use the notion of *test adequacy* to measure the testing progress regarding to what degree each descriptive term of task requirements (i.e., task terms vector) has been tested.

TestAdeq: the degree of testing for each descriptive term t_j in task terms vector. It is measured as follows:

$$TestAdeq(t_j) = \frac{number\ of\ bug\ reports\ with\ t_j}{number\ of\ received\ bug\ reports\ in\ a\ task} \quad (6.4)$$

where $t_j \in task\ terms\ vector$. The larger $TestAdeq(t_j)$, the more adequate of testing for the corresponding aspects of the task. This definition enables the learning of underlying knowledge to match workers' expertise or preference with inadequate-tested terms at a finer granularity.

(2) Resource Context

Based on the crowd worker's characterization in Sect. 4.2, *activeness*, *preference*, *expertise*, and *device* of crowd workers are integrated to model the resource context of a general crowdsourced testing platform. This approach reuse the crowd worker's characterization in Sect. 4.2.

6.3.2.2 Learning-Based Ranking

Based on the dynamic testing context model, a learning-based ranking method is developed to derive the ranks of crowd workers based on their probability of detecting bugs with respect to a particular testing context.

Table 6.8 Features for learning to rank

Category	ID	Feature
Activeness indexing	1	LastBug
	2	LastReport
	3–7	NumBugs-8 hours, NumBugs-24 hours, NumBugs-1 week, NumBugs-2 week, NumBugs-all (i.e., in the past)
	8–12	NumReports-8 hours, NumReports-24 hours, NumReports-1 week, NumReports-2 week, NumReports-all (i.e., in the past)
Preference matching	13–14	Partial-ordered cosine similarity, Partial-ordered Euclidean similarity between worker's preference and test adequacy
	15–19	Partial-ordered Jaccard similarity between worker's preference and test adequacy with the cutoff threshold of 0.0, *0.1, 0.2, 0.3, 0.4*
Expertise matching	20-21	Partial-ordered cosine similarity, Partial-ordered Euclidean similarity between worker's expertise and test adequacy
	22–26	Partial-ordered Jaccard similarity between worker's expertise and test adequacy with the cutoff threshold of 0.0, *0.1, 0.2, 0.3, 0.4*

(1) Feature Extraction

26 features are extracted based on the process context and resource context for the learning model, as summarized in Table 6.8. Features #1–#12 capture the ***activeness*** of a crowd worker. Previous work demonstrated the developer's recent activity has greater indicative effect on his/her future behavior than the activity happened long before [121], so we extract the activeness-related features with varying time intervals. Features #13–#19 capture the matching degree between a crowd worker's ***preference*** and the inadequate-tested aspects of the task. Features #20–#26 capture the matching degree between the a crowd worker's ***expertise*** and the inadequate-tested aspects of the task. Note that, since the learning-based ranking method focuses on learning and matching the crowd worker's bug detection capability related to the descriptive terms of a task, we do not include the *device* dimension of resource context.

The first group of 12 features can be calculated directly based on the activeness attributes defined previously. The second and third group of features are obtained in a similar way by examining the similarities. For brevity, we only present the details to produce the third group of features, i.e. #20-#26.

Previous work has proven extracting features from different perspectives can help improve the learning performance, so we extract the similarity-related features from different viewpoints. Cosine similarity, Euclidean similarity, and Jaccard similarity are the three commonly-used similarity measurements and have proven to be efficient in previous researches, therefore we utilize all these three similarities for feature extraction. In addition, a crowdworker might have extra expertise beyond the task's requirements (i.e., the test adequacy), to alleviate the potential bias introduced by the unrelated expertise, we define the partial-ordered similarity (similar as

Chap. 5) to constrain the similarity matching only on the descriptive terms within the task terms vector.

Partial-ordered cosine similarity (POCosSim) is calculated as the cosine similarity between test adequacy and a worker's expertise, with the similarity matching constraint only on terms appeared in task terms vector.

$$POCosSim = \frac{\sum x_i * y_i}{\sqrt{\sum x_i^2}\sqrt{\sum y_i^2}}, \tag{6.5}$$

where x_i is 1.0—$TestAdeq(t_i)$, y_i is $ProbExp(w, t_i)$, and t_i is the ith descriptive term in task terms vector.

Partial-ordered euclidean similarity (POEucSim) is calculated as the euclidean similarity between test adequacy and a worker's expertise, with a minor modification on the distance calculation.

$$POEuc\ Sim = \begin{cases} \sqrt{\sum (x_i - y_i)^2}, & \text{if } x_i >= y_i \\ 0, & \text{if } \quad x_i < y_i \end{cases}, \tag{6.6}$$

where x_i and y_i is the same as in *POCosSim*.

Partial-ordered Jaccard similarity with the cutoff threshold of θ (POJacSim) is calculated as the modified Jaccard similarity between test adequacy and a worker's expertise based on the set of terms whose probabilistic values are larger than θ.

$$POJacSim = \frac{A \cap B}{A}, \tag{6.7}$$

where A is a set of descriptive terms whose (1.0 -$TestAdeq(t_i)$) is larger than θ, and B is a set of descriptive terms whose $ProbExp(w, t_i)$ is larger than θ.

Take the features of preference matching as an example, cosine similarity is calculated as $\frac{\sum x_i * y_i}{\sqrt{\sum x_i^2}\sqrt{\sum y_i^2}}$, where x_i is 1.0—$TestAdeq(t_i)$, y_i is $ProbExp(w, t_i)$, and t_i is the i_{th} descriptive term in task terms vector. Using the same denotation of x_i, y_i, and t_i, Euclidean similarity is calculated as $\sqrt{\sum (x_i - y_i)^2}$. As Jaccard similarity is designed to measure the difference of two sets, we transfer the original probabilistic values into a set of terms with a cutoff threshold. Jaccard similarity with θ is calculated as $\frac{A \cap B}{A \cup B}$, where A is a set of descriptive terms whose (1.0 -$TestAdeq(t_i)$) is larger than θ, and B is a set of descriptive terms whose $ProbExp(w, t_i)$ is larger than θ. We set θ as 0.0, 0.1, 0.3, and 0.5 to obtain four varies of Jaccard similarities.

(2) Ranking

We employ LambdaMART, which is the state-of-the-art learning to rank algorithm and reported as effective in many learning tasks of software engineering [120].

Model Training For every task in the training dataset, at each *recPoint*, we first obtain the process context of the task and resource context for all crowd workers, then extract the features for each crowd worker in Table 6.8. We treat the crowd workers who submitted new bugs after *recPoint* (not duplicate with the submitted reports) as positive instances and label them as 1. As reported by existing work that unbalanced data could significantly affect the model performance [91], to make our dataset balanced, we randomly sample an equal number of crowd workers (who didn't submit bugs in the specific task) with the positive instances and label them as 0. The instances close to the boundary between the positive and negative regions can easily bring noise to the machine learner, therefore, to facilitate the generation of more effective learning model, we choose crowd workers who are different from the positive instances, i.e., to select those majority instances which are away from the boundary.

Ranking Based on Trained Model   At the *recPoint*, we first obtain the process context and resource context for all crowd workers, extract the features in Table 6.8, and apply the trained model to predict the bug detection probability of each crowd worker. We sort the crowd workers based on the predicted probability in a descending order, and treat a ranked list of higher-ranked *recNum* crowd workers (*recNum* is an input parameter since usually only a small set of crowd workers is considered for recommendation) as the output of the learning-based ranking component, i.e., *initial ranking* in Fig. 6.7.

6.3.2.3   Diversity-Based Re-Ranking

To produce less duplicate reports and improve the bug detection performance, we develop a diversity-based re-ranking method to adjust the initial ranking of crowd workers to optimize the diversity among crowd workers.

(1) Diversity Measurement
We first measure the diversity delta of a worker with respect to current re-ranked list of workers S in two dimensions, i.e., expertise diversity delta and device diversity delta.

Expertise diversity delta gives higher score to these workers who have most different expertise from the workers in the current re-ranked list.

$$ExpDiv(w, S) = \sum_{t_j} ProfExp(w, t_j) \times \prod_{w_k \in S} (1.0 - ProfExp(w_k, t_j)) \qquad (6.8)$$

where the later part (i.e., $\prod$) estimates the extent to which t_j is tested by the workers on current re-ranked list.

Device diversity delta gives higher scores to these workers who can bring more new device's attributes (e.g., phone type, operating system, etc.) to those of the workers on current re-ranked list, so as to facilitate the exploration in new testing environment.

$$DevDiv(w, S) = (w's\ attributes) - \cup_{w_k \in S}(w_k's\ attributes) \qquad (6.9)$$

where $w's\ attributes$ is a set of attributes of $w's\ device$, i.e., Samsung SN9009, Android 4.4.2, KOT49H.N9009, WIFI.

(2) Re-ranking

Suppose we have a ranked list of recommended workers (w_1—w_{recNum}) produced by the learning-based ranking method, and an empty list of re-ranked list S, the re-ranking algorithm first moves w_1 to S, then executes the following steps iteratively (suppose current re-ranked list having r workers): ① Calculate $ExpDiv(w, S)$, $DevDiv(w, S)$ for the remaining workers in ranked list; ② Sort the workers respectively based on $ExpDiv(w, S)$ and $DevDiv(w, S)$ descending, and obtain the expertise index $expI(w)$ and device index $expI(w)$ (e.g., $expI(w) = 1$ for the worker with the largest $ExpDiv(w, S)$); ③ Obtain the combined diversity for each worker by $ExpI(w) + divRatio \times DevI(w)$ (where $divRatio$ is an input parameter denoting the relative weight of device diversity compared with expertise diversity), and move the worker with the smallest value into S. The reason why we use *index* rather *the original value* for the combined diversity is to alleviate the influence of extreme value.

6.3.3   Experiment

This section first presents how we design the experiment, followed by the results and analysis.

6.3.3.1   Experiment Design

(1) Experimental Setup

We use the experimental dataset in Chap. 5 for evaluation. To simulate the usage of iRec in practice, we employ a commonly-used longitudinal data setup. For each task in the testing dataset, at the triggered *recPoint*, we run iRec and other approaches to recommend crowd workers. We experimented *recThres* with four representative *recThres* (i.e., 3, 5, 8, and 10). The size of the experimental dataset (i.e., number of total *recPoint*) under the four *recThres* are 676, 479, 345, and 278 respectively.

For the parameter *divRatio*, we tune the optimal value based on the training dataset. In detail, for every candidate parameter value (we experiment from 0.1 to 0.9), we obtain the *FirstHit* metric of the recommendation result on the training set and calculate the median value. We treat the parameter value, under which the smallest median value is obtained, as the best one. The parameter *recNum* is tuned in the same way.

(2) Evaluation Metrics

Given a crowdsourced testing task, we measure the performance of worker recommendation approach based on whether it can find the "right" workers who can detect bugs, and how early it can find the first one. Following previous studies, we use the commonly-used bug detection rate for the evaluation similar with Sect. 6.2.3, with slight difference since this approach focuses on in-process recommendation.

Bug Detection Rate at k (BDR@k) is the percentage of unique bugs detected by the recommended k crowd workers out of all unique bugs historically detected after the *recPoint* for the specific task. Since a smaller subset is preferred in crowd worker recommendation, we obtain *BDR@k* when k is 3, 5, 10, and 20.

Besides, as our in-process recommendation aims at shortening the non-yielding windows, we define another metric to intuitively measure how early the first bug can be detected.

FirstHit is the rank of the first occurrence, after *recPoint*, where a worker from the recommended list actually submitted a unique bug to the specific task.

(3) Ground Truth and Baselines

The Ground Truth of bug detection of a given task is obtained based on the historical crowd workers who participated in the task after the *recPoint*. In detail, we first rank the crowd workers based on their submitted reports in chronological order, then obtain the *BDR@k* and *FirstHit* based on this order.

To further explore the performance of iRec, we compare iRec with four commonly-used and state-of-the-art baselines.

MOCOM (Sect. 6.2): This is a multi-objective crowd worker recommendation approach by maximizing the bug detection probability of workers, the relevance with the test task, the diversity of workers, and minimizing the test cost.

ExReDiv [16]: This is a weight-based crowd worker recommendation approach that linearly combines experience strategy, relevance strategy, and diversity strategy.

MOOSE [17]: This is a multi-objective crowd worker recommendation, which can maximize the coverage of test requirement, maximize the test experience of workers, and minimize the cost.

Cocoon [107]: This crowd worker recommendation approach is designed to maximize the testing quality (measured in worker's historical submitted bugs) under the test coverage constraint.

For each baseline, we conduct worker recommendation before the task begins; then at each *recPoint*, we first obtain the set of worker who have submitted reports in the specific task (denoted as white list workers), and use the recommended workers minus the white list workers as the final set of recommended workers. Note that, the reason why take out the white list workers is because 99% crowd workers only participated one time in a crowdsourced testing task in our experimental dataset; and without the white list, the performance would be worse.

6.3.3.2 Results and Analysis

RQ1: How Effective Is iRec for Crowd Worker Recommendation?

To answer this question, we first present some general views of iRec for worker recommendation. To further demonstrate its advantages, we then compare its performance with four state-of-the-art and commonly-used baseline methods.

Figure 6.8 demonstrates the *FirstHit* of worker recommendation under four representative *recThres* (i.e., *recThres*-sized non-yielding window is observed), i.e., 3, 5, 8, and 10. We can easily see that for all four *recThres*, *FirstHit* of iRec is significantly (p-value is 0.00) and substantially (Cliff's delta is 0.25-0.39) better than current practice of crowdsourced testing. When *recThres* is 5, the median *FirstHit* of iRec and *Ground Truth* are respectively 4 and 8, indicating our proposed approach can shorten the non-yielding window by 50%. For other application scenarios (i.e., *recThres* is 3, 8, and 10), iRec can shorten the non-yielding window by 50% to 58%.

Figure 6.9 demonstrates the *BDR@k* of worker recommendation under four representative *recThres*. iRec significantly (p-value is 0.00) and substantially (Cliff's delta is 0.24-0.39) outperforms current practice of crowdsourced testing for BDR@k (k is 3, 5, 10, and 20). When *recThres* is 5, a median of 50% remaining bugs can be detected with the first 10 recommended crowd workers by our proposed iRec, with 400% improvement compared with current practice of crowdsourced testing (50% vs. 10%). Besides, a median of 78% remaining bugs can be detected with the first 20 recommended crowd workers by iRec, with 160% improvement compared with current practice (78% vs. 30%). This again indicates the effectiveness of our

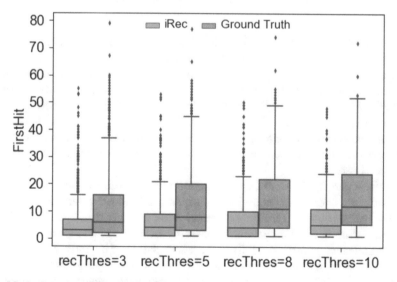

Fig. 6.8 Performance of iRec for FirstHit (RQ1)

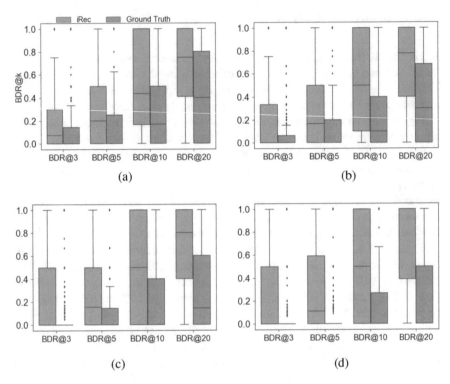

Fig. 6.9 Performance of iRec for BDR@k (RQ1). (**a**) BDR@k for *recThres*=3. (**b**) BDR@k for *recThres*=5. (**c**) BDR@k for *recThres*=8. (**d**) BDR@k for *recThres*=10

approach not only for the power in finding the first "right" workers, but also in terms of the bug detection with the set of recommended workers.

We also notice that for a larger *recThres*, the advantage of iRec over current practice is larger. In detail, when *recThres* is 3, iRec can improve the current practice by 87% (75% vs. 40%) for *BDR@20*, and when *recThres* is 8, the improvement is 460% (80% vs. 14%). This holds true for other metrics. A larger *recThres* might indicate the task is getting tough because no new bugs are reported in quite a long time, and our proposed iRec can help the task get out of the dilemma with new bugs submitted very soon.

Furthermore, for the *recPoint* with larger *FirstHit of Ground Truth*, our proposed approach can shorten the non-yielding window in a larger extent. For example, for the *recPoint* whose *FirstHit of Ground Truth* is larger than 3 (*recThres* is 5), iRec can shorten the non-yielding window by 64% on median (5 vs. 14), while the improvement is 50% (4 vs. 8) in the whole dataset. This further indicates the effectiveness of our approach since for *recPoint* with a larger *FirstHit of Ground Truth*, it is in higher demand for an efficient worker recommendation so that the "right" worker can come soon.

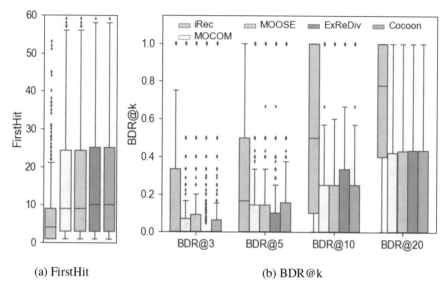

(a) FirstHit   (b) BDR@k

Fig. 6.10 Performance comparison with baselines (RQ1). (**a**) FirstHit. (**b**) BDR@k

In the following sections, we use the experimental setting when *recThres* is 5 for further analysis.

Comparison with Baselines Figure 6.10 demonstrates the comparison results with four baselines. Overall, our proposed iRec significantly (p-value is 0.00) and substantially (Cliff's delta is 0.16–0.23) outperforms the four baselines in terms of *FirstHit* and *BDR@k* (k is 3, 5, 10, and 20). Specifically, iRec can improve the best baseline *MOCOM* by 60% (4 vs. 10) for median *FirstHit*; and the improvement is infinite for median *BDR@k* (e.g., 78% vs. 0 for BDR@20). This is because all the baselines are designed to recommend a set of workers before the task begins and don't consider various context information of the crowdsourced testing process. Besides, the aforementioned baseline approaches do not explicitly consider the activeness of crowd workers which is another cause of performance decline. Furthermore, the baselines' performance are similar to each other which is also due to their limitations of lacking contextual details in one-time worker recommendation.

RQ2: To What Degree iRec Is Sensitive to Different Categories of Context?
The basis of this work is the characterization of the test context model. This research question examines the performance of iRec when removing different sub-category of the context, to understand the context sensitivity of recommendation. Figure 6.11 shows the comparison results between iRec and its six variants. Specifically, *noAct*, *noPref*, *noExp*, and *noDev* are different variants of iRec without activeness, preference, expertise, and device context respectively. Because process context cannot be removed, *noProc* denotes using the process context at the beginning of

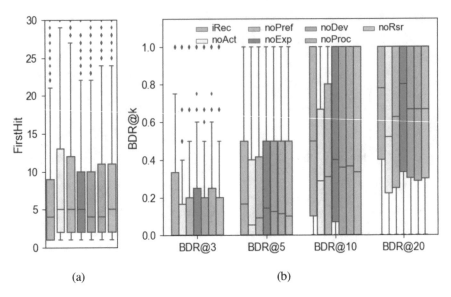

Fig. 6.11 Context sensitivity (RQ2). (**a**) FirstHit. (**b**) BDR@k

a task. We additionally present *noRsr* which denotes using the resource context at the beginning of the task to further demonstrate the necessity of precise context modeling.

We can see that without any type of the resource context (i.e., *noAct*, *noPref*, *noExp*, and *noDev*), the recommendation performance would undergo a decline in both *FirstHit* and *BDR@k*. Without activeness-related context, the *FirstHit* of the recommended workers undergoes a largest variation, i.e., the most sensitive context for recommendation. This might be because this dimension of features is the only one for capturing time-related information, and without them, the model would lack important clues for the crowd workers' time-series behavior. Preference-related context exerts a slightly larger influence on the recommendation performance than expertise-related context, although they are modeled similarly. This might because many crowd workers submitted reports but didn't report bugs, so preference-related context is more informative than experience-related context, thus we can build more effective learning model. The lower performance of *noProc* and *noRsr* compared with iRec further indicates the necessity of the precise context modeling.

RQ3: How Much Is the Diversity Gain by Introducing the Re-Ranking Method in Recommendation?

Besides the learning-based ranking component, we further design a diversity-based re-ranking component to adjust the original ranking. This research question aims at examining its role in recommendation. Table 6.9 first demonstrates the average performance of iRec and *iRec without re-rank*, followed by the distribution of performance increase and decrease of iRec compared with *iRec without re-rank* in all *recPoint*. We can see that with the re-ranking component, the average per-

Table 6.9 Role of re-ranking (RQ3)

	FirstHit	BDR@3	BDR@5	BDR@10	BDR@20
Average performance					
iRec	7.21	21%	32%	48%	67%
iRec without re-rank	8.35	18%	26%	41%	59%
Improvement	13.5%	17.1%	19.6%	15.9%	12.3%
Recommending points					
Performance increase	39%	15%	20%	25%	26%
Performance decrease	27%	9%	12%	15%	12%

formance can be improved by 12%–19%. Specifically, the re-ranking can increase the *BDR@10* in 25% cases, and decrease it in 15% cases. This is because there are large amount of duplicate bugs and increasing the diversity of recommended workers can help decrease the duplicate bugs so as to increase the unique bugs. Furthermore, we can observe that there are more points with performance increase than those with decrease for *BDR@k* with larger *k*. This makes sense because if a crowd worker contributes less to the diversity, he/she would be moved backward so that more unique bugs can be detected earlier; and the larger of examined *k*, the larger possibility for duplicate bugs in terms of the original list, and more room for improvement.

Although the average value for all metrics are increased with re-rank, we admit that the re-ranking component can not always improve the performance. This might be because sometimes the workers ranked earlier are not always those who can detect bugs, and when the re-ranking moves back the similar workers who can actually detect bugs, the bug detection performance would decline. Future work would design more effective re-ranking algorithm to tackle the negative effect on the recommendation performance.

6.3.4 Discussion

6.3.4.1 Benefits of In-Process Recommendation

In-process worker recommendation has great potential to facilitate talent identification and utilization for complex, intelligence-intensive tasks. As presented in the previous sections, the proposed iRec established the crowdsourced testing context model at a dynamic, finer granularity, and constructed two methods to rank and re-rank the most suitable workers based on dynamic testing progress. In this section, we discuss with more details about why practitioners should care about such kind of in-process crowd worker recommendation.

We utilize illustrative examples to demonstrate the benefits of the application of iRec. Figure 6.12 demonstrates two typical bug detection curve using iRec for two *recPoint* of the task in Fig. 6.6a. We can easily see that with iRec, not only

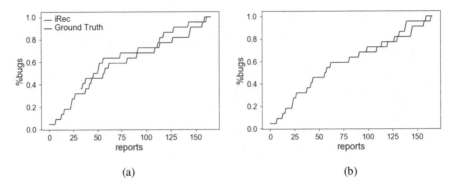

(a)   (b)

Fig. 6.12 Illustrative examples of iRec. (**a**) at report#32. (**b**) at report#86

Table 6.10 Reduced cost with iRec

	recThres=3	recThres=5	recThres=8	recThres=10
1st-quarter	4.8%	4.2%	2.7%	2.8%
median	12.1%	9.8%	8.6%	8.1%
3rd-quarter	21.3%	18.6%	16.7%	16.4%

the current non-yielding window can be shortened, but also the following bug detection efficiency can be improved with the recommended set of workers. In detail, in Fig. 6.12a, we can clearly see that with the recommended workers, the bug detection curve can rise quickly, i.e., with equal number of workers, more bugs can be detected. Also note that, in real-world application of iRec, the in-process recommendation can be conducted dynamically following the new bug detection curve so that the bug detection performance can be further improved. In Fig. 6.12b, although the bug detection curve can not always dominate the current practice, the first "right" worker can be found earlier than current practice. Similarly, with the dynamic recommendation, the current practice of bug detection can be improved.

Based on the metrics in Sect. 6.3.3 that are applied for single *recPoint*, we further measure the **reduced cost** for each crowdsourced testing task if equipped with iRec for in-process crowd worker recommendation. It is measured based on the number of reduced report, i.e., the difference of *FirstHit* value between iRec and *Ground Truth*, following previous work. For a crowdsourced testing task with multiple *recPoint*, we simply add up the reduced cost of each *recPoint*. As shown in Table 6.10, a median of 8% to 12% cost can be reduced, indicating about 10% cost can be saved if equipped with our proposed approach for in-process crowd worker recommendation. Note that, this figure is calculated by simply summing up the reduced cost of single *recPoint* based on the offline evaluation scenario adopted in this work. However, as shown in Fig. 6.12, in real-world practice, the recommendation can be conducted based on the bug arrival curve after the prior recommendation; and the reduced cost should be further improved. Therefore, crowdsourced testing managers could benefit tremendously from actionable insights offered by in-process recommendation systems like iRec.

6.3.4.2 Implication of In-Process Recommendation

Nevertheless, in-process crowd worker recommendation is a complicated, systematic, human-centered problem. By nature, it is more difficult to model than the one-time crowd worker recommendation at the beginning of the task. This is because the non-yielding windows are scattered in the crowdsourced testing process. Although the overall non-yielding reports are in quite large number, some of the non-yielding windows are not long enough to apply the recommendation approach or let the recommendation approach work efficiently. Our observation reveals that an average of 39% cost is wasted on these long-sized non-yielding windows, but the reduced cost by our approach is only about 10% which is far less than the ideal condition. From one point of view, this is because the front part of the non-yielding window (i.e., *recPoint* in the approach) could not be saved because it is needed for determining whether to conduct the worker recommendation. And from another point of view, there is still room for performance improvement.

On the other hand, the true effect of in-process recommendation depends on the potential delays due to interactions between the testing manager, the platform, and the recommended workers. The longer the delays are, the less the benefit can take effect. It is critical for crowdsourced testing platforms, when deploying in-process recommendation systems, to consider how to better streamline the recommendation communication and confirmation functions, in order to minimize the potential delays in bridging the best workers with the tasks under test. For example, the platform may employ instant synchronous messaging service for recommendation communication, and innovate rewarding system to attract more in-process recruitment. More human factor-centered research is needed along this direction to explore systematic approaches for facilitating the adoption of in-process recommendation systems.

Chapter 7
Crowdsourced Testing Task Management

7.1 Introduction

Trade-offs such as "how much testing is enough" are critical yet challenging project decisions in software engineering. Insufficient testing can lead to unsatisfying software quality, while excessive testing can result in potential schedule delays and low cost-effectiveness. This is especially true for crowdsourced testing given the complexity of mobile applications and unpredictability of distributed crowdsourced testing process.

In practice, project managers typically plan for the close of crowdsourced testing tasks solely based on their personal experience. For example, they usually employ duration-based or participant-based condition to close crowdsourced testing tasks through either a fixed period (e.g., 5 days) or a fixed number of participant (e.g., recruiting 400 crowd workers). If either of the criteria is met first, the task will be automatically closed. However, our investigation on real-world crowdsourced testing data reveals that there are large variations in bug arrival rate of crowdsourced testing tasks, and in task's duration and consumed cost for achieving the same quality level. It is very challenging for managers to come up with reasonable experience-based decisions. To avoid insufficient testing, they tend to employ a relatively large threshold for testing period or number of participants. These experience-based decisions could result in ineffective crowdsourced testing process, e.g., an average of 32% wasteful spending in our experimental crowdsourced testing platform. Furthermore, crowdsourced testing is typically treated as a black box process and managers' decisions remain insensitive to its actual progress. This suggests the practical need and potential opportunity to improve current crowdsourced testing practices.

This chapter aims at exploring automated decision support to raise completion awareness w.r.t. crowdsourced testing processes, and manage crowdsourced testing practices more effectively. Particularly, we leverage dynamical bug arrival data associated with crowdsourced testing reports, and investigate whether it is possible to determine that, at certain point of time, a task has obtained satisfactory bug detection level, i.e., being aware of its dynamic completion progress status. The proposed completion-aware crowdsourced testing management approach iSENSE applies incremental sampling technique to process crowdsourced testing reports arriving in chronological order, organizes them into fixed-size groups as dynamic inputs, and integrates Capture-ReCapture (CRC) model and Autoregressive Integrated Moving Average (ARIMA) model to raise awareness of crowdsourced testing progress. It can be utilized for automating crowdsourced testing management and semi-automation of task closing trade-off analysis.

However, iSENSE has one major limitation which seriously effected the practicality of widely deploying this method. It is critically reliant on the manual labeling of duplicate bugs in order to monitor testing progress based on dynamically received crowdsourced testing reports. The labeling processes is time-consuming and error-prone, especially when dealing with large number of reports under the context of crowdsourced testing.

To overcome this limitation, we then propose an extension to iSENSE called iSENSE2.0. This extension improves our prior work in two important ways: (1) Duplicate Tagger which employs semantic analysis technique to automatically determine and label the duplicate status of incoming crowdsourced testing reports; (2) Sanity Checker which integrates coverage-based mechanisms to reduce false alarms in close prediction which contributes to a major cause of performance bottleneck of iSENSE.

Sections 7.2 and 7.3 will respectively introduce these two approaches.

7.2 Completion-Aware Crowdsourced Testing Management

7.2.1 Motivation

To understand the bug arrival patterns of crowdsourced testing in order to better conduct task management, we conduct a pilot study to analyze three metrics, i.e. *bug detection speed*, *bug detection cost*, and *bug detection rate*. The study is conducted based on the dataset described in Sect. 7.2.3.

For each task, we first identify the time when K% bugs have been detected, where K is ranged from 10 to 100. Then, the *bug detection speed* for a task can be derived using the duration (measured in *hours*) between its open time and the time it receives K% bugs. The *bug detection cost* for a task can be derived using the number of submitted reports by reaching K% bugs.

To examine *bug detection rate*, we break the crowdsourced testing reports for each task into 10 equal-sized groups, in chronological order. The rate for each group is derived using the ratio between the number of unique bugs and the number of reports in the corresponding group. In addition, for each crowdsourced testing task,

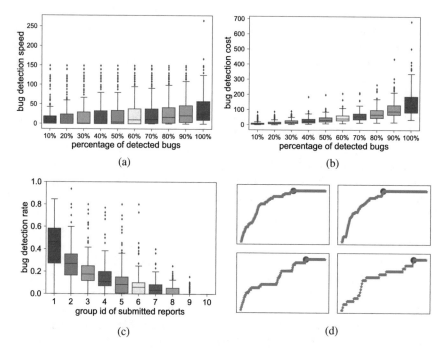

Fig. 7.1 Observations on real-world crowdsourced testing data. (**a**) Bug detection speed. (**b**) Bug detection cost. (**c**) Bug detection rate. (**d**) Bug arrival curve

we also examine the percentage of accumulated bugs (denoted as bug arrival curve) for the previous X reports, where X ranges from 1 to the total number of reports.

The following bug arrival patterns are observed from the analysis results:

(1) Large Variation in Bug Detection Speed and Cost

Figure 7.1a and b demonstrates the distribution of bug detection speed and cost for all tasks. In general, there is large variation in bug detection speed and cost. Specifically, to achieve the same K% bugs, there is large variation in both metrics. This is particularly true for a larger K%. For example, when detecting 90% bugs, the bug detection cost ranges from 3 h to 149 h, and from 27 to 435 reports.

(2) Decreasing Bug Detection Rates Over Time

Figure 7.1c shows the bug detection rate of the 10 break-down groups across all tasks. We can see that the bug detection rate decreases sharply during the crowd-sourced testing process. This signifies that the cost-effectiveness of crowdsourced testing is dramatically decreasing for the later part of the process.

(3) Plateau Effect of Bug Arrival Curve

Figure 7.1d shows typical bug arrival curves for four crowdsourced testing tasks. While they differ, somewhat, note that they all exhibit the same "plateau effect", after which (i.e., red point in Fig. 7.1d) new reports find no new bugs.

We assume the cost spent on these reports after the red point are wasteful spending. In our experimental tasks, there is an average of 32% wasteful spending. The plateau effect together with the large amount of wasteful spending further suggest the potential opportunity and practical need for introducing early closing mechanism (based on the recognition of that plateau) to increase cost-effectiveness of crowdsourced testing.

Needs of Automated Decision Support In addition, an unstructured interview was conducted with the managers, with findings shown below. Project managers commented the black-box nature of crowdsourced testing process. While receiving constantly arriving reports, they are often clueless about the latent bugs, or the required cost to find them. Due to lack of situation awareness, the management of crowdsourced testing is conducted as a guesswork. This frequently results in many blind decisions in task planning and management. Besides, managers typically need to handle large number of crowdsourced testing tasks simultaneously, which is very labor intensive and error-prone in manual planning and management.

In summary, because there are large variations in bug arrival speed and cost, current decision making is largely done by guesswork. This results in low cost-effectiveness of crowdsourced testing. A more effective alternative to manage crowdsourced testing would be to dynamically monitor the crowdsourced testing process and provide actionable decision support for task closing to save unnecessary cost wasting on later arriving reports. Besides, current practice suggests a practical need to empower managers with greater visibility into the crowdsourced testing processes, and ideally raise their awareness about task progress, thus facilitate their decision making.

We intend to address these practical challenges by developing a novel approach for automated decision support in crowdsourced testing management, so as to improve cost-effectiveness of crowdsourced testing.

7.2.2 Approach

Figure 7.2 presents an overview of iSENSE. It consists of three main steps. First, iSENSE adopts an incremental sampling process to model crowdsourced testing reports. During the process, iSENSE converts the raw crowdsourced testing reports arrived chronologically into groups and generates a *bug arrival lookup table* to characterize the bug arrival information. Then, iSENSE integrates two models, i.e. CRC and ARIMA, to predict the total number of bugs contained in the software, and the required cost for achieving certain test objectives, respectively. Finally, iSENSE applies such estimates to support two typical crowdsourced testing decision scenarios, i.e., automating task closing decision, and semi-automation of task closing trade-off analysis. We will present each of the above steps in more details.

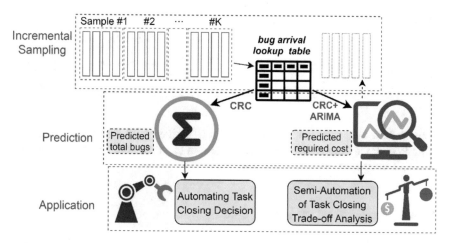

Fig. 7.2 Overview of iSENSE

Table 7.1 Example of bug arrival lookup table

	#1	#2	#3	#4	#5	#6	#7	#8	#9	#10	#11	#12	...
Sample #1	1	1	1	0	0	0	0	0	0	0	0	0	
Sample #2	0	0	1	1	0	0	0	0	0	0	0	0	
Sample #3	0	0	1	0	1	0	0	0	0	0	0	0	
Sample #4	0	0	0	1	1	1	1	1	0	0	0	0	
Sample #5	0	0	1	1	0	0	0	1	1	1	1	0	
Sample #6	1	0	1	0	1	0	0	0	0	0	0	1	
Sample #7							...						

7.2.2.1   Preprocess Data Based on Incremental Sampling Technique

Incremental sampling technique is a composite sampling and processing protocol. Its objective is to obtain a single sample for analysis that has an analytic concentration representative of the decision unit. It improves the reliability and defensibility of sampling data by reducing variability when compared to conventional discrete sampling strategies.

Considering the submitted crowdsourced testing reports of chronological order, when *smpSize* (*smpSize* is an input parameter) reports are received, iSENSE treats it as a representative group to reflect the multiple parallel crowdsourced testing sessions. Remember each report is characterized as: (1) whether it contains a bug; (2) whether it is duplicate of previously submitted reports; if no, it is marked with a new tag; if yes, it is marked with the same tag as the duplicates. During the crowdsourced testing process, we dynamically maintain a two-dimensional *bug arrival lookup table* to record these information.

Table 7.1 provides an illustrative example. After each sample is received, we first add a new row (suppose it is row *i*) in the lookup table. We then go through each report contained in this sample. For the reports not containing a bug, we ignore it. Otherwise, if it is marked with the same tag as existing unique bugs (suppose it is

Table 7.2 Capture-ReCapture models

		Crowd worker's detection capability	
		Identical	Different
Bug detection	Identical	M0 (*M0*)	Mt (*MtCH*)
Probability	Different	Mh (*MhJK, MhCH*)	Mth (*Mth*)

column *j*), record *1* in row *i* column *j*. If it is marked with a new tag, add a new column in the lookup table (suppose it is column *k*), and record *1* in row *i* column *k*. For the empty cells in row *i*, fill it with 0.

7.2.2.2 Predict Total Bugs Using CRC

(1) Background about CRC
The CRC (Capture-ReCapture) model was firstly used to estimate the size of an animal population in biology. In doing so, animals are captured, marked and released on several trapping occasions. The number of marked animals that are recaptured allows one to estimate the total population size based on the samples' overlap. It has also been applied in software inspections to estimate the total number of bugs. Existing CRC models can be categorized into four types according to bug detection probability (i.e. identical vs. different) and crowd worker's detection capability (i.e. identical vs. different), as shown in Table 7.2.

Model *M0* supposes all different bugs and crowd workers have the same detection probability. Model *Mh* supposes that the bugs have different probabilities of being detected. Model *Mt* supposes that the crowd workers have different detection capabilities. Model *Mth* supposes different detection probabilities for different bugs and crowd workers.

Based on the four basic CRC models, various estimators were developed. According to a recent systematic review, *MhJK, MhCH, MtCH* are the three most frequently investigated and most effective estimators in software engineering. Apart from that, we investigate another two estimators (i.e., *M0* and *Mth*) to ensure all four basic models are investigated.

(2) How to Use in iSENSE
iSENSE treats each sample as a capture (or recapture). At the end of each capture, after updating the *bug arrival lookup table*, iSENSE predicts the total number of bugs in the software[1] based on current lookup table. The following subsections provide details about how to utilize the aforementioned five CRC estimators to obtain the estimated bugs.

---

[1] To be precise, what we predict is the total number of potential bugs that are uncovered by crowdsourced testing.

Table 7.3 Variables meaning and computation

Var.	Meaning	Computation based on bug arrival lookup table	Example value
Variables for computing M0			
n_1	Number of bugs in the first round	Count the number of columns with *1* in the first half samples (i.e., sample 1–3)	5
n_2	Number of bugs in the second round	Count the number of columns with *1* in the second half samples (i.e., sample 4–6)	11
m	Number of bugs detected in both rounds	Count the number of columns both with *1* in the first half samples (i.e., sample 1–3) and with *1* in the second half samples (i.e., sample 4–6)	4
Variables for computing Mth, MhJK, MhCH, MtCH			
D	Actual number of bugs captured so far	Number of columns	12
t	Number of captures	Number of rows	6
n_j	Number of bugs detected in each capture	Number of cells with *1* in row j	3, 2, 2, 5, 6, 4
f_k	Number of bugs captured exactly k times in all captures, i.e., $\sum f_k = D$	Count the number of cells with *1* in each column, and denote as r_i; f_k is the number of r_i with value k	1=7, 2=2, 3=2, 5=1
Z_p	Number of bugs captured only in the p_{th} capture, i.e., $\sum Z_p = f_1$	For each row, examine the cell with *1*, if there are no other cells with *1* in the specific column, denote the cell as *true*, otherwise denote as *false*; Z_p is the number of cells with *true* in row p	1=1, 4=2, 5=3, 6=1
Estimated total number of bugs			
	Estimation by M0	with n_1, n_2, m	14
	Estimation by Mth	with D, t, n_j, f_k	24
	Estimation by MhJK	with D, t, f_1	18
	Estimation by MhCH	with D, t, f_1, f_2, f_3	34
	Estimation by MtCH	with D, t, f_2, Z_p	18

Apply M0 Estimators *M0* estimator predicts the total number of bugs based on Eq. 7.1. Table 7.3 shows the meaning of each variable, how to compute its value based on the bug arrival lookup table in Table 7.1. Note that, we simply treat $n_1 \times n_2$ as the total number when m is 0.

$$N_0 = \frac{n_1 \times n_2}{m} \tag{7.1}$$

Apply Mth Estimators *Mth* estimator predicts the total number of bugs based on Eqs. 7.2, 7.3. Table 7.3 shows the meaning of each variable, how to compute its value based on the bug arrival lookup table in Table 7.1.

$$N_{th} = \frac{D}{C} + \frac{f_1}{C}\gamma^2, C = 1 - \frac{f_1}{\sum_{k=1}^{t} k f_k} \tag{7.2}$$

$$\gamma^2 = max\{\frac{\frac{D}{C}\sum_k k(k-1)f_k}{2\sum\sum_{j<k}n_j n_k} - 1, 0\} \tag{7.3}$$

Apply MhJK Estimators *MhJK* estimator is similar with *Mth* method, except its equation for estimating the total number of bugs in Eq. 7.4. Table 7.3 shows the meaning of each variable, how to compute its value based on the bug arrival lookup table in Table 7.1.

$$N = D + \frac{t-1}{t}f_1 \tag{7.4}$$

Note that, the *MhJK* estimation has three other expressions. We use all four expressions, and choose the right estimator through hypothesis testing.

Apply MhCH Estimators *MhCH* estimator is similar with *Mth* method, except its equation for estimating the total number of bugs in Eqs. 7.5, 7.6. Table 7.3 shows the meaning of each variable, how to compute its value based on the bug arrival lookup table in Table 7.1.

$$N = D + \frac{f_1^2}{2f_2} \tag{7.5}$$

or

$$N = D + \frac{[\frac{f_1^2}{2f_2}][1 - \frac{2f_2}{tf_1}]}{1 - \frac{3f_3}{tf_2}}, \text{ if } tf_1 > 2f_2, tf_2 > 3f_3, 3f_1f_2 > 2f_2^2 \tag{7.6}$$

Apply MtCH Estimators *MtCH* estimator is also similar with *Mth* method, except its equation for estimating the total number of bugs in Eq. 7.7. Table 7.3 shows the meaning of each variable, how to compute its value based on the bug arrival lookup table in Table 7.1.

$$N = D + \frac{\sum_{i=1}^{t}\sum_{j=i+1}^{t} Z_i Z_j}{f_2 + 1} \tag{7.7}$$

7.2.2.3 Predict Required Cost Using ARIMA

(1) Background about ARIMA

ARIMA (Autoregressive Integrated Moving Average) model is commonly used to model time series data to forecast the future values. It extends ARMA (Autoregressive Moving Average) model by allowing for non-stationary time series to be modeled, i.e., a time series whose statistical properties such as mean, variance, etc. are not constant over time.

A time series is said to be autoregressive moving average (ARMA) in nature with parameters (p, q), if it takes the following form:

$$y_t = \sum_{i=1}^{p} \phi_i y_{t-i} + \sum_{i=1}^{q} \theta_i \epsilon_{t-i} + \epsilon_t \tag{7.8}$$

where y_t is the current stationary observation, y_{t-i} for $i = 1, ..., p$ are the past stationary observations, ϵ_t is the current error, and ϵ_{t-i} for $i = 1, ..., q$ are the past errors. If this original time series $\{z_t\}$ is non-stationary, then d differences can be done to transform it into a stationary one $\{y_t\}$. These differences can be viewed as a transformation denoted by $y_t = \nabla^d z_t$, where $\nabla^d = (1 - B)^d$ where B is known as a backshift operator. When this differencing operation is performed, it converts an ARMA model into an ARIMA model with parameters (p, q, d).

(2) How to Use in iSENSE

Figure 7.3 demonstrates how ARIMA is applied in predicting future trend of bug arrival. We treat the reports of each sample as a window, and obtain the number of unique bugs submitted in each sample from the bug arrival lookup table (i.e., number of cells in the row whose value is *1* and the corresponding column does not have other *1*). Then we use the former *trainSize* windows to fit the ARIMA model and predict the number of bugs for the later *predictSize* windows. When new window is formed with the newly-arrived reports, we move the window by 1 and obtain the newly predicted results.

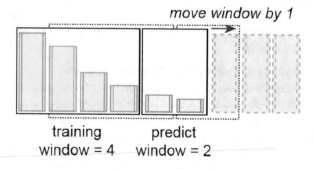

Fig. 7.3 Illustrative example of ARIMA

Suppose one want to know how much extra cost is required for achieving certain test objective (i.e., $X\%$ bugs). As we already know the predicted total number of bugs, we can figure out how many bugs should be detected in order to meet the test objective; suppose it is Y bugs. Based on the prediction of ARIMA, we then obtain when the number of Y bugs can be received, suppose it needs extra K_i reports. In this way, we assume K_i is the required cost for meeting the test objective.

7.2.2.4 Apply iSENSE to Two Decision Scenarios in Crowdsourced Testing

To demonstrate the usefulness of iSENSE, we generalize two typical decision scenarios in crowdsourced testing management, and illustrate its application to each scenario.

(1) Automating Task Closing Decision

The first scenario that can benefit from the prediction of total bugs of iSENSE is decision automation of dynamic task closing. As soon as a crowdsourced testing task begins, iSENSE can be applied to monitor the actual bug arrival, constantly update the bug arrival lookup table, as well as keep tracking of the percentage of bugs detected (i.e., the ratio of the number of submitted reports so far over the predicted total bugs).

In such scenario, different task close criteria can be customized in iSENSE so that it automatically closes the task when the specified criterion is met. For instance, a simple criterion would be to close the task when 100% bugs have been detected in submitted reports. Under this criterion, when iSENSE monitors 100% bugs have received and the prediction remains unchanged for successive two captures, it determines the time, when the last report was received, as the close time; and would automatically close the crowdsourced testing task at run time. Note that the restriction of two successive captures is to ensure the stability of the prediction. We also experimented with other restrictions (i.e., 1–5), results turn out that restriction with 2 can obtain relative good and stable performance; hence we only present these results due to space limit.

iSENSE supports flexible customization of the close criteria. As an example, a task manager can set to close his/her tasks when 80% bugs have been detected. Consequently, iSENSE will help to monitor and close the task by reacting to these customized close criteria.

(2) Semi-Automation of Task Closing Trade-off Analysis

The second scenario that benefits from the prediction of required cost of iSENSE is decision support of task closing trade-off analysis. For example, suppose 90% bugs have been reported at certain time, iSENSE can simultaneously reveal the estimated required cost for detecting an additional $X\%$ bugs (i.e., 5%), in order to achieve a higher bug detection level. Such cost-benefit related insights can provide managers with more confidence in making informed, actionable decision on whether to close immediately, if the required cost is too high to be worthwhile for additional $X\%$

detected bugs; or wait a little longer, if the required cost is acceptable and additional X% detected bugs is desired.

7.2.3 Experiment

This section first describes our experiment design, followed by the results and analysis.

7.2.3.1 Experiment Design

(1) Experimental Setup

We have collected 218 mobile application testing tasks with various domains from a popular crowdsourced testing platform. The minimum, average, and maximum number of crowdtesting reports (*and unique bugs*) per task are 101 (*8*), 175 (*23*), and 798 (*99*), respectively.

For RQ1, we set up 19 checkpoints in the range of receiving 10–100% reports, with an increment interval of 5% in between. At each checkpoint, we obtain the estimated total number of bugs at that time. Based on the ground truth of actual total bugs, we then figure out the MRE in predicting the total bugs for each task.

For RQ2, we also set 19 checkpoints as RQ1. Different from RQ1, the checkpoints of RQ2 is based on the percentage of detected bugs, i.e. from 10% bugs to 100% bugs with an increment of 5% in between. At each checkpoint, we predict the required test cost to achieve an additional 5% bugs, i.e. target corresponding to the next checkpoint. For example, at the checkpoint when 80% bugs have detected, we predict the required cost for achieving 85% bugs. Based on the ground truth of actual required cost, we then figure out the MRE in predicting required cost.

For RQ3, we analyze the effectiveness of task closing automation with respect to five sample close criteria, i.e., close the task when 80%, 85%, 90%, 95%, or 100% bugs have detected, respectively. The reason why we choose these criteria is that we assume it is almost meaningless to close a task when less than 80% bugs being detected.

For RQ4, we use several illustrative cases from experimental projects to show how iSENSE can help trade-off decisions.

For all these experiments, we employ a commonly-used longitudinal data setup as Sect. 5.2.3.

(2) Evaluation Metrics

We measure the **accuracy** of prediction based on Magnitude of Relative Error, a.k.a. *MRE*, which is the most commonly-used measure for accuracy. It measures the relative error ratio between the actual value and predicted value, expressed as follows: It is applied in the prediction of total number of bugs and required cost.

$$MRE = \frac{|actual\ value - predicted\ value|}{actual\ value} \qquad (7.9)$$

We measure the ***cost-effectiveness*** of close prediction based on two metrics, i.e. bug detection level (i.e. %bug) and cost reduction (i.e. %reducedCost).

%bug is the percentage of bugs detected by the predicted close time. We treat the number of historical detected bugs as the total number. The larger *%bug*, the better.

%reducedCost is the percentage of saved cost by the predicted close time. To derive this metric, we first obtain the percentage of reports submitted at the close time, in which we treat the number of historical submitted reports as the total number. We suppose this is the percentage of consumed cost and %reducedCost is derived using 1 minus the percentage of consumed cost. The larger *%reducedCost*, the better.

Intuitively, an increase in %bug would be accompanied with a decrease in %reducedCost. Motivated by the F1 (or F-Measure) in prediction approaches of software engineering, we further derive an analogous metric *F1*, to measure the harmonic mean of %bug and %reducedCost as follows:

$$F1 = \frac{2 \times \%bug \times \%reducedCost}{\%bug + \%reducedCost} \qquad (7.10)$$

(3) Baselines
We compare iSENSE with two baselines.

Rayleigh [41] This baseline is adopted from one of the most classical models for predicting the dynamic defect arrival in software measurement. Generally, it supposes the defect arrival data following the Rayleigh probability distribution. In this experiment, we implement code to fit specific Rayleigh curve (i.e. the derived Rayleigh model) based on each task's bug arrival data, then predict the total bugs and required cost for certain test objectives (with the future bug trend) using the derived Rayleigh model.

Naive This baseline is designed to employ naive empirical results, i.e. the median value of the dataset. Specifically, for the prediction of total bugs, it uses the median total bugs calculated based on the tasks of training set. For required cost, it uses the median required cost from training set, in terms of the corresponding checkpoint.

(4) Parameter Tuning
For each CRC estimator, the input parameter is *smpSize*, which represents how many reports are considered in each capture. We tune the optimal parameter value based on the training set and apply it in the testing set to evaluate the performance. In detail, for every candidate parameter value (we experiment from 1 to 50) and for each checkpoint, we obtain the MRE for the prediction of total bugs for each task in the training set. We then calculate the median of these MRE values, and sum the median across all checkpoints for each candidate parameter value. We treat the

parameter value, under which the smallest sum is obtained, as the best one. For ARIMA model, we use the same method for deciding the best parameter value.

7.2.3.2   Results and Analysis

RQ1: To What Degree Can iSENSE Accurately Predict Total Bugs?
The first two research questions are centered around accuracy evaluation of the prediction of total bugs and required cost. Presumably, to support practical decision making, these underlying predictions should achieve high accuracy. Table 7.4 demonstrates the median and standard deviation for the *MRE* of predicted total bugs for all five CRC estimators. The columns correspond to different checkpoints, and the best two performer under each checkpoint are highlighted (in italic font and red color). We additionally present the detailed performance for *Mth* (the best estimator) in Fig. 7.4.

From Table 7.4 and Fig. 7.4, we can see that, the predicted total number of bugs becomes more close to the actual total number of bugs (i.e., *MRE* decreases) towards the end of the tasks. Among the five estimators, *M0* and *Mth* have the smallest median *MRE* for most checkpoints. But the variance of *M0* is much larger than that of *Mth*. Hence, estimator *Mth* is more preferred because of its relatively higher stability and accurate prediction in total number of bugs. In the following experiments, if not specially mentioned, the results are referring to those generated from iSENSE with *Mth* estimator.

Comparison With Baselines Table 7.5 compares the prediction accuracy of iSENSE and the two baselines, in terms of the median and standard deviation of *MRE*. It shows that iSENSE significantly outperforms the two baselines, especially during the later stage (i.e. after the 40% checkpoint) of the crowdsourced testing tasks.

To summarize, iSENSE with the best estimator *Mth* is accurate in predicting the total bugs in crowdsourced testing, and significantly outperforms the two baselines. Specifically, the median of predicted total bugs is nearly equal with the ground truth

Table 7.4 Statistics for MRE of predicted total bugs (RQ1)

	10%	15%	20%	25%	30%	35%	40%	45%	50%	55%	60%	65%	70%	75%	80%	85%	90%	95%	100%
	Median																		
M0	0.35	*0.25*	0.28	0.21	0.16	0.14	0.09	*0.07*	0.07	*0.05*	*0.04*	*0.03*	*0.03*	*0.00*	*0.00*	*0.00*	*0.00*	*0.00*	*0.00*
MtCH	0.41	0.32	0.28	*0.18*	*0.14*	0.13	0.09	*0.08*	0.08	0.06	0.05	0.04	0.03	0.03	0.03	*0.00*	*0.00*	*0.00*	*0.00*
MhCH	0.38	*0.25*	0.24	0.22	0.19	0.13	0.12	0.09	0.08	0.07	0.06	0.05	0.04	0.03	0.01	*0.00*	*0.00*	*0.00*	*0.00*
MhJK	*0.08*	*0.08*	*0.08*	*0.09*	*0.08*	*0.09*	*0.08*	0.09	0.11	0.10	0.09	0.09	0.10	0.10	0.08	0.07	0.06	0.05	0.04
Mth	*0.32*	0.28	*0.22*	0.18	0.16	*0.12*	*0.09*	0.08	*0.06*	*0.05*	*0.05*	*0.04*	*0.03*	*0.01*	*0.00*	*0.00*	*0.00*	*0.00*	*0.00*
	Standard deviation																		
M0	0.33	0.35	0.33	0.33	0.33	0.32	0.31	0.30	0.27	0.24	0.21	0.17	0.17	0.16	0.12	0.10	*0.06*	*0.07*	*0.04*
MtCH	0.33	0.32	0.31	0.30	0.30	0.27	0.24	0.19	0.16	*0.11*	0.13	*0.09*	*0.10*	*0.09*	*0.09*	0.09	0.09	0.09	0.05
MhCH	0.30	0.33	0.30	0.28	0.29	0.25	0.23	0.19	0.15	0.20	0.20	0.17	0.15	0.15	0.17	0.15	0.17	0.17	0.10
MhJK	*0.14*	*0.14*	*0.14*	*0.13*	*0.13*	*0.12*	*0.12*	*0.11*	*0.11*	0.12	*0.12*	0.12	0.12	0.13	0.13	0.12	0.12	0.10	0.07
Mth	0.27	0.27	0.28	0.27	0.26	0.23	0.19	0.15	0.10	0.09	0.08	0.07	0.06	0.06	0.06	0.05	0.05	0.03	0.03

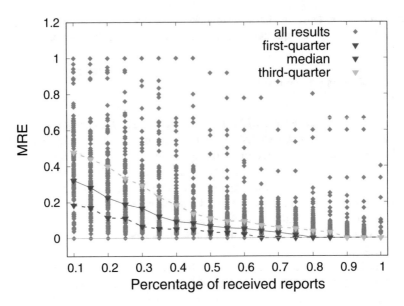

Fig. 7.4 MRE of predicted total bugs of **Mth** (RQ1)

Table 7.5 Comparison with baselines in MRE of predicted total bugs (RQ1)

	10%	15%	20%	25%	30%	35%	40%	45%	50%	55%	60%	65%	70%	75%	80%	85%	90%	95%	100%
Median																			
iSENSE	0.32	*0.28*	*0.22*	*0.18*	*0.16*	*0.12*	*0.09*	0.08	*0.06*	*0.05*	*0.05*	*0.04*	*0.03*	*0.01*	*0.00*	*0.00*	*0.00*	*0.00*	*0.00*
Rayleigh	0.50	0.43	0.35	0.28	0.27	0.27	0.27	0.27	0.26	0.27	0.27	0.27	0.28	0.28	0.28	0.28	0.27	0.17	0.16
Naive	*0.29*	0.29	0.29	0.29	0.29	0.29	0.29	0.29	0.29	0.29	0.29	0.29	0.29	0.29	0.29	0.29	0.29	0.29	0.16
Standard deviation																			
iSENSE	0.27	0.27	0.28	0.27	0.26	0.23	*0.19*	*0.15*	*0.10*	*0.09*	*0.08*	*0.07*	*0.06*	*0.06*	*0.06*	*0.05*	*0.05*	*0.03*	*0.03*
Rayleigh	*0.23*	*0.26*	*0.25*	*0.23*	*0.22*	*0.21*	0.24	0.26	0.28	0.40	0.40	0.51	0.54	0.58	0.58	0.55	0.41	0.39	0.29
Naive	0.40	0.40	0.40	0.40	0.40	0.40	0.40	0.40	0.40	0.40	0.40	0.40	0.40	0.40	0.40	0.40	0.40	0.40	0.20

Table 7.6 Statistics and comparison with baselines for MRE of predicted required cost (RQ2)

	10%	15%	20%	25%	30%	35%	40%	45%	50%	55%	60%	65%	70%	75%	80%	85%	90%	95%	100%
Median																			
iSENSE	*0.33*	*0.25*	*0.15*	*0.13*	*0.13*	*0.10*	*0.08*	*0.06*	*0.07*	*0.06*	*0.04*	*0.03*	*0.04*	*0.04*	*0.05*	*0.04*	*0.05*	*0.06*	*0.06*
Rayleigh	1.01	0.66	0.37	0.33	0.25	0.18	0.14	0.11	0.12	0.10	0.08	0.07	0.08	0.08	0.07	0.08	0.10	0.17	0.14
Empirical	*0.33*	0.40	*0.15*	*0.13*	0.17	0.18	0.10	0.11	0.12	0.13	0.09	0.10	0.10	0.10	0.12	0.12	0.15	0.16	0.18
Standard deviation																			
iSENSE	*0.79*	*0.57*	*0.36*	*0.48*	*0.26*	*0.24*	*0.20*	*0.22*	*0.12*	*0.13*	*0.13*	*0.12*	*0.11*	*0.13*	*0.13*	*0.08*	*0.11*	*0.13*	*0.11*
Rayleigh	1.33	0.93	0.63	0.70	0.39	0.33	0.28	0.29	0.17	0.34	0.30	0.34	0.27	0.38	0.40	0.35	0.38	0.40	0.20
Naive	*0.79*	0.76	*0.36*	*0.48*	0.33	0.33	0.24	0.29	0.17	0.20	0.17	0.16	0.15	0.19	0.22	0.14	0.18	0.30	0.19

(i.e., *MRE* < 0.06) with a standard deviation of less than 10% during the latter half of the process.

RQ2: To What Degree Can iSENSE Accurately Predict Required Cost to Achieve Certain Test Objectives?

Table 7.6 summarizes the comparison of median and standard deviation of the *MRE* of predicted required cost across iSENSE and the two baselines, with columns corresponding to different checkpoints. We highlight the methods with the best performance under each checkpoint.

As indicated by the decreasing median *MRE* in Table 7.6, the prediction of required cost becomes increasingly accurate for later checkpoints. For example, after 50% checkpoint, the median *MRE* of predicted cost is lower than 6%, with about 13% standard deviation. This implies that iSENSE can effectively predict the required cost to target test objectives.

Comparison with Baselines   We can see that the median and standard deviation of *MRE* for two baselines are worse than *iSENSE* during the second half of the task process. This further signifies the advantages of the proposed iSENSE.

To summarize, iSENSE can predict the required test cost within averagely 6% *MRE* for later stage of crowdsourced testing.

RQ3: To What Extent Can iSENSE Help Increase the Effectiveness of Crowd-sourced Testing Through Decision Automation?
The next two research questions are focused on investigating the effectiveness of applying iSENSE in the two typical scenarios, in which iSENSE is expected to facilitate current practices through automated and semi-automated decision support in managing crowdsourced testing tasks. Figure 7.5 shows the distribution of *%bug*, *%reducedCost*, and *F1* for five customized close criteria.

Let us first look at the last series of three boxes in Fig. 7.5, which reflects a close criterion of 100% bugs being detected (i.e., most commonly-used setup). The results indicate that a median of 100% bugs can be detected with 30% median cost reduction. This suggests an additional 30% more cost-effectiveness for managers if equipped with such a decision automation tool as iSENSE to monitor and close tasks

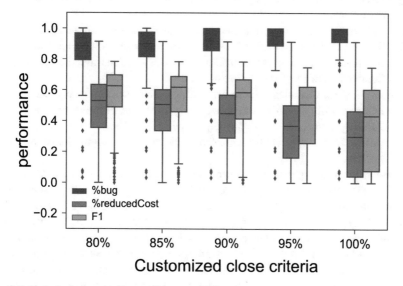

Fig. 7.5   Task closing automation performance (RQ3)

automatically at run-time. The reduced cost is a tremendous figure when considering the large number of tasks delivered in a crowdsourced testing platform. In addition, the standard deviation is relatively low, further signifying the stability of iSENSE.

We then shift our focus on other four customized close criteria (i.e., 80%, 85%, 90%, and 95% in terms of percentage of detected bugs). We can observe that for each close criterion, the median %bug generated from iSENSE is very close to the targeted close criterion, with small standard deviation. Among these close criteria, 36–52% cost can be saved, which further signify the effectiveness of iSENSE.

We also notice that, the median %bug is a little larger than the customized close criterion. For example, if the project manager hopes to close the task when 90% bugs detected, a median of 92% bugs have submitted at the predicted close time. This implies, in most cases, the close prediction produced by iSENSE does not have the risk of insufficient testing. Furthermore, we have talked with the project managers and they thought, detecting slightly more bugs (even with less reduced cost) is always better than detecting fewer bugs (with more reduced cost). This is because %bug is more like the constraint, while %reducedCost is only the bonus.

We also analyze the reason for this phenomenon. It is mainly because, before suggesting close, our approach requires the predicted total bugs remain unchanged for two successive captures. This restriction is to alleviate the risk of insufficient percentage of detected bugs. Besides, this is also because we treat a sample of reports as the unit during the prediction, which can also potentially result in the close time being a little later than the customized close time.

To summarize, the automation of task closing by iSENSE can make crowd-sourced testing more cost-effective, i.e., a median of 100% bugs can be detected with 30% saved cost.

RQ4: How iSENSE Can Be Applied to Facilitate the Trade-off Decisions about Cost-Effectiveness?

Trade-off between investment and outcomes is important for optimizing the resource allocation. To reflect such trade-off context, we randomly pick a time and slice the experimental dataset to retrieve all tasks under testing at that time, then examine the cost-effectiveness of more testing on those tasks.

Figure 7.6 demonstrates 4 trade-off analysis examples across 6 tasks (i.e. *P1-P6*), generated from repeating the above analysis at four different time points (i.e. corresponding to *time1* to *time4* in a sequential order). The y-axis denotes the next test objective to achieve, while x-axis shows the predicted required cost to achieve that objective.

Generally speaking, the crowdsourced testing tasks in the right area are less cost-effective than the tasks in the left area. For example, at *time3*, *P6* is estimated to require additional 14 cost in order to achieve 100% test objective. If the manager is facing budget constraints or trying to improve cost-effectiveness, he/she could choose to close *P6* at *time3*, because it is the least effective one among all tasks.

To facilitate such kind of trade-off analysis on which task to close and when to close, we design two decision parameters as inputs from decision maker: (1) *quality benchmark* which sets the minimal threshold for bug detection level, e.g. the

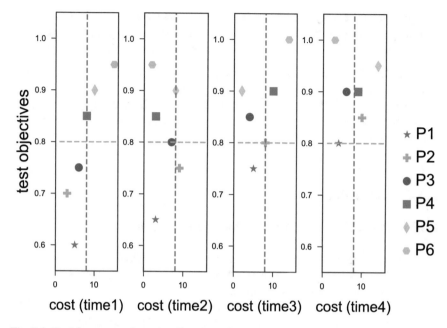

Fig. 7.6 Decision support for trade-off analysis (RQ4)

horizontal red lines in Fig. 7.6; (2) *cost benchmark* which sets the maximal threshold for required cost to achieve the next objective, e.g. the vertical blue lines in Fig. 7.6.

These two benchmarks split the tasks into four regions at each slicing time (as indicated by the four boxes in each subfigure of Fig. 7.6). Each region suggests different insights on the test sufficiency as well as cost-effectiveness for more testing, which can be used as heuristics to guide actionable decision-making at run time. More specifically:

- *Lower-Left (Continue)*: Tasks in this region are low hanging fruits, only requiring relatively less cost to achieve next test objective, and quality level is not acceptable yet; this indicates the most cost-effective option and testing should definitely continue.
- *Lower-Right (Drill down)*: Tasks here have not met the quality benchmark, so continue testing is preferred even though they require significant more cost to achieve quality objective. In addition, it also suggests that the task is either difficult to test, or the current crowd worker participation is not sufficient. Therefore, managers would probably want to drill down in these tasks, and see if more testing guidelines or worker incentives are needed.
- *Upper-Left (Think twice)*: Tasks here already meet their quality benchmark, possibly reaching next higher quality level if with little additional cost investment. Managers should think twice before they take the action.

- *Upper-Right (Close)*: Tasks in this region require relatively more cost to reach next test objective, and current bug detection level is already high enough. This indicates that it is practical to close them considering the cost-effectiveness.

Note that, the two benchmarks in Fig. 7.6 can be customized according to practical needs.

To summarize, iSENSE provides practical insights to help managers make trade-off analysis on which task to close or when to close, based on two benchmark parameters and a set of decision heuristics.

7.2.4 Discussion

7.2.4.1 Best CRC Estimator for Crowdsourced Testing

In traditional software inspection or testing activities, *MhJK*, *MhCH*, and *MtCH* have been recognized as the most effective estimators for total bugs. However, in crowdsourced testing, the most comprehensive estimator *Mth* outperforms the other CRC estimators. This is reasonable because crowdsourced testing is conducted by a diversified pool of crowd workers with different levels of capability, experience, testing devices, and the nature of bugs in the software under test also vary greatly in terms of types, causes, and detection difficulty, etc. In such cases, *Mth*, which assumes different detection probability for both bugs and crowd workers, supposes to be the most suitable estimator for crowdsourced testing.

7.2.4.2 Necessity for More Time-Sensitive Analytics in Crowdsourced Testing Decision Support

As discussed earlier in the background and motivational pilot study, challenges associated with crowdsourced testing management mainly lie in two aspects: uncertainty in crowd worker's performance and lack of visibility into crowdsourced testing progress. We believe there is an increasing need for introducing more time-sensitive analytics during crowdsourced testing process to support better decision making to fully realize the potential benefits of crowdsourced testing.

iSENSE can generate time-based information revealing dynamic crowdsourced testing progress and provide practical guidelines to help managers make trade-off analysis on which task to close or when to close, based on a set of decision heuristics. Besides, iSENSE provides additional visibility into the testing progress and insights for effective task management along with the crowdsourced testing process. The experimental results have proven that a significant portion of crowd-sourced testing cost can be saved through employing our effective decision support approach. This is extremely encouraging and we look forward to more discussion and innovative decision support techniques in this direction.

7.3 Improving Completion-Aware Crowdsourced Testing Management with Duplicate Tagger and Sanity Checker

7.3.1 Motivation

Section 7.2 has analyzed the *bug arrival speed*, *bug arrival cost*, and *bug arrival rate* to explore the bug arrival patterns of crowdsourced testing. This section categorizes the bug arrival curves to further motivate the crowdsourced testing task closing. We employ a two-step rule-based method to group empirical bug arrival curves into three categories to further motivate this study.

In the first step, each bug arrival curve is examined from the start to end, for the existence of a flat-interval and the *knee point* according to an empirically-derived rule (i.e. Rule 1), indicating that during the interval of dozens of reports, the number of detected unique bugs remains unchanged. In another word, all reports received during the flat interval do not involve new bugs. In the second step, we employ three more rules (i.e. Rule 2–4) for comparing actual bug detection rate by knee point with empirically-derived thresholds to categorize a bug arrival curve into its corresponding group. More specifically, the rules are summarized as follows:

- *Rule (1)* If a bug arrival curve contains a flat-interval exceeding a pre-specified value, e.g. 20, the bug reports corresponding to the end of the interval is identified as the knee point of the bug arrival curve;
- *Rule (2)* If all bugs have been revealed at the knee point identified by Rule 1, the task belongs to *Category I Rise-Stay*;
- *Rule (3)* If more than 80% bugs have been revealed by the knee-point, the task belongs to *Category II Rise-Stay-Slight Rise*;
- *Rule (4)* Otherwise, the task belongs to *Category III Rise-Stay-Rise*.

Note that, the number 20 and 80% are empirically-derived thresholds for analyzing and demonstrating the trend, not for study evaluation purpose. The rule-based categorization results show that across the experimental tasks, the proportion is 36% belonging to Category I, 48% belonging to Category II, and 16% belonging to Category III, respectively. Figure 7.7 illustrates 9 example tasks, 3 from each category, denoted in T1–T9 (*Ti* denotes crowdsourced testing task *i*).

T1, T2, and T3 are from the first category *Rise-Stay*. We can see that for these tasks, with the increase of submitted reports, the percentage of detected bugs would first increase sharply and remain unchanged during the latter part of the task.

T4, T5, and T6 are from the second category *Rise-Stay-Slight Rise*. For tasks of this category, with the increase of submitted reports, the percentage of detected bugs would first increase, remain unchanged in the rear part of the task, and increase slightly.

The third category *Rise-Stay-Rise* is more complicated, as shown in the curve of T7, T8, and T9. Unlike the first two categories, bug arrival curves in Category III have multiple sharp increase, connected by flat-intervals in between.

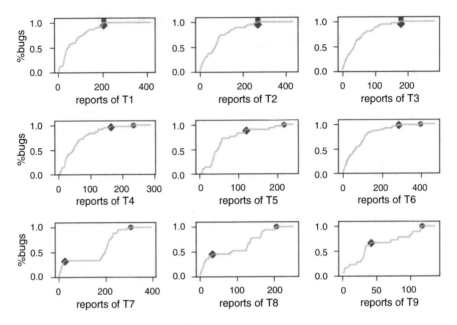

Fig. 7.7 Three categories of bug arrival curve

Challenges in Accurate Task Closing Prediction In Sect. 7.2.1, we mentioned that the plateau point indicates the close time, and the previously proposed iSENSE (in Sect. 7.2) tried to predict the close time based on the auto recognized plateau point. The *knee point* can be treated as the auto recognized plateau point. Through comparing between the knee point (i.e., blue diamonds in Fig. 7.7) and the actual plateau point (i.e., red points in Fig. 7.7), we discuss the drawback of previously proposed iSENSE.

For *Category I*, the plateau point can usually be accurately recognized based on the arrival trend of bugs, i.e., the red dot coincides with the blue diamond. If the crowdsourced testing platform can close the task at this point, a large portion of cost can be saved without sacrifice the testing quality (i.e., number of detected bugs).

Compared with Category I, the tasks of *Category II* exhibit slight increases in the bug numbers after the auto recognized knee point (i.e., blue diamond), i.e., an average of 8.6% bugs found after the knee point in our experimental crowdsourced testing tasks. If the crowdsourced testing platform closes the task in the knee point, the task would be more cost-effective, although a very small portion of bugs would not be detected.

For *Category III*, there is significant increase in bug number after the auto recognized knee point, i.e., an average of 35% bugs found after the knee point in our experimental crowdsourced testing tasks. The existence of Category III can bring "false-alarm" errors with prior proposed approach iSENSE because the knee points (i.e. the blue diamonds) are generally far early than the ideal closing points (i.e. the red dots). Furthermore, the semantic analysis adopted in this approach would potentially increase the ratio of this category; thus could greatly degrade the performance.

In short, the plateau point of the crowdsourced testing tasks in the first category and second category can be easily approximated and recognized based on the dynamics of bug arrival. On the contrary, the identification of the plateau point of the third category is problematic and prone to false alarms which negatively affect the prediction accuracy of iSENSE. This motivates us to develop new strategy to prevent such false-alarms, in order to improve the close prediction performance.

To summarize, iSENSE proposed in previous section leverages dynamical bug arrival data associated with crowdsourced testing reports to support the automation of close decision. However, Category III bug arrival curve indicates that it is insufficient and risky to solely based on the dynamics of bug arrival. There is need to employ additional strategy to reduce false alarms and provide more sensitive closing decision. This section intends to address these practical challenges by developing an extended approach of iSENSE for automated closing decision support in crowdsourced testing management, so as to improve cost-effectiveness of crowdsourced testing.

7.3.2   Approach

Figure 7.8 presents an overview of iSENSE2.0. It contains four main components, i.e. incremental sampling, duplicate tagger, CRC-based close estimator, and coverage-based sanity checker. More specifically, iSENSE2.0 first preprocesses the crowdsourced testing reports employing incremental sampling technique. Second, a semantic-based Duplicate Tagger is designed to automate the labelling of duplicate testing reports, the output from this component is the bug arrival lookup table recording all unique bugs and the occurrence of their duplicates. Third, the CRC-

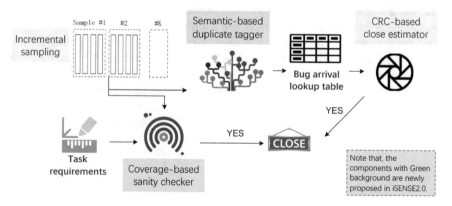

Fig. 7.8 Overview of iSENSE2.0

based close decision is derived based on the bug arrival lookup table and the CRC-based (Capture-ReCapture model) close estimator. Fourth, the coverage-based Sanity Checker verifies the term coverage at the predicted closing time, in order to prevent false-alarms associated with the *Stay* phase, as discussed in the pilot study from Sect. 2.3. The final close decision is constrained on two guarding conditions: one is passing the CRC-based close decision, and the other is passing the coverage-based sanity check. We will present each component in more details at below.

7.3.2.1   Incremental Sampling

Incremental sampling works as it is in iSENSE (Sect. 7.2.2). In detail, considering the submitted crowdsourced testing reports of chronological order, when *smpSize* (*smpSize* is an input parameter) reports are received, iSENSE2.0 treats it as a representative group to reflect the multiple parallel crowdsourced testing sessions.

7.3.2.2   Duplicate Tagger

To overcome the drawback that iSENSE is dependent on manual duplicate labels, in iSENSE2.0, a Duplicate Tagger component is proposed, which applies semantic analysis techniques to automatically identify the duplicate status of the crowd-sourced testing reports.

(1) Semantic Analysis
iSENSE2.0 utilizes word embedding technique to analyze the semantic meaning of crowdsourced testing reports. Word embedding is a feature learning technique in natural language processing where individual words are no longer treated as unique symbols, but represented as d-dimensional vector of real numbers that capture their contextual semantic meanings. The publicly available software[2] is used to obtain the word embedding of a report.

iSENSE2.0 first conducts the natural language processing of the report's descriptions, and represents each report as a set of terms. With the trained word embedding model, each term can be transformed into a d-dimensional vector where d is set to 100 as suggested in previous studies. Meanwhile, each report is transformed into a matrix in which each row represents a term in the report and the each column represents a dimension of word embedding. It then transforms the report matrix into a vector by averaging all the term vectors the report contains, following previous work. Specifically, given a report matrix that has n rows in total, we denote the ith row of the matrix as r_i and the transformed report vector v_d is generated as follows:

$$v_d = \frac{\sum_i r_i}{n} \tag{7.11}$$

---

[2] https://code.google.com/archive/p/word2vec/.

With the above formula, each crowdsourced testing report can be represented as a word embedding vector.

For training the word embedding model, it additionally crawls the textual descriptions and reviews of related applications from application store.[3] It then combines these text with the descriptions of all crowdsourced testing reports, and utilize them for model training. The reason why we use these data is that previous studies have revealed that to train an effective word embedding model, a domain-specific dataset with large size is preferred. The size of our training dataset is 1160 Megabytes.

(2) Duplicate Tagging

For a new coming crowdsourced testing report in the captured sample, duplicate tagger computes the cosine similarity between its word embedding vector and each word embedding vector of the former reports in this task, and obtains the specific former report k with which the maximum similarity *maxSim* is achieved. If the maximum similarity *maxSim* is smaller than the predefined similarity threshold (*simThres*, e.g. 0.80), iSENSE2.0 labels it using a new tag (i.e., a numeric ID value) indicating its duplicate status; otherwise iSENSE2.0 labels the report using the tag of report k.

(3) Bug Arrival Lookup Table

During the crowdsourced testing process of a specific task, iSENSE2.0 will establish and dynamically maintain a two-dimensional *bug arrival lookup table* to record the duplicate status of received reports for that task, similar with iSENSE in Sect. 7.2.2.

7.3.2.3 CRC-Based Close Estimator

iSENSE2.0 treats each sample as a capture (or recapture). At the end of each capture, after updating the *bug arrival lookup table*, iSENSE2.0 predicts the total number of bugs in the software based on current lookup table. The utilization of CRC model for bug prediction is the same as it is in iSENSE, please refer to Sect. 7.2.2 for more details.

7.3.2.4 Coverage-Based Sanity Checker

Recall that one limitation of CRC-based close decision is its performance bottleneck related to the *Rise-Stay-Rise* bug arrival curve. To address that, a coverage-based sanity checker is designed in iSENSE2.0 to reduce probability of false alarms and provide improved decision support. Test code coverage has long been recognized as the indicator of software quality. Various categories of code coverage metrics are proposed, e.g., statement coverage, decision coverage, condition coverage, path

---

[3] https://play.google.com/.

coverage, etc. In crowdsourced testing context, it is unlikely to obtain source code of the application under test due to confidential considerations. Therefore, we propose a new metric of *term coverage* to measure the extent to which the task's requirements are explored under crowdsourced testing environment. In this study, term coverage is defined as the ratio of terms consisted in task's requirements that have been covered in the received testing reports. Term coverage is well applicable in crowdsourced testing context since most crowdsourced testing tasks would have requirements specifying the testing objectives and it should be met by the crowd workers.

Term coverage is defined as the extent to which the terms in task's requirements are covered by the submitted test reports in a crowdsourced testing task. We first represent the task's requirements as well as each submitted report in the vector space of the descriptive terms list. Suppose the task's requirements are denoted as a set of terms L_{req}, suppose we have received K reports and the j_{th} report is denoted as a set of terms L_{pt_j}. Term coverage is measured using the following equation :

$$term\ coverage = 1.0 - \frac{|L_{req} - \cup_j L_{pt_j}|}{|L_{req}|}, where\ j \in [1, K] \tag{7.12}$$

During the crowdsourced testing process, with the arrival of crowdsourced testing reports, iSENSE2.0 constantly update the term coverage, and the close decision of sanity checker is made when the term coverage exceeds *covThres* which is an input parameter.

7.3.3   Experiment

7.3.3.1   Experiment Design

(1) Experimental Setup and Evaluation Metrics
We use the experimental dataset in Sect. 7.2 for the evaluation. And we employ the same longitudinal data setup as Sect. 7.2.3.1. Besides, we measure the effectiveness of close prediction based on two metrics, i.e. bug detection level (i.e. %bug) and cost reduction (i.e. %reducedCost) as Sect. 7.2.3.1.

To evaluate the accuracy of duplicate prediction (RQ2 in Sect. 7.3.3.2), we use recall@k following previous work. Given a query report q, its ground truth duplicate reports set $G(q)$, and the top-k recommended duplicate reports list produced by our approach $R(q)$. **Recall@k** checks whether a top-k recommendation is useful. The definition of *recall@k* for a query report q is as follows:

$$recall@k = \begin{cases} 1, & if\ G(q) \cap R(q) \neq \varnothing \\ 0, & Otherwise \end{cases} \tag{7.13}$$

Given a task, with each report acting as the query report, we compute the averaged $recall@k$ among all query reports to obtain the overall performance. As previous approaches, we set k as 1, 3, 5, and 10.

To evaluate the role of sanity checker in reducing false alarm (RQ3 in Sect. 7.3.3.2), we denote *falseAlarm@* (k is 0.60, 0.65, 0.70, 0.75, 0.80) as the number of crowdsourced testing tasks whose %bug is smaller than k at the close time.

(2) Baselines

To further evaluate the advantages of our proposed iSENSE2.0, we compare it with two baselines.

iSENSE This baseline is the state-of-the-art approach for close prediction of crowdsourced testing tasks which is introduced in Sect. 7.2.

Rayleigh This baseline is adopted from one of the most classical models for predicting the dynamic defect arrival in software measurement, which is utilized in Sect. 7.2.3.1.

(3) Parameter Tuning There are three parameters which needed to be tuned, i.e., *smpSize*, *simThres* and *covThres*. The first parameter represents the sample-size for incremental sampling of dynamically received crowdsourced testing reports, i.e. how many reports are considered in each sample (i.e. each capture in CRC). The second parameter is applied as the minimal similarity score for two testing reports to be considered duplicate. The last parameter controls the termination criteria for the coverage-based sanity checker. In this study, we tune the optimal parameter values based on the training set and apply them in the testing set in order to evaluate the performance of iSENSE2.0.

More specifically, we experiment the value of *smpSize* ranging from 6 to 16 with an incremental interval of 2 in between; the values of *simThres* and *covThres* both ranging from 0.6 to 1.0 with an incremental interval of 0.1 in between. This leads to a total number of 150 combinations of parameter settings. For each candidate combination of these parameter settings, we obtain the %bug and %reducedCost based on the training set. We then select the value combination which produces (1) the largest median %bug and the largest median %reducedCost. In case of multiple equivalent candidates, we pick the one with the largest %bug.

7.3.3.2 Results and Analysis

RQ1: How Effective Is iSENSE2.0 in Automatic Close Prediction?

The purpose of iSENSE2.0 is to facilitate current crowdsourced testing practices through automated decision support. RQ1 is to investigate the effectiveness of iSENSE2.0 in supporting automatic closing decision. Remember that, iSENSE2.0 integrates five CRC estimators for CRC-based close decision, RQ1 also presents the performance of close prediction in terms of the five CRC estimators.

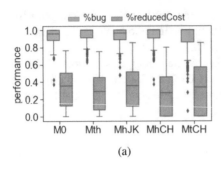 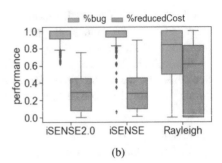

Fig. 7.9 Effectiveness of iSENSE2.0 (RQ1). (**a**) Comparison among five CRC estimators. (**b**) Comparison with baselines

Comparison Across Five CRC Estimators Figure 7.9a illustrates the comparison of the prediction performance of iSENSE2.0 corresponding to each of the five CRC estimators. Overall, all five estimators can achieve relative high and stable performance in close prediction. The median *%bug* obtained by all five estimators is above 96%, and the variance of *%bug* of these five estimators is smaller than 0.14. Besides, the median *%reducedCost* achieved by these five estimators is larger than 27%. There is no significant difference between the close prediction performance of these estimators. Nevertheless, the median *%bug* achieved by *Mth* and *MhCH* can reach 100%, and the variance *%bug* of these two estimators is smaller than others.

In traditional software inspection or testing activities, *MhJK*, *MhCH*, and *MtCH* have been recognized as the most effective estimators for total bugs. However, in crowdsourced testing, the most comprehensive estimator *Mth* outperforms the other CRC estimators. This is reasonable because crowdsourced testing is conducted by a diversified pool of crowd workers with different levels of capability, experience, testing devices, and the nature of bugs in the software under test also vary greatly in terms of types, causes, and detection difficulty, etc. In such cases, *Mth*, which assumes different detection probability for both bugs and crowd workers, supposes to be the most suitable estimator for crowdsourced testing.

In further experiments, if not explicitly mentioned, *Mth* is chosen as default estimator in iSENSE2.0 due to its slight out-performance over others. Consequently, the results of iSENSE2.0 are referring to those generated with *Mth* estimator.

Performance with Best CRC Estimator A median of 100% bugs can be detected with 30% median cost reduction with iSENSE2.0. This suggests an additional 30% more cost-effectiveness for managers if equipped with such a decision automation tool as iSENSE2.0 to monitor and close tasks automatically at run-time. The reduced cost is a tremendous figure when considering the large number of tasks delivered in a crowdsourced testing platform. In addition, the standard deviation (0.7 on *%bug*) is relatively low, further signifying the stability of iSENSE2.0.

Comparison with Baselines Figure 7.9b demonstrates the performance of iSENSE2.0 comparing with two baselines. Table 7.7 presents the results of Mann–

Table 7.7 Results of Mann–Whitney U Test for effectiveness (RQ1)

	%bug	%reducedCost
iSENSE2.0 vs. iSENSE	0.25 (0.05N)	0.67 (0.02N)
iSENSE2.0 vs. Rayleigh	0.00 (0.33M)	0.00 (0.23S)

Note that, the background color denotes the effect size of Large , Median , Small , Negligible .

Whitney Test between iSENSE2.0 and each baseline. Results show that our previous approach iSENSE can also detect a median of 100% bugs with 29% saved effort, which demonstrates no significant difference with iSENSE2.0 proposed in this chapter. However it is worth noting that iSENSE is based on manual duplicate labels, while iSENSE2.0 completely automates the duplicate labelling, which relaxes the burden of manual labelling, and is more practical and flexible. It is promising that iSENSE2.0 can achieve equally good performance with far less human intervention compared with existing work.

Furthermore, the variance *%bug* of iSENSE2.0 is smaller than that of iSENSE (0.7 vs. 1.1). Specifically, the minimum *%bug* of iSENSE2.0 is 62.5%, while the minimum *%bug* of iSENSE is only 6.7% and there are 11 crowdsourced testing tasks whose *%bug* with *iSENSE* is less than 62.5%. These outliers are potentially caused by the 'Rise-Stay-Rise' bug arrival curve. Since we have designed a coverage-based sanity check in iSENSE2.0 to help overcome the performance bottleneck cause by this category of bug arrival curve, there is fewer crowdsourced testing tasks with quite low *%bug* compared with iSENSE.

In addition, iSENSE2.0 significantly outperforms Rayleigh which is based on traditional defect arrival model. The Rayleigh probability distribution has been proven to be effective in modeling the arrival of bugs in traditional software testing. The above results imply that it is not suitable for crowdsourced testing. This might because the bug detection process of crowdsourced testing task is more open and complicated than traditional software testing process.

RQ2: To What Degree the Duplicate Tagger Can Accurately Label Duplicate Report in New Reports?

With the semantic analysis, iSENSE2.0 can automatically label the duplicate status of crowdsourced testing reports, thus consolidate the bug arrival data as input for the CRC-based close estimator. RQ2 is to investigate the accuracy of the duplicate tagger in duplicate reports prediction. We additionally present the accuracy of identified category of bug arrival curve which is derived from duplicate status.

Figure 7.10 demonstrates the results of recall@k of duplicate tagger in duplicate reports prediction. Recall@1 is 0.29–0.84 across all experimental tasks, and the median recall@1 is 0.61. In existing duplicate identification studies studies, the recall@1 are reported as 0.16–0.57. Considering the above existing results, our results support that the proposed duplicate tagger, i.e. with a median of 61% for recall@1, generally outperforms those from existing studies. Although the results are obtained based on different datasets, it is considered to provide a satisfactory performance in automating duplicate bugs in the context of this study.

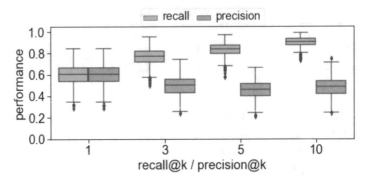

Fig. 7.10 Accuracy of duplicate tagger (RQ2)

Table 7.8 Results of identification of bug arrival curve categories (RQ2)

		Ground truth			
		Category I Rise-stay	Category II Rise-stay-slight rise	Category III Rise-stay-rise	Total
Predicted	Category I	54 (19%)	23 (8%)	4 (1%)	81 (28%)
	Category II	22 (7%)	85 (29%)	15 (6%)	122 (42%)
	Category III	29 (10%)	36 (13%)	20 (7%)	85 (30%)
	Total	105 (36%)	144 (50%)	39 (14%)	

In order to further understand the performance of duplicate tagger, one more question is that whether/how the introduced Duplicate Tagger impacts the shape of the bug arrival curves. To answer this question, we re-produce the rule-based categorization results using predicated labels from Duplicate Tagger, instead of using the actual labels. Table 7.8 summarizes the comparison between the ground truth categorization and that using duplicate tagger predictions. Note that, the figures in Table 7.8 are obtained based on the tasks in testing dataset under the experimental setup, not all tasks. Therefore, there are very slight differences between the categorical distribution as shown in the last row, and those ground truth distribution introduced in Sect. 7.3.1, which was produced on all tasks.

Overall, by summing up the numbers in diagonal cells, we can find that 55% (19%+29%+7%) experimental tasks can be correctly categorized using labels from Duplicate Tagger. We admit that there is a relatively large portion (45%) experimental tasks inaccurately categorized, and Duplicate Tagger tends to lead to more tasks in *Category III Rise-Stay-Rise* (30% vs. 14%), compared with ground truth. This has motivated us to design the coverage-based sanity checker to overcome the performance bottleneck associated with Category III.

RQ3: What Is the Effect Of Sanity Checker on Reducing False Alarm?

The coverage-based sanity checker is proposed to reduce false alarms so as to overcome the performance bottlenecks in *Rise-Stay-Rise* category. RQ3 is to investigate the effect of sanity checker on reducing false alarms. We further investigate the contribution of sanity checker in improving the overall close prediction performance. We also examine the prediction performance in terms of three categories of bug arrival curve to better understand its contribution.

Since the basis of sanity checker is the evaluation of test adequacy by term coverage, we first present the relations between term coverage and bug detection ratio (i.e., the percentage of detected bugs among all bugs) in Fig. 7.11. We can see that the bug detection ratio is positively correlated with the term coverage, which further proves the rationality of our designed term coverage-based sanity checker. When all test requirements are covered (i.e., term coverage is 100%), a median of 85% bugs are detected. This indicates that solely utilizing the term coverage would be ineffective for close prediction, and what we do is integrating it as the sanity checker in our iSENSE2.0.

Table 7.9 presents the number and percentage of falseAlarm@k (k is 0.60, 0.65, 0.70, 0.75, 0.80) respectively for iSENSE2.0 and its variation without applying the coverage-based sanity checker (i.e., only with CRC-based close estimator, denoted as *CRC* in Table 7.9. We can easily see that the coverage-based sanity checker can reduce false alarms in close prediction. Specifically, without sanity checker, there are 26 (9%) experimental tasks whose *%bug* is less than 60%, and this number is zero when equipped with sanity checker. Without sanity checker, there are 52 (18%) experimental tasks whose *%bug* is less than 70%, and this number is 4 (1%) when equipped with sanity checker.

Furthermore, Fig. 7.12 illustrates the comparison between the performance of CRC and iSENSE2.0, as well as three variations of them. *CRC-x* and *iSE-x* respectively denotes the performance of *CRC* or iSENSE2.0 for experimental tasks

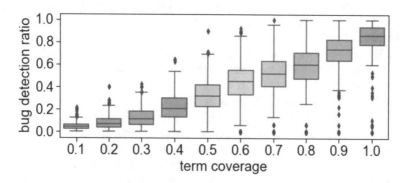

Fig. 7.11 Relation between term coverage and bug detection (RQ3)

Table 7.9 Effect of sanity checker in reducing false alarms (RQ3)

	falseAlarm @0.60	falseAlarm @0.65	falseAlarm @0.70	falseAlarm @0.75	falseAlarm @0.80
CRC	26 (9%)	39 (14%)	52 (18%)	70 (24%)	88 (31%)
iSENSE2.0	0 (0%)	3 (1%)	4 (1%)	11 (4%)	21 (7%)

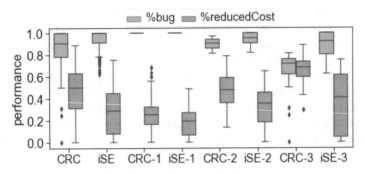

Fig. 7.12 Contribution of coverage-based sanity checker (RQ3)

Table 7.10 Results of Mann–Whitney U Test for contribution of coverage-based sanity checker (RQ3)

	%bug	%reducedCost
CRC vs. iSENSE2.0	0.000 (0.36M)	0.000 (0.44M)
CRC vs. iSENSE2.0 in *Category I Rise-Stay*	1.000 (0.00N)	0.000 (0.26S)
CRC vs. iSENSE2.0 in *Category II Rise-Stay-Slight Rise*	0.000 (0.48L)	0.000 (0.43M)
CRC vs. iSENSE2.0 in *Category III Rise-Stay-Rise*	0.000 (0.81L)	0.000 (0.67L)

Note that, the background color denotes the effect size of Large , Median , Small , Negligible .

from the predicted category x bug arrival curve. Table 7.10 presents the results of Mann–Whitney Test between them.

Let us first look at the first two groups of boxes, i.e. CRC and iSE. It is obvious that the coverage-based sanity checker can increase (or at least maintain) the percentage of bugs detected at the predicted close time. Although it would potentially postpone the close time, i.e., with less reduced cost, even for the tasks which have already detected 100% bugs. This is considered acceptable due to the following two reasons: (1) a sufficient amount of detected bugs are preferred than reduced cost; (2) even with the sanity checker, a median of 30% cost reduction can still be achieved.

We then shift our focus on the performance across the three categories, i.e., the last six series of three boxes in Fig. 7.12. In particularly, as the sanity checker is specifically designed to improve the performance issue associated with *Category III Rise-Stay-Rise*, we can observe a large increase in the median %bug from 0.71 (i.e. CRC-3) to 0.92 (i.e. iSE-3). This indicates, without sanity checker, only a median of 71% bugs can be detected with only CRC model; and with sanity check, a median of 92% bugs can be detected for tasks in *Category III*. This is a clear evidence on improvement attributed to the sanity checker.

As expected, the effect of sanity checker is not as significant on the other two categories as in Category III. For *Category I Rise-Stay*, we can observe that both *iSENSE2.0* and *CRC* can achieve %bug of 1.00; and *CRC* can save more effort than *iSENSE2.0*. As discussed earlier, the optimal close time can be determined solely based on the dynamic arrival of bugs for this category. Therefore, *iSENSE2.0*, which includes sanity check, imposes additional restriction and potentially delays the close time, leading to more cost spending on paying duplicate reports. For *Category II Rise-Stay-Slight Rise*, the sanity checker can slightly increase bug detection rate, i.e. from 0.90 to 0.95, compromised with lower cost reduction. The increase in %bugs can reduce the risk of insufficient testing. Based on feedback from testing managers, detecting more bugs is more favorable than more cost reduction. For crowdsourced testing practitioners, %bug is considered hard objective, while %reducedCost is more like extra bonus.

7.3.4   Discussion

7.3.4.1   Influence of Semantic Analysis on Performance

Our proposed approach is based on the duplicate status derived from the semantic analysis of crowdsourced testing reports. The state-of-the-art duplicate detection techniques can not achieve 100% accuracy, so does our approach. Despite of this, our close prediction can still achieve a median of 100% bugs and 30% reduced cost, which exerts no significant difference with previous work which is based on the human-labeled duplicate tag. This further implies our proposed approach is resistant to noise.

We admit that based on the automatic-labeled duplicate tag, iSENSE2.0 could not provide an accurate prediction of required cost in order for trade-off close analysis as iSENSE, because the predicted total bugs has a large error. When armed with more accurate duplicate detection technique, the accuracy of these prediction can be increased and the usability of iSENSE2.0 can be further improved.

Currently, researchers combined the screenshot and textual descriptions to detect duplicate crowdsourced testing reports which can achieve better performance than solely based on textual description. These new techniques will be investigated and integrated into iSENSE2.0 to further improve its effectiveness.

7.3.4.2   Further Exploration of Sanity Checker

Because the "Stay" stage in the bug arrival curve would mislead the CRC-based prediction to determine it as the close time, we try to employ orthogonal assumption (i.e., coverage-based sanity check) other than the bug arrival trend to help overcome the performance bottleneck. The results indicate that it is beneficial to employ sanity checker based on term coverage, which can potentially break the flat-stay phase of the bug arrival curve, and significantly increase the bug detection rate at the suggested close time. However, the performance in *Rise-Stay* category implies that it can also potentially decrease the cost-effectiveness of crowdsourced testing, i.e., postpone the close time. Therefore, more exploration is needed to carefully design the sanity checker for further lowering the unnecessary cost. Possible improvement is to experiment on new measurement for term coverage, or other term filtering techniques when measuring the term coverage. Another alternative is employing the information from the installation package, besides task requirements, as the indicator in sanity checker.

Other possibilities include developing machine learning based predictors or classifiers to categorize bug arrival trend in advance, and automatically apply the most suitable method in responding to the specific arrival trend. For example, if the bugs arrive following *Category I* and *Category II*, the framework can automatically apply the CRC-based method to predict the close time. However if the bugs arrive following the *Category III Rise-Stay-Rise*, the framework can automatically apply our proposed iSENSE2.0, or alter the project manager to be careful with the prediction.

Part IV
Supporting Technology for Crowdsourced Testing Results

Chapter 8
Classification of Crowdsourced Testing Reports

8.1 Introduction

In order to attract workers, testing tasks are often financially compensated, especially for these failed reports. Under this context, workers may submit thousands of test reports. However, these test reports often have many false positives, i.e., a test report marked as failed that actually involves correct behavior or behavior that was considered outside of the studied software system. Project managers or testers need to manually verify whether a submitted test report reveals fault—true fault. However, such process is tedious and cumbersome, given the high volume workload. Our observation on industrial crowdsourced testing platforms shows that, approximately 100 projects are delivered per month from a typical platform, and more than 1000 test reports are submitted per day on average. Inspecting 1000 reports usually takes almost half a working week for a tester. Thus, automatically classifying *true fault* from the large amounts of test reports would significantly facilitate this process.

Our observation on real industrial data reveals that the projects under crowdsourced testing come from a large variety of domains, ranging from *travel*, *music*, to *safety* and *photo*. Different technical terms are used in the test reports of different domains to describe the software behavior. For instance, reports in *travel* domain would contain such terms as "location", "navigation", and "place", while reports in *music* domain would contain such terms as "play", "lyrics", and "song". Consequently, the textual features derived from these two domains are significantly different in their distributions. The different feature distribution across domains would degrade the performance of machine learning classifiers when utilized for cross-domain classification. This is because most machine learning models are designed under the assumption that training set and test set are drawn from the same data distribution.

Most of the existing approaches toward reports classification directly leveraged the textual features to build models and did not consider the different data distribution problem across domains. This would result in the poor performance for cross-domain classification of crowdsourced reports. Several existing studies simply learned a specific classifier within each domain. The drawback is that usually there are not enough labeled training data for each domain, and obtaining labeled data is cost intensive. Other alternative is by selecting similar data instances from training set to build the classifier. Although it can mitigate the distribution difference problem to some extent, it would fail to take effect when only a small number of similar instances can be found, which is quite common in practice.

To overcome the different data distribution problem and more effectively conduct cross-domain report classification, in this chapter, we propose Domain Adaptation Report claSsification (DARS) approach. It leverages the Stacked Denoising Autoencoders (SDA), which is a powerful representation learning algorithm (also known as deep learning), to learn the high-level features and then utilize these features for classification. In order to abstract the high-level features, SDA discovers the intermediate representation from raw textual terms that is shared across domains. Putting it intuitively, the intermediate representation is learned through the co-occurrence between the aforementioned domain-specific terms and domain-unaware terms (e.g., terms appeared across domains such as "button", "open", and "wrong"). Section 8.2 will present the details of this approach.

The above propose approach and other existing researches proposed to classify the reports using supervised machine learning algorithms. Unfortunately, these approaches often require users to manually label a large number of training data, which is both time-consuming and labor-intensive in practice. Therefore, it is crucial to reduce the onerous burden of manual labeling while still being able to achieve good performance.

We try to adopt active learning to mitigate this challenge. Active learning aims to achieve high accuracy with as few labeled instances as possible. It recommends a small portion of instances which are most informative, and asks user their labels. These labeled reports are then used to train a model to classify the remaining reports. However, existing active learning techniques generate poor and unstable performances on these crowdsourced testing data because of the different feature distribution problem across domains as mentioned above.

We propose LOcal-based Active ClassiFication approach (LOAF) to effectively classify the reports with few or none labeled training data. The idea behind is to query the most informative instance within local neighborhood, then learn classifiers based on local neighborhood. Section 8.3 will present the details of this approach.

8.2   Domain Adaptation for Testing Report Classification

8.2.1   Motivation

Most of the existing test report classification approaches assume that the training set and test set are drawn from the same data distribution. This means that the

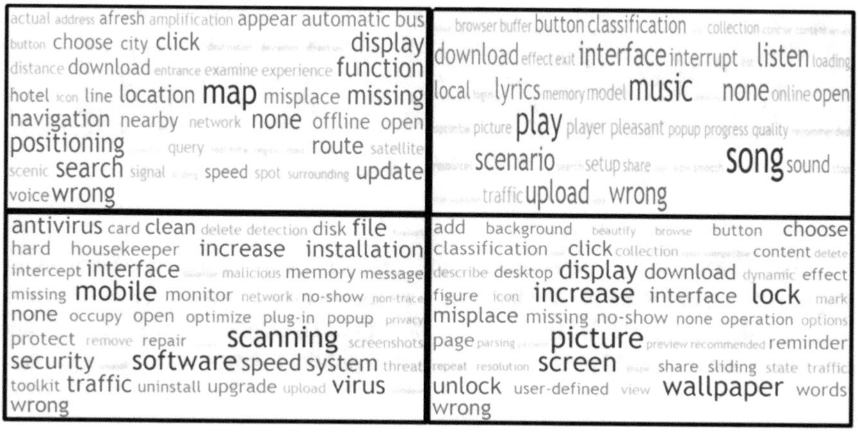

Fig. 8.1 Illustrative examples for the different data distribution of crowdsourced testing reports

performance would decline rapidly when using these approaches to classify the new coming test reports that have different distributions with the training set.

However, our observation on real industrial data reveals that crowdsourced reports across domains are under different distributions. The main reason is as follows. The projects under crowdsourced testing come from a large variety of domains, ranging from travel, music, to safety and photo. Moreover, different domains focus on different functional and technical aspects. Test reports from different domains usually use specific technical terms to describe the software behavior.

We present the term clouds of the textual descriptions of test reports for four randomly selected domains, i.e., *travel, music, safety,* and *photo,* to illustrate the distribution difference and its influence in Fig. 8.1. We can easily observe that the technical terms exert significant differences among different domains. For instance, reports in the *travel* domain (the upper left subfigure of Fig. 8.1) contain such terms as "location", "navigation", and "place", while reports in the *music* domain (the upper right subfigure of Fig. 8.1) contain such terms as "play", "lyrics", and "song". Consequently, textual features derived from these two domains are significantly different in their distributions. Taken in this sense, models with textual features, built on the reports from *travel* domain, may fail to effectively classify the reports from *music* domain. To mitigate this problem, new features and approaches are required.

In Fig. 8.1, we also notice that projects across domains share a certain amount of common terms. For example, many projects contain such behavioral terms like "display", "setup", and "download", or describable terms like "none", "wrong", and "missing". These shared terms could help bridge the gap across domains. More specifically, in *travel* domain, there are descriptions like "display location of building", while in *music* domain, descriptions like "display lyrics of song" are quite common. With the help of representation learning algorithm, such terms as "lyrics", "song" and term "location" would establish a relationship through the shared term

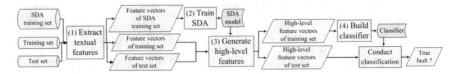

Fig. 8.2 Overview of DARS

"display". Based on the co-occurrence, the representation learning algorithm would map the raw terms to high-level features. The more similar context two terms share, the more similar their high-level features would be. The high-level features can then be used as input to build prediction models and predict the crowdsourced reports.

8.2.2 Approach

Figure 8.2 illustrates the overview of Domain Adaptation Report claSsification (DARS) approach. Generally speaking, DARS first trains the Stacked Denoising Autoencoders (SDA) to effectively encode the input features. Then the training set and test set are fed into the trained SDA to generate high-level features. The classification is then conducted based on the high-level features.

DARS consists of four major steps: (1) extract textual features, (2) train the SDA, (3) leverage the SDA to generate high-level features based on textual features, and (4) build classifiers and conduct classification using the learned high-level features.

8.2.2.1 Extracting Textual Features

The goal of feature extraction is to obtain features from crowdsourced reports which can be used as input to train the SDA. We extract these features from the text descriptions of crowdsourced reports.

We first collect different sources of text descriptions together (input and operation steps, result description). Then we conduct the commonly-applied natural language processing operations, i.e., word segmentation, stopwords removal, synonym replacement. Each of the remaining terms corresponds to a feature. For each feature, we take the frequency it occurs in the description as its value. We use the TF (term frequency) instead of TF-IDF because the use of the inverse document frequency (IDF) penalizes terms appearing in many reports. In our work, we are not interested in penalizing such terms (e.g., "break","problem") that actually appear in many reports because they can act as discriminative features that guide machine learning techniques in classifying reports. We organize these features into a *feature vector*, with each feature value being the corresponding term frequency.

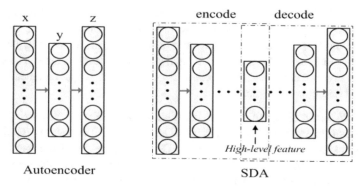

Fig. 8.3 Autoencoder and stacked denoising autoencoders

8.2.2.2 Training SDA

(1) Bakcground of Stacked Denoising Autoencoder (SDA) SDA is an artificial neural network for unsupervised learning of effective representation, which consists of multiple layers of denosing autoencoders.

An *autoencoder* (shown in Fig. 8.3) takes an input vector $x \in [0, 1]^d$, and codes it to a hidden representation $y \in [0, 1]^{d'}$ through a deterministic mapping $y = f_\theta(x) = s(Wx + b)$, parameterized by $\theta = W, b$. W is a $d' \times d$ weight matrix and b is a bias vector. The resulting latent representation y is then decoded to a "reconstructed" vector z in input space $z = g_{\theta'}(y) = s(W'y + b')$ with $\theta' = W', b'$. The weight matrix W' of the reverse mapping is constrained by $W' = W^T$. The parameters of this model are optimized to minimize the *average reconstruction error*:

$$argmin \frac{1}{n} \sum_{i=1}^{n} L(x(i), g_{\theta'}(f_{\theta(x(i))})) \tag{8.1}$$

where L is a loss function of *reconstruction cross entropy*. The autoencoder is trained by stochastic gradient descent, in which *number of training iterations* is an input parameter to balance the time cost, and error rate between the reconstructed vector and the input vector.

The ***Denoising Autoencoder (DA)*** incorporates a slight modification to the autoencoder, i.e., corrupts the inputs before coding them into the hidden representation. It is trained to reconstruct (or denoise) the original input x from its corrupted version $\tilde{x}$ by minimizing $L(x, g(h(\tilde{x})))$.

A typical choice of corruption is binary masking noise. It sets a fraction of the features of each input to zero, in which the *level of noise* is an input parameter. This is natural for the textual features of crowdsourced test reports, where person-specific term preferences can influence the existence or absence of words.

The *Stacked Denoising Autoencoder (SDA)* stacks a series of DAs together to build a deep architecture, by feeding the hidden representation of the tth DA as input into the $(t + 1)$th DA. The training is performed greedily, layer by layer. The latent representation in the last DA is treated as the high-level features. The *number of hidden layers* and *the number of nodes in each layer* are input parameters which can be set based on users' demand.

(2) How to Train SDA To generate the high-level features for classifying crowdsourced reports, we need to first train the SDA using the SDA training set. Existing researches showed that the larger size of SDA training set, the better performance can be achieved. Moreover, the representation learning technique does not involve the class information (i.e., whether the report is a true fault or not). Hence, common practice would utilize all available data instances in the training process. To train a SDA is to determine the weights w and the biases b, so that the trained SDA can effectively encode the input features.

To train an effective SDA for generating the high-level features, we need to tune four parameters, which are: (1) *the number of hidden layers*, (2) *the number of nodes in each hidden layer*, (3) *the level of noise*, and (4) *the number of training iterations*. Existing work that leveraged the SDA to generate features for natural language processing and image recognition reported that the performance of the SDA-generated features is sensitive to these parameters.

The nodes in the input and output layers are equal to the size of feature vector. For other layers, we set the number of nodes to be the same to simplify our model. Besides, the SDA requires the input vectors be the same length. To use the SDA to generate high-level features, we first collect all the features appeared in the SDA training set and organize them into a joint feature vector. Then we transform the original feature vectors to the the joint feature vectors. In detail, for a feature contained in the original feature vector, we use its original value as the value in the joint feature vector. Otherwise, we set its value to zero. Adding zeros does not affect the results, because it simply means that the specific term does not appear in the report.

Note that, the SDA requires the values of input data ranging from 0 to 1. As the input vector represents the term frequency of each feature, its value can be larger than 1. To satisfy this requirement, we normalize the values in the feature vectors of the SDA training set using min-max normalization.

8.2.2.3   Generating High-Level Features

After we have trained a SDA, both the weights w and the biases b are fixed. For the feature vectors of training set and test set, we first map them into the joint feature vector. Then we use min-max normalization to normalize them into the range between 0 and 1.

The normalized joint feature vectors of the training set and test set are fed into the SDA respectively. The representations in last hidden layer of SDA are then treated as the high-level features.

8.2.2.4   Building a Classifier

After we obtain the generated high-level features for each crowdsourced report in both the training set and test set, we build a machine learning classifier based on the training set. Then we use the test set to evaluate the performance of the built classifier.

To better assist the manual inspection, the classifier will provide the probability for the reports being true faults. The bigger the probability value, the more likely the report contains a true fault. To compute the F1, we use 0.5 as cutoff value, denoting that reports with a probability value larger than 0.5 are treated as true faults, and vice versa.

8.2.3   Experiment

8.2.3.1   Experimental Desgin

(1) Experimental Dataset
We collect 58 crowdsourced testing projects with 31,508 reports from a popular crowdsourced testing platform. We group these projects into domains based on the domain name recorded in the platform. Table 8.1 provides details of these domains with the number of projects, the number of submitted reports, the number of reported *failed* reports, and the number and the ratio of *true faults* in failed reports.

Note that, our classification is conducted on *failed* reports, not the complete set. We exclude the *passed* reports because of the following reason. As we mentioned, failed reports can usually involve both correct behaviors and true faults. However, through talking with testers in the company, we find that almost none of the passed reports involve true faults. This maybe because that the compensation favors the faults, so the crowd workers are very unlikely to miss the faults.

Additionally, we randomly collect three other projects (belonged to three domains) to conduct the case study in RQ3, as shown in Table 8.1.

(2) Experiment Setup
As we mentioned above, training a SDA does not involve the class information. Following previous studies, we treat all the experimental crowdsouced reports as *SDA training set*, denoting that we use these data to extract the *feature vectors of SDA training set* and train the SDA model. For all the domains under investigation, we use all crowdsourced reports of one domain as the *test set* and extract the

Table 8.1 Projects under investigation

Domain	# Project	# Report	# Failed report	# True fault	%True fault
Efficiency	9	4237	2198	884	40.2%
Entertainment	8	6423	4913	2700	54.9%
Music	4	2160	1497	450	30.0%
News	6	2740	2517	1112	44.1%
Photo	4	2207	1498	564	37.6%
Read	7	2042	3136	875	27.9%
Safety	3	2216	1916	762	39.7%
Shopping	3	2280	1836	842	45.8%
Tool	10	5320	4409	1628	36.9%
Travel	4	1883	1644	529	32.1%
Summary	58	31,508	25,564	10,346	40.4%
C1 (shopping)	1	231	177	87	49.1%
C2 (tool)	1	690	455	182	40.0%
C3 (efficiency)	1	1428	1004	392	39.0%

feature vectors of test set. We randomly select K number of crowdsourced reports from the other nine domains to act as the *training set* and extract the *feature vectors of training set.* K is set as 100, 200, 500, 1000, 1500, 2000, 3000, and 5000 respectively to investigate the influence of training set size on the model performance. The experiment for each K is repeated 50 times to ensure the stability of the results.

(3) Baselines
To further explore the performance of our proposed approach, we compare DARS with three typical baseline approaches.

Domain-Unaware Classification (DUC) It is the most straightforward prediction approach and does not consider the distribution difference among different domains. It builds the machine learning classifiers using all the crowdsourced reports in the training set and conducts classification on the test set.

Transfer Component Analysis (TCA+) [62] It is the state-of-the-art technique for domain adaptation. TCA aims to find a latent feature space for both the training set and test set by minimizing the distance between the data distributions while preserving the original data properties. TCA+ extends TCA with automatically normalization, and can yield better performance than TCA.

Cluster-Based Classification Approach (CURES) [97] It is the state-of-the-art technique to classify crowdsourced reports which can also mitigate the difference of data distribution in crowdsourced reports. It first clusters similar reports of training set together, and builds classifiers based on the reports of each cluster. Then it selects the most similar clusters with the test set, and conducts classification.

Both DARS and these baselines involve utilizing different machine learning classification algorithms to build classifiers. In this work, we experiment with Linear Regression (LR), which is widely reported as effective in many different classification tasks in software engineering.

(4) Evaluation Metrics

To evaluate our proposed approach, we use two metrics: ***F1*** and ***AUC***.

F1 is a widely adopted metric to evaluate issue report classification techniques. It is the harmonic mean of precision and recall of classifying true fault. AUC is the most popular and widely used metric for evaluating classification performance on imbalanced data. As the dataset of crowdsourced reports is usually imbalanced (i.e., less true faults), we specifically use this metric. It is the area under ROC curve,[1] which measures the overall discrimination ability of a classifier. The AUC for a perfect model would be 1, and for a model predicting all instances as true or false would be 0.

(5) Parameter Settings for Training a SDA Model

Many SDA applications report that an effective SDA needs well-tuned parameters, i.e., (1) the number of hidden layers, (2) the number of nodes in each hidden layer, (3) the level of noise, and (4) the number of training iterations. In this study, since we leverage the SDA to generate the high-level features, we need to consider the impact of the four parameters. We tune these parameters by conducting experiments with different values of the parameters on our experimental data.

We use all the crowdsourced reports to train the SDA with respect to the specific values of the four parameters. Then, we use the trained SDA to generate high-level features for all the crowdsourced reports. After that, we use the original labelled reports to build a classifier and apply it to the unlabeled reports. Lastly, we evaluate the specific values of the parameters by the AUC score.

Setting the Number of Hidden Layers and the Number of Nodes in Each Layer

Since the number of hidden layers and the number of nodes in each hidden layer interact with each other, we tune these two parameters together. For the number of hidden layers, we experiment with 8 discrete values including 1, 2, 3, 4, 5, 10, 20, and 50. For the number of nodes in each hidden layer, we experiment with 8 discrete values including 20, 50, 100, 200, 300, 500, 800, and 1000. When we evaluate these two parameters, we set the level of noise to 0.1 and number of training iterations to 200, and keep it constant.

Figure 8.4 illustrates the AUC for tuning the number of hidden layers and the number of nodes in each hidden layer together. When the number of nodes in each layer is fixed, with the increase number of hidden layers, the AUC are convex curves. Most curves peak at the point where the number of hidden layers is 3. If the number of hidden layers remains unchanged, the best AUC happens when the number of nodes in each layer is 200 (the top line). As a result, we choose the number of

---

[1] The ROC curve is created by plotting the true positive rate.

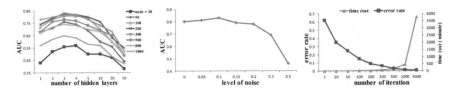

Fig. 8.4 Performance with different parameters

hidden layers as 3 and the number of nodes in each hidden layer as 200. Thus, the number of high-level features is 200.

Setting the Level of Noise The level of noise is also an important parameter for the SDA. We experiment with 7 discrete values ranging from 0 to 0.5. Noise level of 0 denotes the input features remain unchanged, while level of 0.5 denotes that 50% of original features would be randomly set to zero. Figure 8.4 shows the AUC for tuning this parameter. We can see that training the model without noise cannot reach the best performance. Instead, the best performance is achieved when the level of noise is 0.1, denoting that 10% of original features would be randomly set as zero. Therefore, we choose the level of noise as 0.1.

Setting the Number of Iterations The number of iterations is another important parameter for building an effective SDA. During the training process, the SDA adjusts weights to narrow down the error rate between reconstructed input data and original input data in each iteration. In general, the bigger the number of iterations, the lower the error rate. However, there is a trade-off between the number of iterations and the time cost. To balance the number of iterations and the time cost, we conduct experiments with 9 discrete values, ranging from 1 to 5000. We use error rate to evaluate this parameter. Figure 8.4 demonstrates that, as the number of iterations increase, the error rate decreases slowly with the corresponding time cost increases exponentially. In this study, we set the number of iterations to 200, with the error rate is about 0.09 and the time cost is about 23 min. Note that, we only need to conduct the SDA training process once, then we can utilize the trained SDA to generate the high-level features for different training set and test set. This is why we suppose the time for training SDA (23 min) is acceptable.

8.2.3.2   Results and Analysis

RQ1: How Effective Is DARS in Classifying Crowdsourced Reports?
We investigate the performance of DARS in classifying crowdsourced reports under different experimental settings. Figure 8.5 demonstrates the F1 and AUC of DARS for the 50 experiments of all experimental domains, under different training set size. We can see that with the increase of training set size, both the F1 and AUC would first improve and then remain almost unchanged.

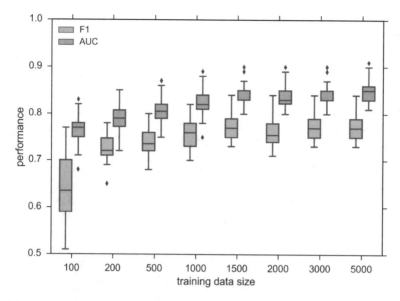

Fig. 8.5 The effectiveness of DARS (RQ1)

We then conduct Mann–Whitney Test for the performance of classification under each adjacent training set sizes. Results reveal that when the training set size is smaller than 1500, the p-value of both F1 and AUC for each adjacent train sets are less than 0.05. When the train set size is larger than 1500, the p-value of both F1 and AUC for each adjacent training sets are more than 0.05. This illustrates that a training set with less than 1500 instances would decrease the performance, and a training set with more than 1500 instances cannot increase the performance significantly. Thus, 1500 is the relative optimal train set size.

We focus on the performance with the training set size as 1500. The F1 ranges from 0.72 to 0.82, with the median F1 as 0.77. The AUC ranges from 0.80 to 0.90, with the median AUC as 0.84.

This implies that DARS merely needs 1500 labeled data instances for achieving relatively satisfactory performance. It benefits from the learned high-level features, which can be learned based on the unlabeled data. There are usually large amounts of unlabeled data and they are relatively easy to collect. Our approach provides a way to effectively utilize these unlabeled data.

Table 8.2 demonstrates the classification performance for each domain acting as test set, with training set size as 1500. We can easily observe that the performance for different domains might vary to some extent. The median F1 ranges from 0.71 to 0.83 for different domains, while the AUC varies from 0.79 to 0.89.

The worst performance occurs in such domains as safety and music. We further analyze the underlying reason. There are large amounts of new terms appearing in the crowdsourced reports of these two domains, e.g., terms for song name. These terms would bring noise when establishing the intermediate representation.

Table 8.2 Performance for each test domain (RQ1)

Domain	F1			AUC		
	Min	Max	Median	Min	Max	Median
Efficiency	0.741	0.761	0.752	0.825	0.835	0.831
Entertainment	0.751	0.820	0.785	0.824	0.859	0.840
Music	0.720	0.747	0.735	0.798	0.813	0.809
News	0.814	0.846	0.832	0.877	0.907	0.896
Photo	0.727	0.763	0.740	0.806	0.823	0.814
Read	0.761	0.795	0.780	0.847	0.859	0.854
Safety	0.709	0.730	0.713	0.783	0.799	0.794
Shopping	0.762	0.816	0.802	0.840	0.862	0.853
Tool	0.726	0.758	0.739	0.802	0.815	0.810
Travel	0.700	0.811	0.758	0.781	0.845	0.819

Table 8.3 Comparison of performance with baselines (RQ2)

		F1				AUC			
		100	500	1500	3000	100	500	1500	3000
Min	DARS	0.507	0.682	0.731	0.728	0.684	0.747	0.800	0.809
	DUC	0.122	0.166	0.222	0.248	0.298	0.318	0.402	0.382
	TCA+	0.272	0.305	0.345	0.502	0.462	0.502	0.498	0.442
	CURES	0.305	0.355	0.435	0.502	0.474	0.512	0.603	0.635
Max	DARS	0.765	0.801	0.837	0.837	0.825	0.869	0.901	0.907
	DUC	0.625	0.667	0.717	0.783	0.783	0.793	0.793	0.808
	TCA+	0.770	0.724	0.754	0.781	0.797	0.811	0.802	0.805
	CURES	0.661	0.711	0.803	0.801	0.688	0.721	0.799	0.831
Median	DARS	0.636	0.738	0.773	0.771	0.767	0.802	0.831	0.834
	DUC	0.356	0.398	0.441	0.456	0.485	0.501	0.572	0.582
	TCA+	0.526	0.559	0.602	0.627	0.647	0.670	0.682	0.698
	CURES	0.504	0.543	0.638	0.646	0.626	0.663	0.704	0.736
Var.	DARS	0.075	0.029	0.031	0.031	0.031	0.028	0.026	0.026
	DUC	0.113	0.121	0.109	0.086	0.100	0.112	0.071	0.074
	TCA+	0.114	0.115	0.114	0.060	0.097	0.085	0.079	0.082
	CURES	0.086	0.087	0.070	0.094	0.058	0.056	0.051	0.062

RQ2: Can DARS Outperform Existing Techniques in Classifying Crowdsourced Reports?

To demonstrate the advantages of DARS, we compare its performance with three baseline methods.

Table 8.3 illustrates the performance of DARS and three baselines. Due to space limit, we only present 4 of the 8 training set sizes (shown in Fig. 8.5) with intervals. We randomly choose the crowdsourced reports to act as the training set and repeat 50 times for each training set size. We present the minimum, maximum, and median performance of the random experiments for these methods. The value with dark background denotes the best F1 or AUC for each training set size.

At first glance, we can find that DARS can achieve the highest median F1 and AUC with the smallest variances, for every training set size. We also conducted Mann–Whitney Test for both F1 and AUC between DARS and each baseline. The p-value for all the tests are less than 0.05. This further illustrates the effectiveness and advantages of our approach.

Table 8.4 Participant of case study (RQ3)

Group A		Group B
A1	2–5 years' experience in testing	B1
A2	1–2 years' experience in testing	B2
A3	0–1 years' experience in testing	B3

Among the three baselines, the performance of DUC is the worst, denoting that classifiers without considering the data distribution difference across domains would result in quite bad performance.

The performance of TCA+ is worse than DARS in both F1 and AUC for all the training set sizes. It is reasonable because existing domain adaption methods (i.e., TCA+) generate the new features based on linear projections of raw features. However, deep learning techniques (e.g., SDA) could learn the high-level features from the non-linear mapping of the raw features, thus can encode complex data variations. Furthermore, SDA has been proven to be more effective than existing domain adaptation methods in other tasks.

Our approach also outperforms CURES, which is the state-of-the-art technique to classify the crowdsourced reports. This is because CURES relies on the historical similar reports to construct the classifier. When the training set is not large enough, CURES's performance would be degraded.

RQ3: Is DARS Useful for Software Testers?

We conduct a case study and a survey in an industrial crowdsourced testing group to further evaluate the usefulness of our approach. We randomly select three projects for our case study. Six testers from the crowdsourced testing group are involved. We divide them into two groups according to their experience, with details summarized in Table 8.4.

The goal of this case study is to evaluate the usefulness of DARS in classifying *true faults* from the crowdsourced test reports. Firstly, we utilize the trained SDA to generate the high-level features for all the reports of the three experimental projects. We then use the originally labeled reports to build a classifier. Through conducting classification for the three projects, we obtain the probability of each report being a true fault.

For both groups, we ask the practitioners to label each report with "yes" or "no", denoting whether the report involves a true fault. For practitioners in Group B, we only present them the crowdsourced test reports under classification. For practitioners in Group A, besides the crowdsourced reports, we provide them with the predicted probability for each report being a true fault. More than that, the reports are displayed by the probability values in descending order.

To build the ground truth, we gather all the classification outcomes from the practitioner. Follow-up interviews are conducted to discuss the differences among them. Common consensus is reached on all the difference and a final edition of classification is used as the ground truth.

We mentioned that we only require the practitioners to assign the label of "yes" or "'no", because the probability of being true faults is complex to measure by manual.

Table 8.5 Results of case study (RQ3)

Project	Results from Group A			Results from Group B		
	C1	C2	C3	C1	C2	C3
Precision	0.90,0.94	0.80,0.86	0.76,0.88	0.90,0.94	0.86,0.90	0.80,0.90
Recall	0.96,1.00	0.94,0.98	0.91,0.98	0.96,0.99	0.93,0.99	0.90,0.96
F1	0.93,0.97	0.86,0.91	0.82,0.92	0.93,0.97	0.89,0.94	0.84,0.92
Time (min)	40,52	80,112	128,164	72,86	186,232	360,394

Note: The two numbers in one cell represent the minimum and the maximum values from the three practitioners

Table 8.6 Results of survey (RQ3)

Questions	Strongly disagree	Disagree	Neither	Agree	Strongly agree	Total
Q1. Do you think DARS is useful to help classify "true fault" from crowdsourced test report?	0	2	1	5	13	21
Q2. Would you like to use the probability provided by DARS to help with the classification task?	0	3	2	3	13	21
If Disagree for either of the question, please give the reason.	Still need much effort; Worry the accuracy on other projects; The recall is unsatisfying;					3

Hence, we do not present the AUC which requires the probability to compute. Instead, besides F1, we present the precision, recall, and the time taken for the classification in Table 8.5.

The classification assisted with the probability provided by DARS (Group A) can find as many true faults as the classification without assistance (Group B), with far less time. In particular, with the increase of project size, the consumed time of manual classification without assistance can dramatically increase, while its accuracy (F1) does not show the fundamental difference.

In addition, we design a questionnaire and conduct a survey to ask testers about the usefulness of DARS. The questionnaire first demonstrates a short description about DARS, what DARS can provide for the classification and the summarized evaluation results on 58 projects. Then it asks three questions shown in Table 8.6. We provide five options for the first two questions, and allow respondents freely express their opinion for the third question.

We send invitation emails to the testers who are involved in the report classification in Baidu crowdsourced testing group. We totally receive 21 responses out of 47 requests.

As indicated in Table 8.6, of all 21 respondents, 16 of them (76%) agree that DARS is useful for report classification and they would like to use it. This means testers agree the usefulness of DARS in general. Only 2 hold conservation options and 3 disagree. When it comes to the reason for disagreement, they mainly worry about its flexibility on new projects, the unsatisfactory recall, as well as the effort still needed to take. In addition, the project manager shows great interest in DARS, and is arranging to deploy it on their platform to assist the classification process.

8.2.4   Discussion

8.2.4.1   Why Does It Work?

We have mentioned that the major challenge for crowdsourced reports classification is the different data distribution of reports across domains. Simply utilizing the reports in other domains to build the classifier can easily result in low accuracy.

We suppose the representation learning algorithm could make the feature distributions across domains more similar, thus reduce the noise introduced by the domain-specific information. To intuitively demonstrate it, we examine the A-distance between the feature distributions of each pair of domains. A-distance is a measure of similarity between the probability distribution of two datasets. We hypothesize that it should be more difficult to discriminate between different domains after the representation learning, which implies the effectiveness of domain adaptation. This can be illustrated by more similar feature distributions. Common practice for obtaining A-distance would compute the generalization error ϵ of a classifier trained to discriminate between two domains. Then A-distance is measured as $2(1 - 2\epsilon)$.

Figure 8.6 reports the A-distance for raw features and high-level features for every domain pair. As expected, A-distance is decreased for high-level features, which implies that the feature distributions between domains become more similar after the representation learning. This is why the classification based on high-level features can achieve higher performance.

8.2.4.2   Lessons Learned

Based on the aforementioned studies and an un-structured interview, which is conducted with the test manager of our experimental crowdsourced testing platform and involved practitioners of the case study, the following lessons can be learned.

(1) Testers Care False Negative More Than False Positive In terms of the classification performance, we found that the testers care more about false negatives (i.e., reports with true faults that are misclassified as reports without faults) than false positives (i.e., reports without faults that are misclassified as reports with

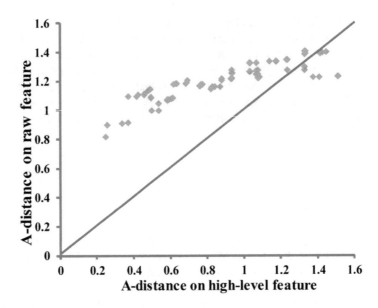

Fig. 8.6 A-distance for every domain pair

faults). In other words, a higher recall is expected, even at the expense of lower precision. This is rational because missing a true fault might introduce serious quality issues in the future, and require extra budget to debug and fix it.

Moreover, for the reports with quite high or low predicted probability as being true faults, the practitioners tend to classify them consistent with the provided probability. Specifically, by observing the manually labelling process of testers, we found that in most cases the testers will label a test report as a true fault without any consideration, if its probability is large enough (e.g., larger than 0.8). That is to say, for the reports which are actually not faults but have high probability, the practitioners would just label them as true faults. Similarly, for the faults which are assigned with quite low probability, there would be hardly any chance for them to be classified correctly. This is the root cause of low performance in Table 8.5. The testers also mentioned that, it would be preferred if an approach can help remove a portion of reports which are definitely not faults. To address this challenge, we would like to explore other approaches to help filter this kind of reports.

(2) Providing the Probability for a Report Is More Actionable and Scalable
The testers also mentioned that the prediction outcomes should be actionable to make DARS more practical. They supposed that tagging each report with its probability is a good choice, as this kind of information suggested them the uncertainty of the prediction. If an automated approach labels each report as binary category, i.e., whether it is a true fault, it would be hard to decide which reports need more human inspection.

Furthermore, they thought that the results in the form of probability values are more scalable than results with binary category. Users can set up the cutoff point, e.g., reports with probability larger than 0.7 are treated as true faults, according to their demands when utilizing these probability values for classification. In this way, based on the same set of prediction results, the testers can customize different kinds of manual classification designs considering the planned time and effort. Testers need some evidences to prove the effectiveness of DARS.

We have attached the summarized evaluation results of DARS on the questionnaire. The testers mentioned that these results played an important role in convincing them that DARS is useful and they would like to use it. They supposed it would be better to provide some video materials to demonstrate how the probability can be utilized in the manual classification process.

(3) DARS Might Also Be Useful to Crowd Workers The tester manager also suggested that it would be useful to show the prediction results to the crowd workers before they submit reports. If their reports suffered from low predicted probability, the crowd workers might choose to conduct the testing again or not to submit the report. Both practices can help improve the quality of test reports and the efficiency of crowdsourced testing.

8.3 Local-Based Active Classification of Testing Report

Previous section presented DARS, which can achieve good classification performance, yet it requires large number of labeled training data, which is time-consuming to collect. To overcome this issue, this section introduces LOAF which can reduce the onerous burden of manual labeling while still being able to achieve good performance.

8.3.1 Approach

Figure 8.7 demonstrates the overview of our approach. We first employ the same method as introduced in Sect. 8.2.2.1 for feature extraction, and organize each report into a *feature vector*. We then conduct the crowdsourced test report classification with our proposed LOcal-based Active ClassiFication (LOAF).

LOAF is based on the general framework of active learning. The primary focus of active learning techniques is measuring the informativeness of unlabeled data, in order to query the most informative instance to help build effective classifier. The design of existing techniques is based on such assumption that data are identically distributed. However, crowdsourced reports are usually differently distributed, so existing techniques would generate poor and unstable performance on these data. This is why we propose LOAF. Its main idea is to query the most informative

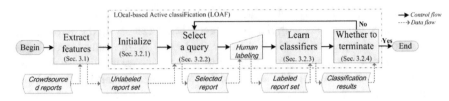

Fig. 8.7 Overview of LOAF

instance within local neighborhood, then learn classifiers based on local neighborhood. Local neighborhood is defined as one or several nearby (with smallest distance) labeled instances. To cope with the local bias in the investigated dataset, the informativeness in our approach is measured within local neighborhood—denoted as '*local informativeness*'. In details, we first obtain the local neighborhood for each unlabeled instance, and measure its local informativeness. We then select the most local informative unlabeled instance and query its label.

Algorithm 1 and Fig. 8.7 summarize the process of LOAF. LOAF first chooses the initial instance and asks user its label. After that, LOAF would iteratively select one instance, ask user its label, and learn classifiers from the labeled instances. LOAF then leverages the up-to-date labeled information to choose which instance to select next. The process will continue until satisfying one of the termination criteria. We will illustrate the process in more detail in the following subsections.

Algorithm 1 Local-based active classification (LOAF)

Input:
  Unlabeled report set U; Labeled report set L = null;
  Tag for termination TM = true; Parameter pr_local and pr_stop;
Output:
  Classification results C;
 1: //*Initialize*
 2: Choose the initial report UR_i according to Eq. (8.1) and query its label;
 3: $L = L \cup UR_i, U = U - UR_i$;
 4: **while** (TM) **do**
 5: //*Select a query*
 6: Select unlabeled report UR_i from U according to Eq. (8.2) and query its label;
 7: $L = L \cup UR_i, U = U - UR_i$;
 8: //*Learn classifiers*
 9: **for** each unlabeled report UR_i in U **do**
 10: Choose pr_local labeled report LR_j according to Eq. (8.3), learn classifier and obtain the classification result C_i for report UR_i.
 11: **end for**
 12: //*Whether to terminate*
 13: Judge whether can terminate based on pr_stop, if yes, set TM as false.
 14: **end while**

---

(1) Initializing This step is to choose the initial test report and ask user its label. Because of the existence of local bias, randomly choosing the initial instance in existing active learning techniques cannot work well. Hence, our approach proposes a new initial selection method to choose the initial test report for labeling. This can mitigate the influence of initial instance and obtain stable good performance.

LOAF first computes the distance between each pair of report, then obtains the nearest distance for each report. Second, LOAF selects the report whose nearest distance is the largest among all reports. This is to ensure the most sparse local region can also build effective classifiers.

In detail, the chosen initial instance is computed as follows:

$$\arg\max_{i \in U} \{ \min_{j \in U, j \neq i} (distance(UF_i, UF_j)) \} \tag{8.2}$$

where U represents the initial unlabeled dataset, UF_i and UF_j denote the feature vector of i_{th} and j_{th} test report in U, respectively. We apply cosine similarity between two feature vectors to measure their distance. This is because prior study showed that it performs better for high-dimensional text documents than other distance measures (e.g., euclidean distance, manhattan distance).

(2) Selecting a Query This step aims at selecting the most informative test reports and asking user their labels. In each iteration, given a set of labeled reports and unlabeled reports, LOAF will select an unlabeled report based on its local informativeness. In detail, firstly, LOAF obtains the local neighborhood for each unlabeled report, and measures its local informativeness. This is done through computing the distance between the unlabeled report and every labeled report. The labeled report with nearest distance is treated as the local neighborhood for each unlabeled report, and the local informativeness is measured using the nearest distance. Secondly, LOAF selects the unlabeled report whose local informativeness is the largest, which can better serve the local-based classification. This is done by selecting the unlabeled report whose nearest distance is the largest, among all unlabeled reports.

The rationale behind is as follows: to serve as the local-based classification in the next step, it should be guaranteed that each unlabeled instance has nearby reports which can be used to classify itself. Hence, if one instance's nearest neighbor has already been labeled, the local-based classifier would have the higher probability of correctly classifying it. On the other hand, if the nearest labeled instance turns out to be far away, this might imply big uncertainty in model building and classification. From this point of view, the farthest of the nearest labeled instance turns out to be the most informative one for local-based classification.

In detail, the selected instance is computed as follows:

$$\arg\max_{i \in U} \{ \min_{j \in L} (distance(UF_i, LF_j)) \} \tag{8.3}$$

where U and L represent the unlabeled dataset and labeled dataset in this iteration, respectively. UF_i and LF_j denote the feature vector of i_{th} unlabeled report and feature vector of j_{th} labeled report, respectively. Similarly, we apply cosine similarity to measure the distance of two feature vectors.

(3) Learning Classifiers This step aims at learning classifiers to classify unlabeled reports, using labeled reports. Since our investigated dataset has local bias, LOAF uses the local-based classification, i.e., utilizing the reports in one's local neighborhood to conduct the classification. In detail, for each unlabeled report, LOAF uses the pr_local most nearest labeled test reports to build classifier.

The pr_local labeled reports are chosen as follows:

$$\arg_{pr\_local}\{\min_{j \in L}(distance(UF_i, LF_j)\} \tag{8.4}$$

where UF_i denotes the feature vector of i_{th} unlabeled report which needs to be classified. LF_j represents the feature vector of j_{th} labeled report, and L represents the labeled dataset in this iteration. Note that, if the size of L is smaller than pr_local, then pr_local is set as the size of L. Similarly, we apply cosine similarity to calculate the distance of the two feature vectors.

(4) Whether to Terminate This step is to judge whether the labeling process could be terminated. Our approach considers two different scenarios of termination. The first one is that user can input the maximum effort (e.g., number of labeling instances) they can afford. When the effort is reached, the labeling process will be terminated. The second one is that the approach will decide whether to terminate according to the classification results. If the classification for each unlabeled report remains unchanged in the successive pr_stop iterations, LOAF would suggest termination. For both scenarios, the performance in the last iteration is treated as the final classification results.

Note that, as the classification performance in the first scenario is unguaranteed, this chapter only evaluates the effectiveness of LOAF under the second scenario.

8.3.2 Experiment

8.3.2.1 Experimental Design

(1) Experimental Datasets
We use 34 crowdsourced testing projects for evaluation. Table 8.7 provides details with total number of crowdsourced reports submitted (#), number of `failed` reports (#Fa), number and ratio of reports assessed as `true fault` (#TF, %TF). Additionally, we have three other projects to conduct the case study in RQ3.

Table 8.7 Projects under investigation

	#	#Fa	#TF	%TF		#	#Fa	#TF	%TF
P1	321	267	183	68.5	P2	874	717	144	20.1
P3	302	168	125	74.4	P4	216	144	31	21.5
P5	492	455	280	61.5	P6	403	304	25	8.2
P7	688	647	253	39.1	P8	1094	727	447	61.4
P9	504	394	157	39.8	P10	320	163	61	37.4
P11	637	537	220	40.9	P12	436	232	165	71.1
P13	297	223	129	57.8	P14	217	157	46	29.3
P15	423	272	250	91.9	P16	556	398	251	63.1
P17	815	667	262	39.3	P18	307	180	122	67.8
P19	632	545	183	33.5	P20	580	323	112	34.7
P21	802	672	177	26.3	P22	466	402	102	25.3
P23	1414	1034	500	48.3	P24	1502	1152	583	50.1
P25	342	181	76	41.9	P26	824	503	131	26.0
P27	524	424	163	38.4	P28	391	317	253	35.2
P29	390	334	87	26.0	P30	495	417	83	19.9
P31	832	754	465	61.7	P32	806	522	199	38.1
P33	358	93	49	52.7	P34	452	284	58	20.4

Summary

#		#Fa		#TF		%TF	
19,712		14,609		6,372		43.4	

Projects for case study

C1	231	177	87	49.1	C2	690	455	182	40.0
C3	1428	1004	392	39.0					

(2) Baselines

To demonstrate the advantages of LOAF, we first compare our approach to three *active learning techniques*, which are commonly-used or the state-of-the-art techniques:

Margin Sampling Randomly choose the initial test report to label. Use all current labeled reports to build classifier, and query a report for which the classifier has the smallest difference in confidence for each classification type (true fault or not). Label it and repeat the process.

Least Confidence Randomly choose the initial test report to label. Use all current labeled reports to build classifier, and query a report that the classifier is least confident about. Label it and repeat the process.

Informative and Representative [31] Randomly choose the initial test report to label. Use all current labeled reports to build classifier. Then query a report which can both reduce the uncertainty of classifier and represent the overall input patterns of unlabeled data. Label it and repeat the process. This is the state-of-the-art technique.

To alleviate the influence of initial report on model performance, for each method, we conduct 50 experiments with randomly chosen initial reports.

As there might be some historical data which can be utilized for model building, we also compare our approach with **supervised learning technique**. Inspired by the cross-project prediction in defect prediction and effort estimation, our experimental design is as follows: for each project under testing, we choose the most similar project from all available crowdsourced testing projects, then build a classifier based on the reports of that selected project. The similarity between two projects is measured based on the marginal distribution of training set and test set.

Both our approach and these baselines all involve utilizing machine learning classification algorithm to build classifier. We have experimented with Support Vector Machine (SVM), Decision Tree, Naive Bayes, and Logistic Regression. Among them, SVM can achieve good and stable performance. Hence, we only present the results of SVM in this chapter, due to space limit.

(3) Evaluation Metrics

As the main consideration for active learning is cost-efficient, we utilize **accuracy** and **effort** to evaluate the classification performance.

The F-Measure of classifying true fault after termination, which is the harmonic mean of precision and recall, is used to measure the **accuracy**. The reason we do not use precision and recall separately is because most of the F-Measure in our experiments is 1.00, with 100% precision and 100% recall.

We record the percentage of labeled reports among the whole set of reports after termination, to measure the **effort** for the classification.

8.3.2.2   Results and Analysis

RQ1: How Effective Is LOAF in Classifying Crowdsourced Reports?

We first investigate the performance of LOAF in classifying crowdsourced report for each experimental project. Then we study the influence of parameter pr_local and pr_stop on model performance, as well as suggest the optimal pr_local and pr_stop. Finally, we explore the influence of initial instance on model performance and further demonstrate the effectiveness of our initial selection method.

RQ1.1: What Is the Performance of LOAF in Classifying Crowdsourced Reports?

Table 8.8 demonstrates the accuracy and effort of LOAF for each experimental project (under the optimal pr_local (15) and pr_stop (10)), as well as the statistics. Results reveal that in 70% projects (24/34), LOAF can achieve the accuracy of 1.00, denoting 100% precision and 100% recall. In 85% projects (29/34), the accuracy is above 0.98. Furthermore, the minimum accuracy attained by LOAF is 0.95, with precision and recall both above 0.90.

For effort, LOAF merely requires to label 10% of all test reports on median for building effective classifier. Besides, for 88% (30/34) projects, LOAF only needs to

Table 8.8 Comparison of classification performance with different active learning techniques (RQ1.1 & RQ2.1)

	LOAF		Margin Samp.		Least Conf.		Infor. Repre.	
	acc.	eff.	acc.	eff.	acc.	eff.	acc.	eff.
P1	1.00	13	0.74,0.94	28,55	0.74,0.97	27,42	0.75,0.97	34,45
P2	1.00	15	0.62,0.97	26,42	0.84,0.95	16,32	0.80,0.96	16,42
P3	1.00	52	0.85,0.95	29,56	0.87,0.95	25,58	0.87,0.95	28,40
P4	1.00	8	0.18,0.98	43,73	0.22,0.98	20,44	0.20,0.93	20,56
P5	1.00	13	0.30,0.99	38,88	0.43,0.95	32,44	0.40,0.94	17,54
P6	0.97	14	0.07,0.96	15,24	0.12,0.95	20,34	0.10,0.95	26,40
P7	1.00	6	0.32,0.96	28,78	0.42,0.99	32,54	0.31,0.99	33,65
P8	1.00	2	0.58,0.96	24,51	0.82,0.98	11,24	0.76,0.97	13,24
P9	1.00	3	0.61,0.96	34,54	0.84,0.98	38,49	0.80,0.95	37,49
P10	1.00	11	0.47,0.95	49,89	0.41,0.99	48,53	0.40,0.98	47,66
P11	1.00	2	0.92,0.97	41,81	0.92,0.98	32,53	0.86,0.99	56,80
P12	1.00	10	0.90,0.99	44,84	0.88,0.98	26,34	0.88,0.97	32,38
P13	1.00	14	0.92,0.99	45,95	0.92,0.98	27,45	0.92,0.98	32,80
P14	0.98	25	0.78,0.97	48,68	0.78,0.98	48,72	0.76,0.98	51,71
P15	0.96	22	0.84,0.95	26,38	0.86,0.99	22,35	0.84,0.95	25,36
P16	0.98	14	0.52,0.95	36,86	0.60,0.98	36,78	0.52,0.96	19,64
P17	1.00	4	0.38,0.98	38,68	0.36,0.99	35,52	0.31,0.96	17,23
P18	0.99	25	0.90,0.98	28,98	0.90,0.99	27,54	0.92,0.99	27,34
P19	1.00	2	0.47,0.97	34,84	0.64,0.97	26,74	0.40,0.96	26,43
P20	1.00	3	0.80,0.99	34,84	0.76,0.97	22,46	0.80,0.99	32,68
P21	0.99	12	0.04,0.98	13,44	0.43,0.97	17,37	0.26,0.97	13,32
P22	1.00	7	0.17,0.97	12,32	0.68,0.97	26,38	0.34,0.96	21,38
P23	1.00	1	0.86,0.98	56,86	0.90,0.94	43,63	0.88,0.97	47,62
P24	1.00	1	0.72,0.92	37,57	0.76,0.95	35,45	0.78,0.96	35,43
P25	1.00	11	0.90,0.93	36,90	0.91,1.00	36,52	0.90,0.98	47,62
P26	1.00	3	0.44,0.94	28,56	0.64,0.97	30,53	0.50,0.98	34,50
P27	1.00	3	0.30,0.97	31,81	0.37,0.99	21,46	0.22,0.99	24,59
P28	1.00	4	0.90,0.98	17,47	0.92,0.98	24,32	0.90,0.98	24,42
P29	0.95	20	0.59,0.98	28,80	0.56,0.98	23,47	0.44,0.98	24,42
P30	0.99	14	0.90,0.96	20,60	0.89,0.96	23,50	0.88,0.98	35,54
P31	1.00	2	0.82,0.99	30,40	0.80,0.98	25,42	0.82,0.98	24,38
P32	0.95	9	0.90,0.97	45,78	0.94,0.97	41,56	0.90,0.95	44,62
P33	1.00	15	0.96,1.00	62,98	0.96,0.98	37,64	0.96,0.99	46,64
P34	0.95	15	0.40,0.96	33,48	0.64,0.98	22,35	0.52,0.97	32,42
min	0.95	1	0.04,0.92	13,24	0.12,0.94	11,24	0.10,0.93	13,23
max	1.00	52	0.96,0.99	62,98	0.96,1.00	48,78	0.96,0.99	56,80
med.	1.00	10	0.67,0.97	33,70	0.77,0.98	26,46	0.77,0.97	30,47
avg.	0.99	11	0.61,0.96	33,67	0.69,0.97	28,48	0.64,0.96	30,50

Note: The two numbers in one cell represent minimum and maximum value of 50 random experiments

label less than 20% of all reports, which can support classifying all the remaining test reports effectively.

The above analysis indicates that LOAF can facilitate the report classification with high accuracy and little effort.

RQ1.2: What Is the Impact Of Parameter *pr_local* on Model Performance and What Is the Optimal *pr_local* for LOAF?

We use *pr_local* to control the local neighborhood when conducting local-based classification. To answer this question, we vary *pr_local* from 2 to 50 with *pr_stop* as 10, and compare the classification performance (Fig. 8.8). We find that for all experimental projects, there are two patterns of performance trend under changing

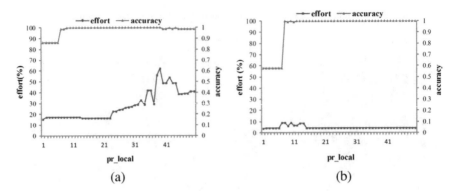

Fig. 8.8 Influence of *pr_local* on performance (RQ1.2). (**a**) Project 3. (**b**) Project 10

pr_local. Due to space limitation, we only present the performance trend of one random-chosen project for each pattern.

We can observe that *pr_local* indeed could influence the model performance, which indicates the need for finding the optimal *pr_local*. In the first pattern, the performance would remain best from *pr_local* is 15, thus the optimal *pr_local* ranges from 15 to 50. In the second pattern, only when *pr_local* is between 13 and 23, the accuracy is highest while the effort is lowest, thus the optimal *pr_local* is in a narrower range (from 13 to 23). The reason why performance keeps unchanged in the first pattern is that the actual labeled instances are fewer than *pr_local*, so that the actual *pr_local* used in such scenario is the number of labeled instances, not the demonstrated *pr_local*. Generally speaking, too small and too large *pr_local* can both result in low accuracy and high effort. This may be because small *pr_local* will result in the overfitting of classifiers, while large *pr_local* can easily bring noise to the model.

To determine the optimal *pr_local* in our approach, we first obtain the value of optimal *pr_local* for each experimental project. Then we count the occurrence of each value and consider the value with most frequent occurrence as optimal *pr_local*, which is 15, 16, and 17 in our context. We simply use 15 in the following experiments for saving computing cost.

RQ1.3: What Is the Impact of Parameter *pr_stop* on Model Performance and What Is the Optimal *pr_stop* for LOAF?

In our work, we use *pr_stop* to decide whether to terminate. To answer this question, we use the optimal *pr_local* obtained earlier, which is 15, and vary *pr_stop* from 2 to 20 for experiments. Through examining the performance trend for all experimental projects, we find that there are also two patterns of performance trend under changing *pr_stop*. We only present the performance trend of one random-chosen project for each pattern in Fig. 8.9, because of space limitation.

Similarly, we can observe that *pr_stop* indeed could influence the model performance, thus suggesting the optimal *pr_stop* would be helpful. It is easily understood that with the increase of *pr_stop*, the effort would increase corre-

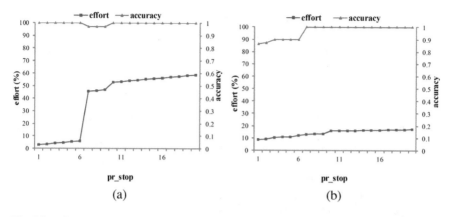

Fig. 8.9 Influence of *pr_stop* on performance (RQ1.3). (**a**) Project 3. (**b**) Project 10

spondingly. From the first pattern, we can observe that accuracy might occasionally decrease with the increase of *pr_stop*, but can recover when *pr_stop* is 10. The second pattern shows that the accuracy can reach the highest and remain unchanged, from *pr_stop* is 7.

To determine the optimal *pr_stop*, we first obtain the value of *pr_stop* when the accuracy reach the highest and keep stable for each project (10 and 7 for the two demonstrated projects). We then consider the maximum among these values as optimal *pr_stop*, which is to ensure all the projects can reach the highest accuracy. In our experimental context, the optimal *pr_stop* is 10.

RQ1.4: What Is the Impact of Initial Instance on Model Performance and How Effective of Our Initial Selection Method?

To answer this question, we experiment with random-chosen report acting as the initial instance, and repeat N times (N is set as half of project size). Figure 8.10 demonstrates the min, average and max value of model performance for random selection of initial report.

Nearly 40% (13/34) projects would undergo quite low accuracy (min value is less than 0.2) when randomly choosing initial report. For effort, nearly 60% (20/34) projects would involve quite high effort (max value is more than 30%) when

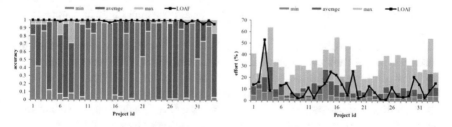

Fig. 8.10 Influence of initial instance on model performance (RQ1.4)

choosing some random report for initial labeling. This reveals that random selection of initial instance can usually fall into low performance. The results further indicate the great necessity to design a method for the selection of initial instance to ensure a stable performance.

We then compare the performance of our initial selection method with the statistics of random selection. For accuracy, in 70% (24/34) projects, our method of initial selection can achieve the maximal value which the random selection can ever achieve. For other projects, the difference between our method and the maximal value of random selection is almost negligible, ranging from 0.008 to 0.04. These findings reveal that our initial selection method can achieve high and stable accuracy even compared with the best accuracy which random selection can ever reach.

For effort, in 97% (33/34) projects, our method of initial selection requires less effort than the maximal effort which random selection would require. In 55% (19/34) projects, our method requires less effort than the average effort required by random selection. In 86% (13/15) of remaining projects, the difference between the effort of our method and the average effort of random selection is smaller than 10%. These illustrations further reveal that our initial selection method is superior to random selection, considering its stable results, high accuracy, and little effort.

RQ2: Can LOAF Outperform Existing Techniques in Classifying Crowdsourced Reports?

To demonstrate the advantages of our approach, we compare the performance of LOAF with both active learning techniques and supervised learning technique.

RQ2.1: How Does LOAF Compare To Existing *Active Learning Techniques* in Classifying Crowdsourced Reports?

Table 8.8 illustrates the performance of LOAF and three active learning baselines. As we mentioned above, we conduct 50 experiments for each active learning method because their random initialization can effect the final performance. We present the minimum and maximum performance of the random experiments for these methods. LOAF has well-designed initial selection step, so its performance is unique. The value with dark background denotes the best accuracy or effort for each project.

At first glance, we can find that all the three baseline methods can occasionally fall into quite low accuracy and more effort, for most of the projects. On the contrary, as we have well-designed method to choose the initial report, LOAF can achieve high and stable performance. We also noticed that even the state-of-the-art method ('Infor. Repre.' method in Table 8.8) can not perform well for crowdsourced testing reports. This may stem from the fact that it does not consider the local nature of the dataset.

We then compare the performance of LOAF with the best performance which the baselines can ever achieve (highest accuracy or least effort). We can observe that all statistics (min, max, median and average) of accuracy for LOAF is higher than the best performance of baselines, denoting our approach can achieve a more accurate classification performance (the median value is 1.00). In addition, these statistics for effort of our approach are all less than the baselines (10% vs. 26% for median value).

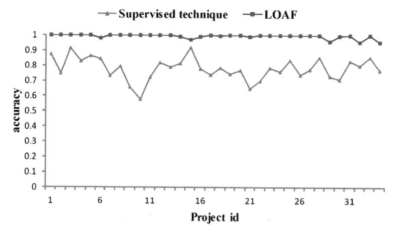

Fig. 8.11 Comparison of classification performance with supervised learning technique (RQ2.2)

We then shift our focus to the performance of each project. For more than 85% of all projects (29/34), our approach can attain both the highest accuracy and least effort, even compared with the best performance of baselines. Besides, for one of the remaining projects, our approach can achieve much higher accuracy, with 27% more effort at worst (P3), than the best baseline approach. For other four projects, our approach has slight decline in accuracy but with least effort. We also noticed that the decline is quite small with the maximum being 0.03 (0.95 vs. 0.98), and all the accuracy of our approach is above 0.95.

When it comes to the time and space cost of the mentioned techniques, it takes less than 1.0 seconds and less than 4.0 MB memory for each step. Due to space limit, we would not present the details.

RQ2.2: How Does LOAF Compare to Existing *Supervised Learning Technique* in Classifying Crowdsourced Reports?

Figure 8.11 illustrates the accuracy of LOAF and supervised prediction technique. We do not present the effort because supervised learning relies on historical data for classification, thus the effort is labeling all the training data.

We can easily observe for all the projects, the accuracy of LOAF is higher than the accuracy obtained by supervised learning. The median accuracy of supervised learning for all projects is 0.77, which is much smaller than that of LOAF (1.00). This indicates that LOAF can perform even better than supervised classification, which built on the large amount of historical labelled data. The reason might be originated from the fact that existing techniques cannot well deal with the local bias of crowdsourced testing data.

Chapter 9
Duplicate Detection of Crowdsourced Testing Reports

9.1 Introduction

The benefit of crowdsourced testing must be carefully assessed with respect to the cost of the technique. At first place, crowdsourced testing is a scalable testing method under which large software systems can be tested with appropriate results. This is particular true when the testing is related with the feedback on GUI systems, or subjective opinions about different features.

One aspect of crowdsourced testing which is not received enough attention is the confusion factors in crowdsourced testing results. Our observation on real industrial data shows that an average of 82% crowdsourced testing reports are duplicate, which suggests much of the crowdsourced testing work can be optimized. A significant problem with such a large number of duplicate reports is that the subsequent analysis by software testers becomes extremely complicated. For example, we find that merely working through 500 crowdsourced testing reports to find the duplicate ones takes almost the whole working day of a tester. This chapter mostly removes that effort by a novel method for detection of duplicate reports.

The issue of duplicate reports has been studied in terms of textual descriptions. However, in practice, it is common that different people might use different terminologies, or write about different phenomena to describe the same issue, which makes the descriptions often confusing. Because of this, most existing approaches for duplicate report detection suffer from low accuracy. However, when dealing with crowdsourced testing reports of GUI systems, besides the textual descriptions, often the feedback is in the form of images. Our observation on real industrial crowdsourced testing data reveals that an average of 94% crowdsourced testing reports are accompanied with an image, i.e., screenshot of the app. We suppose this is another valuable source of information for detecting duplicate crowdsourced testing reports. Compared with the textual description, a screenshot can reflect the real context of the bug and is not affected by the variety of natural languages.

We propose SETU which combines information from the ScrEenshots and the TextUal descriptions to detect duplicate crowdsourced testing reports. We first extract two types of features from screenshots (i.e., image structure feature and image color feature), and two types of features from textual descriptions (i.e., TF-IDF feature and word embedding feature). We then obtain the screenshot similarity and textual similarity through computing the similarity scores based on the four types of features. To decide the duplicates of a query report, SETU adopts a hierarchical algorithm. Specifically, if the screenshot similarity between the query report and candidate report is higher than a threshold, we treat the candidate report as the first class and rank all reports in the first class by their textual similarity. Otherwise, we treat it as the second class (follow behind the first class) and rank all reports in this class by their combined textual similarity and screenshot similarity. Finally, we return a list of candidate duplicate reports of the query report, with the ranked reports of the first class followed by the ranked reports of the second class. Section 9.2 will present the details of this approach.

9.2   Combining Textual Description and Screenshot Information for Duplicate Reports Detection

9.2.1   Motivation

In this section, we present two examples from real-world crowdsourced testing to motivate the need of using both the screenshots and the textual descriptions in duplicate crowdsourced testing report detection. These examples draw from a sport application, i.e., JIAJIA Sport. It can automatically record and analyze users' sport-related information such as running, rope skipping, etc. To better test this application, its testers distribute the testing task on crowdsourced testing platform, and 462 crowdsourced testing reports are submitted by the crowd workers. By analyzing these crowdsourced testing reports, we find the following two motivating examples.

9.2.1.1   Motivating Example 1: Descriptions Could Be Confusing

Crowdsourced testing reports *Rope-145* and *Rope-270* are about the sharing function (Fig. 9.1). Their descriptions are as follows:

Rope-145: I press the qzone[1] sharing button in the bottom and want to share my rope skipping record, but nothing happens.

---

[1] qzone is a popular social networking website in China.

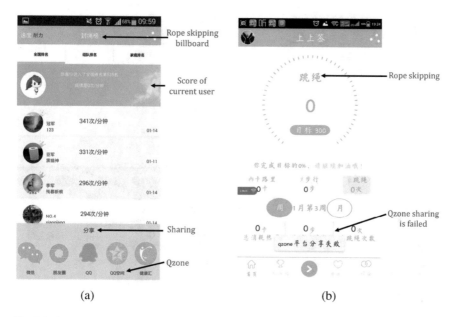

Fig. 9.1 Motivating example 1. (**a**) Rope-145. (**b**) Rope-270

Rope-270: I press the sharing button and want to share my rope skipping record to qzone, but nothing happens except a failure notice.

Both descriptions contain such words as "sharing button", "rope skipping record", and "qzone". Using traditional duplicate detection approaches, these two reports would be identified as duplicates with a high probability. However, if the screenshot information is considered, they can be easily determined as non-duplicates, which is the ground truth. The screenshot of *Rope-145* is about the billboard of rope skipping record, and the crowdsourced testing report reveals a bug about sharing the ranking of rope skipping record. For the screenshot of *Rope-270*, it demonstrates the detail page of rope skipping record, and the report reveals a bug about sharing the detailed record. In this sense, the screenshot provides the context-related information and can help better detect duplicate reports. One may argue that the above information should be in the *operation steps* submitted by the crowd workers. However, the crowd workers are far from professional testers, and in our datasets only few reports contain the detailed and correct operation steps.

Finding 1: The textual descriptions of crowdsourced testing reports may easily lead to confusing understanding. With the help of context-related information provided by screenshots, the duplicate crowdsourced testing reports can be detected more accurately.

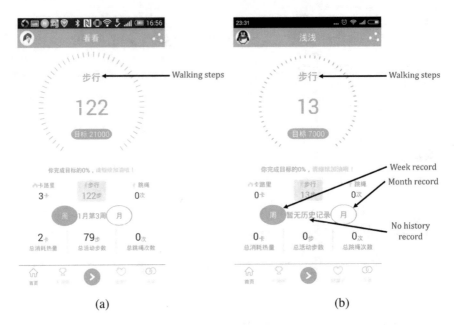

(a)   (b)

Fig. 9.2 Motivating example 2. (**a**) Rope-62. (**b**) Rope-217

9.2.1.2   Motivating Example 2: Screenshots Usually Lack Details

In this example, crowdsourced testing reports *Rope-62* and *Rope-217* have similar screenshots (Fig. 9.2). If the duplicate detection is only based on the screenshot information, these two reports would be determined as duplicates with a high probability. However, the ground truth is just the opposite. Their descriptions are as follows:

> *Rope-62: I walked for 10 min, but the steps only increased by 10. An hour later, i just sat on my chair, but the steps increased sharply.*

> *Rope-217: In the detail page, there is indeed step record for today, but there is no step record for this week.*

From the descriptions, we can easily observe that these two crowdsourced testing reports involve two different bugs, although under the same function which is denoted by the two highly similar screenshots. In this sense, a screenshot merely demonstrates the context-related information about a crowdsourced testing report. We still need to refer to the textual descriptions to finally determine whether they are duplicates.

Finding 2: Screenshots of crowdsourced testing reports mainly demonstrate the context-based information. Under a specific context, only with the detailed illustration provided by the textual description, the duplicated reports can be accurately detected.

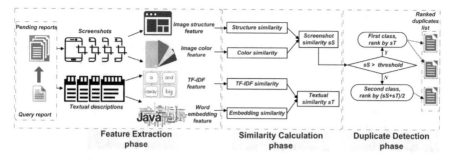

Fig. 9.3 Overview of SETU

9.2.2 Approach

Motivated by the two examples, we propose a duplicate detection approach (SETU), which combines information from both the ScrEenshots and the TextUal descriptions to detect duplicate crowdsourced testing reports. Figure 9.3 illustrates the overview of SETU, which is organized as a pipeline comprising three phases: feature extraction, similarity calculation, and duplicate detection.

In the feature extraction phase, for the screenshots, we extract two types of features, i.e., image structure feature and image color feature. For the textual descriptions, we also extract two types of features, i.e., TF-IDF (Term Frequency and Inverse Document Frequency) feature and word embedding feature.

In the similarity calculation phase, based on the four types of features, we compute four similarity scores between the query report and each of the pending reports, and obtain the screenshot similarity and textual similarity. Cosine similarity, which is commonly used for measuring distance, is employed in our approach.

In the duplicate detection phase, we design a hierarchical algorithm. In detail, if the screenshot similarity between the query report and pending report is larger than a specific threshold, we treat the pending report as first class and rank all reports in the first class by their textual similarity. Otherwise, we treat it as second class (follow behind the first class) and rank all reports in this class by their combined textual similarity and screenshot similarity. Finally, we return a list of candidate duplicate reports of the query report, with the ranked reports of the first class followed by the ranked reports of the second class. The reason why we separate reports in two classes is to take the advantages of the information provided by screenshots. As described previously, the screenshots can provide the context-related information, and reports with different screenshots are very unlikely to be duplicate with each other. We will further discuss the performance of other combinations of the screenshot similarity and textual similarity.

9.2.2.1 Extracting Screenshot Features

We extract screenshot features from the image of screenshot accompanied with each crowdsourced testing report. Note that, in our experimental projects, all the crowdsourced testing reports contain zero or one screenshot. For reports which do not have a screenshot, we use a default blank picture to extract the features. Future work will consider the situation that one report contains several screenshots. We use the following two types of features.

(1) Image Structure Feature The geometric structure of an image exhibits fundamental information for distinguishing screenshots. Images with highly similar geometric structures (e.g., line segments) would be probably the same screenshot.

Gist descriptor can capture the spatial structure of an image through the segmentation and processing of individual regions. Its general idea is as follows: propose a set of perceptual dimensions (naturalness, openness, roughness, expansion, ruggedness) to represent the dominant spatial structure of an image; estimate these dimensions based on the spectral and coarsely localized information; generate a multidimensional space in which scenes sharing membership in semantic categories are projected closed together.

We use the publicly available package[2] with default parameters to extract image structure feature. It results in a 128-dimensional image structure feature vector for each image.

Figure 9.4 shows the image structure features for the four screenshots in Figs. 9.1 and 9.2. The x axis is the feature's dimension (i.e., 128), while the y axis is the value of the feature in each dimension. We can easily find that the image structure feature vectors of *Rope-145* and *Rope-270* are obviously different with each other, while the structure feature vectors of *Rope-62* and *Rope-217* are almost the same. This coincides with our visual perception.

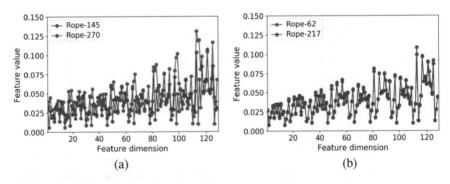

Fig. 9.4 Image structure features. (**a**) Rope-145 and Rope-270. (**b**) Rope-62 and Rope-217

---

[2] http://people.csail.mit.edu/torralba/code/spatialenvelope/.

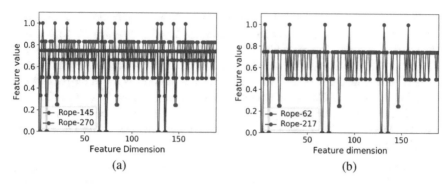

Fig. 9.5 Image color features. (**a**) Rope-145 and Rope-270. (**b**) Rope-62 and Rope-217

(2) Image Color Feature Color is another basic indicator of visual contents, and is often used to describe and represent an image. Images with highly similar color distributions are probably the same screenshot.

MPEG-7 descriptor can capture the representative colors on a grid superimposed of an image based on segmentation and clustering. Its general idea is as follows: use the edge flow algorithm to segment image; perform color clustering on each segmented region to obtain its representative colors and calculate the percentage of these colors; each representative color and its corresponding percentage form a pair of attributes that describe the color characteristics in an image.

We also use the publicly available software[3] to extract the image color feature. It results in a 189-dimensional image color feature vector for each image.

Figure 9.5 demonstrates the image color feature vectors for the four screenshots in Figs. 9.1 and 9.2. The x axis is the feature's dimension (i.e., 189), while the y axis is the value of the feature in each dimension. The image color feature vector of *Rope-145* exerts obvious difference with the vector of *Rope-270*, while the color vector of *Rope-62* is quite similar with the vector of *Rope-217*. Just as the image structure feature, this coincides with our visual perception.

Both structure feature and color feature are widely used in image processing tasks, so we adopt both of them in the duplicate crowdsourced testing report detection and explore their performance.

9.2.2.2 Extracting Textual Features

We extract textual features from the textual descriptions of crowdsourced testing reports, and use them to extract the following two types of features.

(3) TF-IDF Feature TF-IDF (Term Frequency and Inverse Document Frequency) is one of the most popular feature for representing textual documents in information

---

[3] http://www.semanticmetadata.net/.

retrieval. The main idea of TF-IDF is that if a term appears many times in one report and a few times in the other report, the term has a good capability to differentiate the reports, and thus the term has high TF-IDF value. Specifically, given a term t and a report r, $TF(t, r)$ is the number of times that term t occurs in report r, while $IDF(t)$ is obtained by dividing the total number of reports by the number of reports containing term t. TF-IDF is computed as: $TF - IDF(t, r) = TF(t, r) \times IDF(t)$.

With the above formula, the textual description of a report r can be represented as a TF-IDF vector, i.e., $r = (w_1, w_2, \ldots, w_n)$, where w_i denotes the TF-IDF value of the ith terms in report r.

(4) Word Embedding Feature   Word embedding is a feature learning technique in natural language processing where individual words are no longer treated as unique symbols, but represented as d-dimensional vector of real numbers that capture their contextual semantic meanings.

We use the publicly available software[4] to obtain the word embedding of a report. With the trained word embedding model, each word can be transformed into a d-dimensional vector where d is set to 100 as suggested in previous studies. Meanwhile a crowdsourced testing report can be transformed into a matrix in which each row represents a term in the report. We then transform the report matrix into a vector by averaging all the word vectors the report contains as previous work did. Specifically, given a report matrix that has n rows in total, we denote the ith row of the matrix as r_i and the transformed report vector v_d is generated as follows:

$$v_d = \frac{\sum_i r_i}{n} \tag{9.1}$$

With the above formula, each crowdsourced testing report can be represented as a word embedding vector.

The TF-IDF feature focuses on the similarity of reports considering the term matching, while the word embedding feature concerns more on the relationship of terms considering the context they appear. We adopt both of them in our approach and investigate their performance in duplicate report detection.

9.2.2.3   Conducting Duplicate Report Detection

Following the previous studies, our duplicate crowdsourced testing report detection problem is formulated as follows: Given a query report of a crowdsourced testing project, our approach would recommend a list of duplicate reports from all the pending reports of the project and rank them by their probabilities to be duplicates. We design a hierarchical algorithm (Algorithm 2) to detect the duplicate reports.

In the algorithm, the screenshot similarity can be seen as a filter because the screenshot provides the context-related information. If two crowdsourced testing

---

[4] https://code.google.com/archive/p/word2vec/.

Algorithm 2 Duplicate report detection algorithm

Input:
    Pending crowdsourced testing report set R;
    Query report q; Threshold $thres$
Output:
    A list of duplicate reports D;
1: **for** each report r in R and q **do**
2:     Extract the image structure feature vector and image color feature vector from its screenshot;
3:     Extract the TF-IDF feature vector and word embedding feature vector from its textual description;
4: **end for**
5: **for** each report r in R **do**
6:     **for** $fType$ in $[structure, color, tfidf, embedding]$ **do**
7:         Compute the cosine similarity between the $fType$ vector of q and r, and denote as s_fType;
8:     **end for**
9:     $s\_screenshot = (s\_structure + s\_color)/2$;
10:    $s\_textual = (s\_tdidf + s\_embedding)/2$;
11:    $s\_total = (s\_screenshot + s\_textual)/2$
12:    **if** $s\_screenshot > thres$ **then**
13:       put r in D_first
14:    **else**
15:       put r in D_second
16:    **end if**
17: **end for**
18: Rank D_first based on reports' $s\_textual$ and put them in D sequentially
19: Rank D_second based on reports' s_total and put them in D sequentially (follow behind the reports of D_first)

---

reports have different screenshots, they are unlikely to be duplicate even if the textual similarity between them is high. In addition, if two crowdsourced testing reports are accompanied with the same screenshot, whether they are duplicate reports mainly depends on the similarity of their textual descriptions.

The threshold to determine whether two screenshots are the same one is an input parameter. We explore the influence of this parameter on the detection performance.

We have also experimented with different weights for $s\_structure$ and s_color when combining them to obtain $s\_screenshot$ (Line 9 in Algorithm 2), the weights for s_tfidf and $s\_embedding$ when combining them to get $s\_textual$ (Line 10 in Algorithm 2), as well as the weights for $s\_screenshot$ and $s\_textual$ when combining them to obtain s_total (Line 11 in Algorithm 2). Results turned out that when the two similarities have an equal weight, SETU can achieve a relative good and stable performance. Due to space limit, we do not present the detailed results. Note that, this does not imply the screenshot and textual descriptions are equally important, because the weights for $s\_screenshot$ and $s\_textual$ are only used in the second class of reports (Line 10 and 19 in Algorithm 2). Another note is that, for the reports in the second class, we have experimented with other ranking manners, i.e., by *s_screenshot*, by *s_textual*, and results turned out that with the ranking manner shown above, the detection performance is relative good and stable.

9.2.3 Experiment

9.2.3.1 Experimental Design

(1) Experimental Dataset

9.2.4 Experimental Dataset

We use 12 crowdsourced testing projects for evaluation. Table 9.1 presents the detailed information of the projects with the application domain, the number of reports (i.e., *# report*), the number and percentage of reports which have screenshots (i.e., *# screenshots* and *% screenshots*).

There is a label accompanied with each report. It signifies a specific type of bug assigned by the tester in the company. Reports with the same label denote they are duplicates of each other. In this sense, we treat the pair of reports with the same label as duplicates, while the pair of reports with different labels as non-duplicates.

Table 9.1 also presents the percentage of duplicates (i.e., *% duplicates*) and percentage of duplicate pairs (i.e., *% duplicate pairs*).

(2) Baselines

To explore the performance of our proposed SETU, we compare it with three state-of-the-art and typical baseline approaches. Note that, since there is no approach

Table 9.1 Projects under investigation

	Domain	# report	# screenshot	% screenshot	# duplicates	% duplicates	% duplicate pairs
P1	Music	213	188	88%	208	97%	31%
P2	Weather	215	200	93%	168	78%	7%
P3	Beauty	230	216	94%	214	93%	22%
P4	News	243	236	97%	210	86%	18%
P5	Browser	252	237	95%	190	75%	14%
P6	Medical	271	255	94%	207	76%	3%
P7	Safety	282	270	96%	249	87%	23%
P8	Education	284	278	98%	233	82%	4%
P9	Health	317	307	97%	246	77%	3%
P10	Language	344	317	97%	236	68%	2%
P11	Sport	462	425	93%	391	84%	2%
P12	Efficiency	576	547	95%	490	85%	11%
Summary		78,738		94%		82%	12%

designed for duplicate *crowdsourced testing report* detection, we choose the approaches for duplicate *bug report* detection as our baselines.

Information retrieval with word embedding (IR-EM) [110]: It is the state-of-the-art technique for duplicate bug report detection. This approach first builds TF-IDF vector and word embedding vector and calculates two similarity scores based on them respectively. Meanwhile, it calculates a third similarity score based on bug product field and component field. Finally, it combines the three similarity scores into one final score and makes similar bug recommendation with it.

Similarity based on bug components and descriptions (NextBug) [74]: It is another state-of-the-art similarity-based approach for duplicate bug report detection. This approach first checks whether two reports have the same bug component field, if yes, processes the reports with standard information retrieval technique, calculates the cosine similarity of the reports, and ranks the reports with the similarity value.

Note that, for these two baselines, because the crowdsourced testing reports do not have the product or component fields, we use the most similar field, i.e., *test task id* for substitution.

Information retrieval with topic modeling (DBTM) [65]: It is the commonly-used technique for detecting duplicate bug reports. DBTM supposes a report as a textual document describing one or more technical issues, and duplicate reports as the documents describing the same technical issues. It then utilizes term-based and topic-based features to detect duplicates.

(3) Evaluation Metrics

We use three evaluation metrics, i.e., recall@k, mean average precision (MAP), and mean reciprocal rank (MRR), to evaluate the performance of duplicate detection. These metrics are commonly-used to evaluate the duplicate detection approaches.

Given a query report q, its ground truth duplicate reports set $G(q)$, and the top-k recommended duplicate reports list produced by duplicate detection approach $R(q)$.

Recall@k checks whether a top-k recommendation is useful. The definition of *recall@k* for a query report q is as follows:

$$recall@k = \begin{cases} 1, & if \ G(q) \cap R(q) \neq \varnothing \\ 0, & Otherwise \end{cases} \tag{9.2}$$

According to the formula, if there is at least one ground truth duplicate report in the top-k recommendation, the top-k recommendation is useful for the query report q. Given a set of query reports, we compute the proportion of useful top-k recommendations by averaging the *recall@k* of all query reports to get an overall *recall@k*. As previous approaches, we set k as 1, 5, and 10 to obtain the performance.

MAP (Mean Average Precision) is defined as the mean of the Average Precision (AP) values obtained for all the evaluation queries. The AP of a single query q is calculated as follows:

$$AP(q) = \sum_{n=1}^{|G(q)|} \frac{Precision@k(q)}{|G(q)|} \tag{9.3}$$

In the above formula, $Precision@k(q)$ is the retrieval precision over the top-k reports in the ranked list, i.e., the ratio of ground truth duplicate reports of the query report q in the top-k recommendation:

$$Precision@k(q) = \frac{\#\, ground\, truth\, in\, top\, k}{n} \tag{9.4}$$

MRR (Mean Reciprocal Rank) is defined as the mean of the Reciprocal Rank (RR) values obtained for all the evaluation queries. RR of a single query q is the multiplicative inverse of the rank of first correct recommendation $first_q$ (i.e., first ground truth duplicate report in the recommendation list):

$$RR(q) = \frac{1}{first_q} \tag{9.5}$$

9.2.4.1   Results and Analysis

RQ1: How Effective Is SETU in Detecting Duplicate Crowdsourced Testing Reports?

Figure 9.6 presents the *recall@1*, *recall@5*, *recall@10*, *MAP*, and *MRR* for SETU and three baselines. We can see that, our approach SETU can achieve the highest performance in all experimental projects for all five evaluation metrics. *recall@1* is 0.44 to 0.79 across all experimental projects, denoting in 44% to 79% circumstances, our approach can find the duplicate report in the first recommendation. *recall@5* is 0.66 to 0.92 across all experimental projects, denoting in 66% to 92% circumstances, our first five recommendations contain the duplicate report. *MAP* is 0.21 to 0.58 across all experimental projects. The reported *recall@1* in existing duplicate bug report detection approach is 0.16 to 0.67, and the reported MAP is 0.26 to 0.53. Since our experiment is conducted on crowdsourced testing reports which is different from bug reports in open source projects, these figures are not comparable. However, the fact that these figures being the same order of magnitude proves the effectiveness of our approach.

Compared with the three baselines, SETU brings great improvement in all five evaluation metrics for all experimental projects. The improvement of *recall@1* is 20% to 211% compared with the three baselines, while the improvement of MAP is 28% to 241% in all experimental projects. Other evaluation metrics also undergo similar improvements.

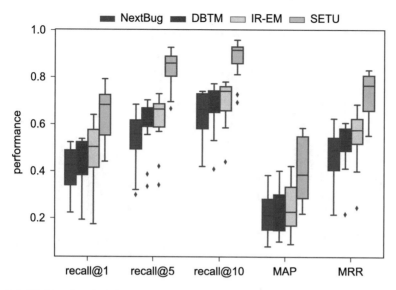

Fig. 9.6   SETU vs. baselines (RQ1)

We further conduct Mann-Whitney U Test for the five metrics between SETU and each baseline. Compared with the three baselines, SETU statistically significantly (i.e., p-value for all tests is less than 0.05) achieves a better performance in terms of all the evaluation metrics for all experimental projects. This further indicates the effectiveness and advantage of our approach.

Among the three baselines, the *IR-EM* and *NextBug* employ the *product* field or *component* field to help detect duplicate reports. We use a different field *test task id* in this experiment. The reason is that the crowdsourced testing reports do not have the field *product* or *component*, and *test task id* is the most similar field. Moreover, we also experiment with four other fields, i.e., *phone type, operation system, ROM information*, and *network environment* and the performance is even worse.

The performance of *NextBug* is almost the worst. This might because the reports from different test tasks are already distinguishable in their textual descriptions. Therefore, the utilization of the *test task id* field could not provide extra information in detecting duplicate reports. The low performance of *IR-EM* in our crowdsourced testing reports dataset might due to the similar reason. As the *test task id* almost could not contribute to duplicate detection, the baseline *IR-EM* degenerates to, to some extent, the approach of only using textual descriptions (i.e., the TF-IDF and word embedding features).

The *DBTM* utilizes term-based and topic-based features for duplicate detection. The low performance of this baseline might because, unlike the large-scale open source projects, the reports of one crowdsourced testing project only have very few topics. The optimal topic number is about 100 to 300 for Eclipse, OpenOffice, and Mozilla. However, the optimal topic number for our experimental projects is about

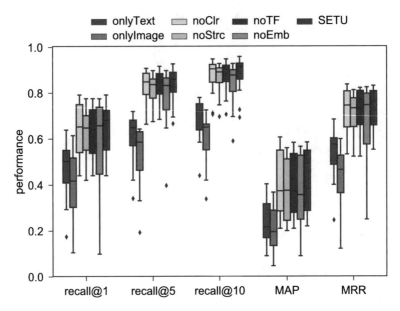

Fig. 9.7 SETU vs. its alternatives (RQ2, RQ3)

5 to 10. The tiny number of topics cannot effectively help distinguish duplicate reports.

RQ2: Are Both Screenshots and Textual Descriptions Necessary in Detecting Duplicate Crowdsourced Testing Reports?

For answering RQ2, we employ two additional experiments, i.e., *onlyText* and *onlyImage*, to investigate whether both screenshots and textual descriptions are necessary in duplicate reports detection. In detail, *onlyText* denotes ranking the reports only based on the textual similarity, while *onlyImage* denotes ranking the reports only based on the screenshot similarity. Figure 9.7 presents the performance for SETU and its two variations.

We can observe that the performance obtained by *onlyText* or *onlyImage* is worse than SETU. The improvement in *recall@1* of SETU is 23% to 211% compared with *onlyText*, and 17% to 319% compared with *onlyImage*. The improvement in *MAP* of SETU is 31% to 241% compared with *onlyText*, and 40% to 552% compared with *onlyImage*.

We further conduct Mann-Whitney U Test for the five metrics between SETU and *onlyText*, *onlyImage*. Compared with only using screenshots or textual descriptions (i.e., *onlyText*, *onlyImage*), SETU significantly (i.e., p-value for all tests is less than 0.05) achieves a better performance in terms of all the evaluation metrics for all experimental projects. This further indicates that only using screenshots or textual descriptions is not effective enough, and combining these two sources of information is a sensible choice for duplicate crowdsourced testing report detection. To make our presentation more catchy, we do not provide the detailed results either.

The performance of *onlyImage* is a little lower than the performance of *onlyText*. This might because the screenshot mainly provides the context-related information. Without the assistance of textual descriptions, the screenshot can not distinguish the duplicate reports in many circumstances. Moreover, duplicate detection with only textual descriptions can neither achieve equivalent performance with SETU, denoting the screenshot plays an indispensable role in detecting duplicate crowdsourced testing reports.

RQ3: What Is the Relative Effect of the Four Types of Features (i.e., TF-IDF, Word Embedding, Image Color, and Image Structure) in Detecting Duplicate Crowdsourced Testing Reports?
We use another four experiments, i.e., *noTF*, *noEmb*, *noClr*, and *noStrc*, to investigate the relative effect of the four types of features utilized in duplicate detection. Each experiment denotes conducting the duplicate detection by removing one specific type of feature. For example, *noTF* denotes applying other three features except TF-IDF (i.e., only use word embedding, image color and image structure feature) for duplicate detection. Figure 9.7 presents the performance for SETU and its four variations.

We can observe that, in most circumstances, performance obtained by SETU is better than or equal with the performance obtained by using three features (i.e., *noClr*, *noStrc*, *noTF*, or *noEmb*). In rare cases, the performance obtained by using three features is a little better than the performance of SETU.

We further conduct Mann-Whitney U Test for the five metrics between SETU and *noClr*, *noStrc*, *noTF*, *noEmb*. SETU significantly (i.e., p-value for all tests is less than 0.05) achieves a better performance than other four variations in terms of all the evaluation metrics for all experimental projects. This further indicates our proposed approach of combining these four types of features is effective.

Among the four experiments with three types of features, we can see that *noEmb* achieves relatively worse results. This might because the word embedding feature focuses on the relationship of terms by considering the context they appear. Without this feature (i.e., *noEmb*), simply matching the occurrence of terms, which is done by TF-IDF feature, cannot effectively detecting the duplicate reports. This implies word embedding feature is the least replaceable feature, i.e., the performance would undergo a relatively large decline if removing this feature.

We can also see that *noClr* achieves relatively better results among the four experiments with three types of features. This indicates image color feature is the most replaceable feature, i.e., the performance would undergo a relatively small decrease if removing this feature. This also implies that image color feature would sometimes bring noise in the duplicate detection.

Chapter 10
Prioritization of Crowdsourced Testing Reports

10.1 Introduction

In Chaps. 8 and 9, we have mentioned that it is often time-consuming and tedious to manually inspect all received test reports. Besides automatic classification of test reports introduced in Chap. 8 and duplicate detection of test reports introduced in Chap. 9, this chapter seeks for other alternatives for managing these test reports, i.e., to prioritize test reports for manual inspection.

Past research has produced test-case prioritization techniques (e.g., [20, 39, 46, 77, 104, 114]) in which test *cases* from a regression test suite are prioritized so that they execute in an order that reveals faults earlier. Although such techniques do not address the concept of prioritizing test *reports*, these techniques' motivating principles provide inspiration for our approach to prioritize test reports: namely, diversification of test behavior to help identify multiple faults.

Another body of existing research attempts to automatically classify bug reports in a bug-reporting system by their level of severity (e.g., [70, 79, 100]). Although such techniques do not address the concept of prioritizing test reports, which are less structured and report both passing and failing behavior, they inspire another motivating principle of our approach: namely, recognizing patterns of risk factors that may foretell reports that reveal faults.

In this chapter, we propose approaches to prioritize test reports for use in crowd-sourced testing. In Chap. 10.2, we first introduce a natural language processing based test report prioritization technique. This technique utilizes two key strategies: (1) a diversity strategy to help developers inspect a wide variety of test reports and to avoid duplicates and wasted effort on falsely classified faulty behavior, and (2) a risk strategy to help developers identify test reports that may be more likely to be fault-revealing based on past observations. Together, these strategies form our **DivRisk** strategy to prioritize test reports in crowdsourced testing.

© The Author(s), under exclusive license to Springer Nature Singapore Pte Ltd. 2022
Q. Wang et al., *Intelligent Crowdsourced Testing*,
https://doi.org/10.1007/978-981-16-9643-5_10

Furthermore, in the mobile testing domain, test reports often consist of screen-shots and shorter descriptive text. Therefore, the text-based technique may be ineffective or inapplicable. The shortage and ambiguity of natural-language text information and the well defined screenshots of activity views within mobile applications motivate our second technique based on using image understanding for multi-objective test-report prioritization. Therefore, in Chap. 10.3, we present a multi-objective optimization-based prioritization technique to assist inspections of crowdsourced testing reports, by taking the similarity of screenshots into consideration.

10.2   Test Report Prioritization with Diversity and Risk Strategies

10.2.1   Motivation

We have collected the crowdsourced testing reports of three applications from Baidu[1] as described follows.

P1: The first project is Baidu-Input[2] on Android, which can support several input methods. Testers in the company provide 10 functionality sets. One crowd worker can select one functionality set, and each functionality set can be selected by at most two crowd workers, who use different mobile phones and different versions of Android.

P2: The second project is Baidu-Browser[3], which is a web browser. Testers in the company provide seven functionality sets for regression testing. One crowd worker can select three functionality sets.

P3: The third project is Baidu-Player[4], which is a multimedia player. Testers in the company provide three performance testing scenarios. One crowd worker should cover all of these three scenarios.

Workers can report other problems, such as usability and compatibility problems, in test reports.

There are over 2000 test reports submitted for the three applications, among which 757 were labeled as "failed" and as such were gathered for manual inspection. Upon manual inspection of all test reports that were labeled as failed, 462 of the 757 failed test reports were false positives. In other words, 462 out of 757 test reports described behavior that was either correct behavior or behavior that was considered

---

[1] baidu.com.

[2] http://shurufa.baidu.com/.

[3] http://liulanqi.baidu.com/.

[4] http://player.baidu.com/.

outside the behavior of the studied software system (e.g., external problems such as advertisements).

Through informal and extensive discussions with professional test engineers at Baidu, a number of observations and lessons were learned:

1. The number of test reports submitted by crowdsourced workers quickly became challenging to manually inspect. A larger crowdsourced testing session would have produced prohibitively many reports to manually inspect.
2. The number of false positives were more numerous than would have been expected, and presented challenges for inspection.
3. Many of the true positives and false positives were duplicates of the same underlying behavior.
4. Many crowdsourced workers performed many easy tasks and reported shallow bugs, presumably due to the incentive structures that reward quantity of submitted reports.
5. The word choice among the true positive and false positive test reports were sufficiently consistent, when accounting for word variations and synonyms.

Based on these observations by test engineers at Baidu and informed by our discussions with them, we attempted to assist with the processing and inspection of test reports, particularly for the scenario of crowdsourced testing for which the plethora of reports would be even greater. Lessons 1 and 2 simply motivate the need for some automated assistance. Lessons 3 and 4 motivate the need for looking for *diversity* in test reports—test reports that are duplicate (whether true positives or false positives) present the opportunity for wasted inspection effort and delayed identification of new true faults. Lesson 5 motivates the use of natural-language techniques to categorize test reports in an effort to automatically infer duplicate test reports.

As such, our experiences and interactions with our industrial partners motivate us to use natural language techniques (i.e., NLP) to cluster test reports. Lessons 3 and 4 have motivated the need to prioritize these clusters to account for diversity (i.e., our **Div** strategy).

However, because the goal of such prioritization is to reveal as many faults as early as possible, we have incorporated an additional strategy that we are calling **Risk**. The **Risk** strategy learns from already inspected test reports that were manually assessed as *true positive*, i.e., true failures that revealed true faults in the software system under test. As such, the **Risk** strategy guides the prioritization order toward other test report clusters that include similar words.

Finally, we note and recognize that the motivations for **Div** and **Risk** are, in a way, at odds—**Div** seeks to find the next test-report cluster most dissimilar from the already inspected ones, whereas **Risk** seeks to find the next test-report cluster most similar to already-inspected true positives. To account for these contrasting motivations, we created a hybrid strategy, **DivRisk**, that incorporates both **Div** and **Risk** to both maximize the distance from inspected test reports (and thus reduce inspection of duplicates and false positives) and guide the search toward riskier software behavior (and thus increase discovery of new true positives).

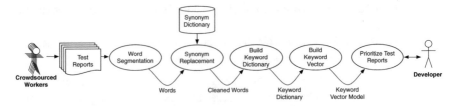

Fig. 10.1 The framework of test report prioritization

10.2.2   Approach

In this section, we present our test report prioritization methods in detail. Figure 10.1 shows the framework of test report prioritization, which mainly contains four steps: (1) test report collection, (2) test report processing, (3) keyword vector modeling, and (4) prioritizing test reports.

10.2.2.1   Test Report Collection

We collect the crowdsourced testing reports of a task, and extract the *input* and *description* of these reports for further processing.

Running Example In order to demonstrate our methods, we sample seven test reports (*Input* and *Description*) in P2, as shown in Table 10.1. TR1, TR5, TR6 and TR7 are false positive test reports. That is, workers mark them as failed test reports, but testers inspect them and judge that they are not. TR2 and TR4 reveal the same fault, denoted by "Fault1". TR3 reveals another fault, denoted by "Fault2". Please note that all test reports are written in Chinese, and our implementation is written to handle Chinese test reports. In order to facilitate understanding, we translate them into English, as shown in Table 10.1.

10.2.2.2   Test Report Processing

As shown in Fig. 10.1, test report processing contains two steps: word segmentation and synonym replacement.

Word Segmentation Word segmentation is a basic NLP task. There are many efficient tools of word segmentation for different languages [42]. We adopted ICTCLAS[5] for word segmentation, which is a widely used Chinese NLP platform. *Input* and *Description* of test reports were segmented into words marked with their Part-Of-Speech (POS) in the context, and then the POS tagging was applied. Hidden

---

[5] http://ictclas.org/.

Table 10.1 Seven test reports from P2

No.	Input	Description	Result
TR1	Login renren.com in compatibility mode, click on "Personal Homepage" or "Send a Gift"(to friends), then after clicking the back button, click the forward button.	The page content is not consistent before clicking the back button with the content after clicking the forward button.	Non-fault
TR2	Enter compatibility mode, login renren.com, click one of the friend links, then click the "Personal Homepage" button, click the back button after loading.	It can go back to friend page only after clicking the back button twice.	Fault1
TR3	Open the browser, select tools→options→security, set "ad block" enhanced, input "http://soudu.org/" in the address bar.	Ads on the lower right of the page are not blocked successfully.	Fault2
TR4	In the input box in Baidu homepage, search "group buying" in compatibility mode. Next, search "ice cream" and the "red bull", double click the back button and then click the forward button once.	The page content is not consistent before clicking the back button with the content after clicking the forward button.	Fault1
TR5	Open the browser, in maximized mode, wait for the program to load and then switch the program, which means rapid and continual full-screen switch.	Sometimes the bug appears when taskbar at the bottom of the system do not disappear, especially when open other browser simultaneously. When the system is busy, the bug is more likely to occur. Move the cursor onto some task and after the appearance of the task, the system operates correctly.	Non-Fault
TR6	Select menu→options in the browser, set "ad block" closed in the security page, open the link "http://www.narutom.com/" and pop-up ads are found while loading; select menu→options in the browser, set "ad block" enhanced in the Security page, open the link "http://www.narutom.com/" to check again.	Ads blocking failed.	Non-Fault
TR7	Select menu→options in the browser, set "ad block" closed in the Security page, open the link "http://www.qidian.com/Default.aspx", and floating ads or ads around the edge of the web page are found; select menu→options in the browser, set "ad block" enhanced in the security page, open the link to check; switch the browser mode, refresh the page to check again.	When the blocking mode is switched, the number of blocked ads is not consistent with the previous one.	Non-Fault

Markov models were used in the POS tagging [3]. Finally, the bi-gram model [7] was introduced to count the classes of words.

Synonym Replacement In crowdsourced testing, test reports are committed by part-time workers or self-identified volunteers, who are often from different workplaces. Workers have different preferences of words and different habits of expression. Some words in test reports are meaningless for revealing faults. Hence, we filtered out these useless words (often referred to as "stop words" in the NLP literature). Prior studies show that verbs and nouns are most important to reflect the content of a document. Hence, we retained only verbs and nouns as candidate keywords of test reports and filtered out other words. Also, workers often use different words to express the same concept. For example, "thumb keyboard" and "nine-grids keyboard" refer to the same layout of keyboard in Chinese. We introduced the synonym replacement technique in NLP to alleviate this problem. In our method, we adopted the synonym library of Language Technology Platform (LTP) [13], which is largely considered as one of the best cloud-based Chinese NLP platforms.

Example In our example, keywords are extracted from test reports, shown in Table 10.2. For example, "compatibility" indicates that TR1, TR2 and TR4 may report some compatibility problems; "menu" indicates that TR6 and TR7 may report some problems related to menu options.

Table 10.2 Keywords from 7 test reports

No.	Keywords
TR1	compatibility/n, mode/n, login/v, click/v, person/n, homepage/n, friend/n, gift/n, back/v, button/n, forwad/v, page/n, content/n
TR2	enter/v, compatibility/n, mode/n, login/v, click/v, friend/n, link/n, person/n, homepage/n, button/n, load/v, back/v, page/n
TR3	open/v, browser/n, tool/n, options/n, security/n, ads/n, block/v, select/v, address/n, input/v, page/n, corner/n, not/v
TR4	compatibility/n, mode/n, input/v, groupon/v, click/n, search/v, button/n, icecream/n, redbull/n, back/v, forward/v, result/n
TR5	open/v, browser/n, maximize/v, condition/n, wait/v, program/n, load/v, finish/v, do/v, switch/v, fullscreen/n, appear/v, system/n, task/n, miss/v, possibility/n, mouse/n, thumbnail/n, restore/v
TR6	browser/n, click/n, menu/n, options/n, security/n, page/n, ads/n, block/v, close/v, open/v, link/n, load/v, find/v, strength/n, check/v, fail/v
TR7	browser/n, click/n, menu/n, options/n, security/n, page/n, ads/n, block/v, closed/v, open/v, link/n, appear/v, floating/v, strength/n, check/v, switch/v, mode/n, refresh/v, button/n, select/v, change/v, number/n

Table 10.3 Keyword dictionary

No.	Word	Freq.	No.	Word	Freq.
K1	button	4	K2	strength	2
K3	homepage	2	K4	input	2
K5	person	2	K6	switch	2
K7	browser	4	K8	friend	2
K9	options	3	K10	login	2
K11	check	2	K12	back	3
K13	mode	4	K14	block	3
K17	click	5	K18	ads	3
K19	load	3	K20	menu	2
K21	security	3	K22	select	2
K23	link	3	K24	page	5
K25	forward	2	K26	compatibility	3

10.2.2.3   Keyword Vector Modeling

The next step is to build the keyword vector model KV. We then create the risk vector RV and the distance matrix DM based on KV.

Keyword Dictionary Keywords extracted from test reports play an important role in test report prioritization. In order to summarize the information contained within the keywords, we count the frequencies (i.e., the number of occurrence) of keywords. In practice, we set a threshold ε to remove some keywords with low frequency to improve the effectiveness. As a result, a keyword dictionary is built.

Example Table 10.3 shows the keyword dictionary of the 7 test reports. In the example, $\varepsilon = 2$, i.e., all keywords with frequency < 2 in Table 10.2 are removed to produce Table 10.3.

Keyword Vector Based on the keyword dictionary, we construct a keyword vector for each test report $tr_i = (e_{i,1}, e_{i,2}, \cdots, e_{i,m})$, in which m is the number of keywords in keyword dictionary. We compute that $e_{i,j} = 1$ if the ith test report contains the jth keyword in keyword dictionary; and $e_{i,j} = 0$ otherwise.

Example Table 10.4 shows the keyword vector model KV of the seven test reports, in which the ith row is the keyword vector of TRi, i.e., $KV(i, *) = tr_i$. KV is an $n \times m$ matrix for n test reports and m keywords in keyword dictionary.

Risk Vector Keywords in a test report reflect their values of revealing faults to some extent. For example, the most frequent word is "click" in Table 10.3. However, we cannot claim that "click" is the most important one for revealing faults, because "click" is a common operation in a browser. We can simply count the number of "1"s in the keyword vector as the risk value of test report, denoted by $RV(i) = \sum_{j=1}^{m} e_{i,j}$. RV is an $n \times 1$ vector for n test reports, as shown in Table 10.5.

Table 10.4 Keyword vector model: KV

No.	1	2	3	4	5	6	7	8	9	10	11	12	13	14	15	16	17	18	19	20	21	22	23	24	25	26
TR1	1	0	1	0	1	0	0	1	0	1	0	1	1	0	0	0	1	0	0	0	0	0	0	1	1	1
TR2	1	0	1	0	1	0	0	1	0	1	0	1	1	0	0	0	1	0	1	0	0	0	1	1	0	1
TR3	0	0	0	1	0	0	1	0	1	0	0	0	0	0	1	1	0	0	1	0	0	1	1	0	1	0
TR4	1	0	0	1	0	0	0	0	0	0	0	1	1	0	0	0	1	0	0	0	0	0	0	0	1	1
TR5	0	0	0	0	0	1	1	0	0	0	0	0	0	0	1	0	0	0	1	0	0	0	0	0	0	0
TR6	0	1	0	0	0	0	1	0	1	0	1	0	0	1	1	1	1	1	1	1	1	0	1	1	0	0
TR7	1	1	0	0	0	1	1	0	1	0	1	0	1	1	1	1	1	1	0	1	1	1	1	1	0	0

Table 10.5 Distance Matrix DM and Risk Vector RV

DM	TR1	TR2	TR3	TR4	TR5	TR6	TR7	RV
TR1	0	3	18	6	15	21	20	11
TR2	3	0	19	9	14	18	19	12
TR3	18	19	0	14	9	9	10	9
TR4	6	9	14	0	11	19	18	7
TR5	15	14	9	11	0	12	15	4
TR6	21	18	9	19	12	0	5	14
TR7	20	19	10	18	15	5	0	17

Distance Matrix Based on the keyword vector matrix KV, we can calculate the distances of each pair of test reports. In this work, we adopt the Hamming distance. That is, for two keyword vectors tr_i and tr_k, we count the number of different $e_{i,j}$ and $e_{k,j}$ in the corresponding position j, as the distance $\mathcal{D}(tr_i, tr_k)$. The inverse distance indicates the similarity of test reports.

Example As a result, we construct an $n \times n$ distance matrix for n test reports. For example, the distance matrix of the seven test reports is shown in Table 10.5. $\mathcal{D}(tr_1, tr_2) = 3$, for TR1 and TR2 have 3 different keywords; $\mathcal{D}(tr_1, tr_7) = 20$, for TR1 and TR7 have 20 different keywords in the keyword dictionary.

10.2.2.4   Prioritization Strategy

In this section, we present three prioritization strategies: ***Risk***, ***Div*** and ***DivRisk***, based on the risk vector RV and the distance matrix DM.

Risk In order to reveal faults as early as possible, it is natural to give the top priority to inspect the most risky test report, i.e., the test report TRi with the highest risk value $RV(i)$. If multiple test reports share the highest risk value, one of them is selected for inspection. Let QTR be the *ordered set* of already inspected test reports.

Example Based on the risk values in Table 10.5, TR7 ($RV(7) = 17$) is first selected for inspection. Then TR6 ($RV(6) = 14$) is selected for inspection, followed by TR2 ($RV(2) = 12$). At this point of processing, $QTR = \{\text{TR7, TR6, TR2}\}$.

Algorithm 3 updateKV(KV, δ, k)

1: **for all** j **do**
2:    **if** $KV(k, j) > 0$ **then**
3:       **for all** i **do**
4:          $KV(i, j) := KV(i, j) + \delta$
5:       **end for**
6:    **end if**
7: **end for**
8: **return** KV

We adopt a dynamic prioritization strategy based on the risk values and the inspection results. That is, if TRk is inspected and determined to be a true failure, all keywords of TRk in KV are increased by δ ($\delta = 0.2$ in our projects). The algorithm of updating KV is shown in Algorithm 3. Based on the new KV, the risk values in RV are updated. That is, for each i, $RV(i) = \sum_{j=1}^{m} KV(i, j)$.

Example Because TR2 is determined to be a true failure, the risk values of TR1, TR3, TR4 and TR5 are updated to 13(11+0.2*10), 9.2(9+0.2*1), 8.0(7+0.2*5) and 4.2(4+0.2*1), respectively. That is, for TR1, TR3, TR4 and TR5, there are 10, 1, 5 and 1 same keywords as TR2, respectively. In this way, we can get the final prioritization result of test reports: $QTR = \{TR7, TR6, TR2, TR1, TR3, TR4, TR5\}$.

Div The Div strategy is based on the diversity principle of test selection [12, 58]. We prefer to select the test report tr_i with the maximal distance to QTR. Without confusion, QTR is also used to denote the set of keyword vectors $\{tr_i\}$ of already inspected test reports. The distance of tr and QTR, denoted by $\mathcal{D}(tr, QTR)$, is defined by the maximum distance between tr and each tr_i in QTR, i.e., $\mathcal{D}(tr, QTR) = Max_{tr_i \in QTR}\{\mathcal{D}(tr, tr_i)\}$.

Example We use the seven test reports to demonstrate **Div** based on the distance matrix in Table 10.5. Initially, the most risky test report TR7 is selected, thus $QTR = \{TR7\}$. For the next test report, since the maximum distance is $\mathcal{D}(tr_1, QTR) = 20$, TR1 is selected. Thus, $QTR = \{TR7, TR1\}$. And then TR5 is selected, because $\mathcal{D}(tr_5, QTR) = 15$ is the maximum distance for the remained test reports. In this way, we can get the final prioritization result of test reports: $QTR = \{TR7, TR1, TR5, TR3, TR4, TR6, TR2\}$.

DivRisk In order to reveal faults as early as possible and as many as possible, *Risk* and *Div* are combined to a hybrid strategy *DivRisk*. The algorithm of *DivRisk* is shown in Algorithm 4. The risk value vector RV and distance matrix DM can be calculated based on KV (Line 1–2). Initially, the most risky test report is selected for inspection (Line 4–6). Then, a candidate set CTR is constructed by selecting n_c test reports with maximum distance(s) $\mathcal{D}(tr_i, QTR)$ (Line 8). The most risky test report in CTR is selected for inspection (Line 9–11). If the inspected test report is a failed one and $\delta > 0$, the keyword vector KV will be updated by Algorithm 3 and the risk value vector RV will also be updated (Line 12–15). Finally, the prioritization result QTR is returned.

Algorithm 4 DivRisk(KV, n_c, δ)

1: For each i, j, $DM(i, j) := \mathcal{D}(KV(i, :), KV(j, :))$
2: For each i, $RV(i) := \sum_{j=1}^{m} KV(i, j)$
3: $TR\{1, 2 \cdots, n\}$: n is the number of rows in KV
4: $QTR := \{\text{TR}k\}$: TRk with the highest risk value $RV(k)$ in TR
5: $QTR := QTR \cup \{\text{TR}k\}$
6: $TR := TR - \{\text{TR}k\}$
7: **while** $|TR| \neq 0$ **do**
8:      $CTR :=$ Select n_c reports TRi with the largest distances $\mathcal{D}(tr_i, QTR)$
9:      Select the test report TRk with the highest risk value in CTR for inspection
10:     $QTR := QTR \cup \{\text{TR}k\}$
11:     $TR := TR - \{\text{TR}k\}$
12:     **if** TRk is a failed test report by inspection AND $\delta > 0$ **then**
13:         $KV := updateKV(KV, \delta, k)$
14:         For each i, $RV(i) := \sum_{j=1}^{m} KV(i, j)$
15:     **end if**
16: **end while**
17: **return** QTR

Example We use the seven test reports to demonstrate **DivRisk**. Initially, TR7 is selected for inspection, for it is most risky. $QTR = \{\text{TR7}\}$. Since the number of test reports is small in this example, we set $n_c = 2$ to facilitate demonstration. The candidate set $CTR = \{\text{TR2, TR1}\}$, for $\mathcal{D}(tr_2, QTR) = 20$ and $\mathcal{D}(tr_1, QTR) = 19$ are the two largest ones. TR2 is selected for inspection, for TR2 is more risky than TR1, i.e. $RV(2) = 12 > RV(1) = 11$. In this way, we can get the final prioritization result $QTR = \{\text{TR7, TR2, TR3, TR4, TR6, TR1, TR5}\}$.

The hybrid strategy *DivRisk* will be reduced to the risk strategy *Risk* if $n_c \geq |TR|$, and it will be reduced to the diversity strategy *Div* if $n_c = 1$. Hence, we need to set a modest number to n_c ($n_c = 8$ in our projects) for a reasonable hybrid result.

10.2.3   Experiment

10.2.3.1   Experiment Design

(1) Experimental Dataset
In this study, we evaluated our test report prioritization methods: **Risk**, **Div** and **DivRisk** with the three crowdsourced testing projects described in Sect. 10.2.1. In our projects, $\delta = 0.2$ and $n_c = 8$ as described above.

All test reports in our experimental projects were manually inspected by testers without any prioritization method. We carefully checked the inspection results again and get the final inspection results, as summarized in Table 10.6.

Table 10.6 Summary of test reports

Project	P1	P2	P3
# Report	274	231	252
# F-Report	186	47	62
% F-Report	67.88%	20.35%	24.60%
# Fault	27	22	18

In Table 10.6, "# Report" is the number of test reports marked as failed by workers. These test reports were collected in the test report bucket. Testers inspected these test reports to judge whether they could reveal faults. "# F-Report" and "% F-Report" are the number and the percentage of test reports judged as failed ones by testers, respectively. In practice, some tests may reveal same faults. "# Fault" is the number of faults revealed by these test reports.

(2) Baselines

In order to verify the effectiveness of our prioritization methods, three baselines for comparison are selected. The first baseline of comparison was the **Random** strategy, which is widely used in software testing. Given a set of finite number of test reports, all possible orderings of test reports could be enumerated in theory. Supposing that we know which test reports are truly fault revealing in advance, the **Best** and the **Worst** prioritization results could be determined. For example, {TR2, TR3, TR4, TR1, TR5, TR6, TR7} is one of the best prioritization results and {TR7, TR1, TR5, TR6, TR2, TR4, TR3} is one of the worst prioritization results. In order to fairly compare these prioritization methods, the experiment was repeated 50 times to collect experimental data.

(3) Evaluation Metrics

In order to measure the effectiveness of prioritization methods, we adopt the APFD (Average Percentage of Fault Detected), which is a widely used evaluation metric in test case prioritization. For each fault, we mark the index of the first test report which reveals it. Based on the order of the test reports and information about which test reports revealed which faults, we can calculate the APFD values to measure the effectiveness of the prioritization methods. A higher APFD value indicates a better prioritization result. That is, it can reveal more faults earlier than the other methods do. APFD is formalized as follows.

$$APFD = 1 - \frac{T_{f1} + T_{f2} + \ldots + T_{fM}}{n \times M} + \frac{1}{2 \times n} \qquad (10.1)$$

in which, n denotes the number of test reports and M denotes the total number of faults revealed by all test reports. T_{fi} is the index of the first test report that reveals fault i.

APFD indicates the fault detection rate of all test reports. However, testers cannot inspect a large number of test reports in limited time. In practice, testers will stop inspecting test reports when the limited resource is used up. At that time, testers may only inspect 25% or 50% test reports. Therefore, we should evaluate how APFD varies for permutations of the same set of test reports. We use the linear interpolation [46] as follows.

- M denotes the total number of faults revealed by all test reports.
- $p \in \{25\%, 50\%, 75\%\}$, the percentage used in our experiment.
- $Q = M \times p$, which is the number of faults corresponding to a percentage. Let $int(Q)$ and $frac(Q)$ be the integer part and fractional part of Q, respectively. If $frac(Q) = 0$, the linear interpolation is needed.
- i, j are the indexes of reports that reveal at least Q and $Q+1$ faults respectively. The linear interpolation is calculated as $i + (j - i) \times frac(Q)$

The linear interpolation value indicates the cost of testing to detect the given number of faults. Hence, a lower value of linear interpolation indicates a better prioritization result.

10.2.3.2 Result Analysis

RQ1: Can Our Prioritization Methods Improve the Effectiveness of Test Report Inspection?

If we have no prioritization method on-hand, testers will inspect test reports in a random order. That means, testers would be motivated to adopt a prioritization method only if it can outperform the **Random** strategy. RQ1 evaluates the effectiveness of our prioritization methods **Risk**, **Div** and **DivRisk**.

The results of all prioritization methods are shown in Fig. 10.2. Figure 10.2a, c, and e shows the box-plots of APFD results of the three projects (P1–P3) for the 50 experimental runs. The prioritization methods are shown on the horizontal axis, and the APFD values are shown on the vertical axis. The blue horizontal line in Fig. 10.2a, c, and e denotes the **Best** APFD value, in theory.

Figure 10.2b, d, and f shows the average growth curves of the three projects (P1–P3). The percentage of the inspected test reports is shown on the horizontal axis, the percentage of revealed faults is shown on the vertical axis.

Based on the results shown in Fig. 10.2a, c, and e, we can find that all of our prioritization methods outperform **Random**. In particular, **DivRisk** can outperform **Random** significantly. The hybrid strategy **DivRisk** can also improve the single strategies **Risk** and **Div**. Moreover, the box-plots show that our methods are substantially more stable than **Random**. Figure 10.2b, d, and f show the average growth curves. The line charts in Fig. 10.2b and d show that **DivRisk** presents smooth curves to the top (**Best**).

In order to further investigate our test report prioritization methods, we do Bonferroni means separation tests for all results in Table 10.7. All F-values are very large and the all p-values are much smaller than 0.001 in Table 10.7. Compared with the **Random** strategy, the percentage of improvement of **DivRisk** ranges 14.29%–34.52%. In summary, the experimental results are encouraging for the use of the hybrid **DivRisk** strategy in practice.

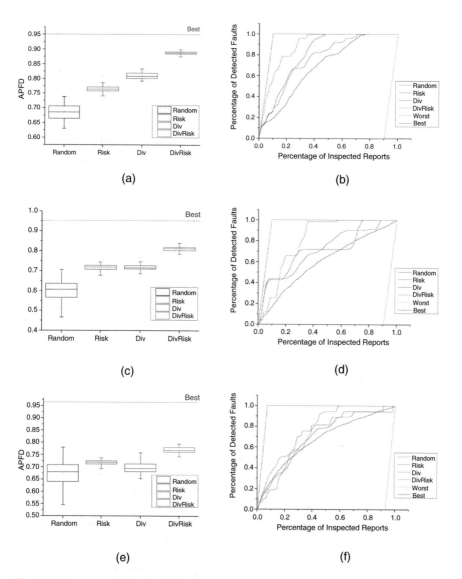

Fig. 10.2 Experimental Results (50 times). (**a**) APFD on P1. (**b**) Average Fault Detection Rates on P1. (**c**) APFD on P2. (**d**) Average Fault Detection Rates on P2. (**e**) APFD on P3. (**f**) Average Fault Detection Rates on P3

Summary   We find that our prioritization methods can improve the effectiveness of test report inspection.

RQ2: How Large Is the Gap Between Our Prioritization Methods and Best?

In practice, it is difficult to design one method that can work well in all cases. Hence, it is valuable to know the gap between the on-hand methods and the best one in theory. RQ2 evaluates the room for improvement of our prioritization methods.

Table 10.7 Bonferroni
means separation tests

Method	APFD Means	Improvement $\frac{X-Random}{Random}$	Gap $\frac{Best-X}{X}$
P1: $F(3, 200) = 1549.27$, p-value ≤ 0.0001			
DivRisk	0.8879	29.66%	7.07%
Div	0.8094	18.20%	17.46%
Risk	0.7639	11.55%	24.45%
Random	0.6848	–	38.83%
Best	0.9507	38.83%	–
P2: $F(3, 200) = 474.15$, p-value ≤ 0.0001			
DivRisk	0.8113	34.52%	17.39%
Div	0.7167	18.84%	32.89%
Risk	0.7158	18.69%	33.05%
Random	0.6031	–	57.92%
Best	0.9524	57.92%	–
P3: $F(3, 200) = 90.42$, p-value ≤ 0.0001			
DivRisk	0.7686	14.29%	25.46%
Risk	0.7165	6.54%	34.58%
Div	0.6962	3.52%	38.51%
Random	0.6725	–	43.39%
Best	0.9643	43.39%	–

Figure 10.2 shows that the hybrid strategy **DivRisk** provides the best approximation of the **Best** result in P1 and P2. For P3, **DivRisk** provides one of the best results, but there is a larger gap between its results and the **Best** result than we found for P1 and P2. For more details, we can observe the growth curves in Fig. 10.2. The curves of **Best** grow very fast. The curves of **DivRisk** reach the curves of **Best** when we have inspected nearly 30% test reports in P1–P2 and nearly 60% test reports in P3.

Table 10.7 shows the gaps between our prioritization methods and **Best**. The gap between **DivRisk** and **Best** on P1 is small (7.07%). Please recall that the results of **Best** are purely hypothetical and based on an unrealistically omniscient best-case analysis. Hence the result of **DivRisk** may be, or at least approximate, the best one in practice. The gaps on P2 and P3 may be, thus, acceptable (17.79% and 25.49%) in practice, and moreover, do improve the ordering of unordered or random ordering.

In order to explain the results more clearly, we calculate the linear interpolations shown in Table 10.8. Table 10.8 shows the average numbers of inspected test reports in the cases of detecting 25%, 50%, 75% and 100% faults. If we need to reveal 25% or 50% faults, **DivRisk** is near to **Best**. However, if we need to reveal more faults, there may be room for additional improvement. A strange phenomenon is worthy of attention: **Risk** outperforms **DivRisk** for the 25% level of inspected faults for P2

Table 10.8 Linear Interpolation (the average number of inspected test reports)

Pro.	Tech.	25%	50%	75%	100%
P1	Random	35.34	75.83	116.96	196.6
	Risk	21.12	51.64	94.19	190.7
	Div	22.39	46.80	81.27	123.5
	DivRisk	**8.885**	**20.38**	**43.09**	**99.20**
	Best	6.750	13.50	20.25	27.00
P2	Random	33.37	74.86	138.3	217.5
	Risk	**8.780**	56.22	106.4	201.2
	Div	9.200	47.46	121.2	170.1
	DivRisk	21.97	**36.24**	**66.93**	**98.30**
	Best	5.500	11.00	16.50	22.00
P3	Random	22.25	61.72	122.2	226.8
	Risk	32.90	57.14	**83.01**	230.2
	Div	23.88	61.16	104.4	246.4
	DivRisk	**14.90**	**42.44**	95.94	**145.3**
	Best	4.500	9.000	13.50	18.00

and the 75% level of inspected faults for P3. This result may be due to the heuristic nature of these methods and will be a subject of additional investigation in the future.

Summary We find that our prioritization methods can provide a reasonable approximation for the theoretical *Best* result for some software subjects, and for other subjects provide some of the smallest gaps. In all cases that we studied, it provided better than the unordered or random ordered test reports.

10.2.4 Discussion

10.2.4.1 Method Selection

The idea of prioritization is widely used in software engineering, especially in software testing. Crowdsourced testing is usually conducted in rapidly iterative software development. In this situation, we can only inspect a subset of test reports for revealing and fixing faults before software release. Hence, test report prioritization plays a key role for a cost-effective result of crowdsourced testing. Our prioritization methods contain two key parts: the risk strategy (**Risk**) and the diversity strategy (**Div**). In software development, we need to reveal as many faults as possible, i.e., **Div**. In contrast, we need to inspect the most probable "true failure" test reports early, i.e., **Risk**. These two requirements of crowdsourced testing drive us to design a hybrid prioritization method **DivRisk** by combining **Risk** and **Div**. Therefore, it is not surprising that **DivRisk** can outperform the random prioritization technique significantly.

10.2.4.2   Mobile Application Testing

DivRisk shows different effectiveness in different crowdsourcing projects. The P1 project involves mobile application testing. The effectiveness of **DivRisk** in P1 was very encouraging and approximated **Best**. We reviewed the test reports in P1 and discussed with testers in Baidu. Since workers used different mobile phones and different versions of Android, they reported many compatibility problems of the application under test. The compatibility problems were easier to identified than other problems for mobile applications. Moreover, part-time workers (crowd workers here) preferred to select testing tasks of mobile applications, because it could be done anywhere and any time. Therefore, it is not surprising that the prioritization results of P1, as shown in Table 10.6, were more effective than on P2 and P3. Workers committed more test reports and revealed more faults on P1 than on P2 and P3. The percentage of useful test reports (i.e., F-report) is 67.88%, which was better than P2 (20.35%) and P3 (24.60%). The high quality test reports can help our test report prioritization methods, because our methods rely on keywords from test reports. As such, such crowdsourced testing and prioritization methods may be a good fit for mobile application testing.

10.2.4.3   Cost and Scalability

The total cost of test report processing in our projects is less than 10 min. Please note that our prioritization algorithms only involve numerical calculation on KV, RV and DM. Hence, the cost of test report prioritization methods may be negligible. The **DivRisk** algorithm is flexible. For example, we can set $\delta = 0$ in Algorithm 4, and as a result, the dynamic prioritization strategy are reduced to a static prioritization strategy. The static prioritization strategy does not rely on inspection. Hence, it can be fully automated and be more efficient, although the results may be worse. Moreover, **DivRisk** does not rely on the languages of test reports. **DivRisk** can also be used for test reports written in other languages by using other NLP tools for other natural languages. For example, we can adopt Stanford CoreNLP[6] for word segmentation [40] and WordNet[7] for synonym replacement [57] to process English test reports, and build keyword vector model KV. Based on KV, we can use the **DivRisk** algorithm for English test report prioritization.

---

[6] http://nlp.stanford.edu/software/corenlp.shtml.

[7] http://wordnet.princeton.edu/wordnet/.

10.3 Multi-Objective Test Report Prioritization Using Image Understanding

In this section, by taking the similarity of screenshots into consideration, we present a multi-objective optimization-based prioritization technique to assist inspections of crowdsourced test reports. In this technique, we employ the Spatial Pyramid Matching (SPM) technique to measure the similarity of the screenshots, and apply the natural-language processing technique to measure the distance between the text of test reports.

10.3.1 Motivation

In almost all existing techniques, the test reports are captured and analyzed based on their textual similarity (e.g., [87, 88, 93]) or based on their execution traces (e.g., [18, 70, 105]). For software designed for a desktop computer, such techniques are likely sufficient. However, for mobile software, writing long and descriptive test reports may be more challenging on a mobile-device keyboard. In fact, test reports written from mobile devices tend to be shorter and less descriptive, but also to include more screenshots (primarily due to the ease of taking such screenshots on mobile platforms). Due to this paucity of textual information for test reports, and also due to the ambiguity of natural language and prevalence of badly written reports [124], utilizing the screenshots to assist with such mobile crowdsourced testing techniques is appealing. Moreover, the activity views of typical mobile applications often provide distinguishable aspects of the software interface and feature set, and provide more motivation for utilizing such screenshots. Therefore, we aim at proposing an approach to test-report prioritization that utilizes a hybrid analysis technique, which is both text-based and image-based.

10.3.2 Approach

In this section, we propose an automatic diversity-based prioritization technique to assist the inspection of crowdsourced mobile application test reports. We capture textual and image information and measure the similarity among the reports. For the image analyses, we employed the Spatial Pyramid Matching (SPM) [45] technique to measure the similarity of screenshots. For the textual analyses, we used natural-language textual analysis techniques to measure the similarity of textual descriptions within test reports. Finally, we combine these similarity results using a multi-objective optimization algorithm to produce a hybrid distance matrix among all test reports. Based on these results, we prioritize the test reports for inspection using a

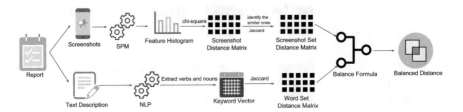

Fig. 10.3   Test-report processing framework

diversity-based approach, with the goal of assisting developers of finding as many unique bugs as possible, as quickly as possible.

This section elaborates the details of our method. We assume the test reports only consist of two parts: text description and screenshots, which we will handle separately and finally generate the balanced distance. Figure 10.3 shows the framework of calculating the distance between the test reports, which mainly contains three steps: (1) screenshot-set distance calculation, (2) test-description distance calculation, and (3) distance balancing. After we compute the distance matrix from the test-report set, we apply various strategies to prioritize test reports.

Even though, in practice, there could be other multi-media information that exists in the mobile test reports, such as the short operation videos and voice messages, our experience indicates that text descriptions and screenshots are the most widely used types of information. In this section, we focus on the processing of mobile screenshots to assist the test-report prioritization procedure. We assume each of the test reports only consists of two parts: a text description and a set of screenshots, i.e., the test report set $R(r) = \{r(S_i, T_i)|i = 0 \dots n\}$, in which, S denotes the screenshots (i.e., images) containing the views that may capture symptoms of the bug being reported, and T denotes the text describing the buggy behavior.

10.3.2.1   Text Processing

The processing of text is similar to the procedure we introduced in the Sect. 10.2. It consists of two steps: (1) keywords set building and (2) distance calculation.

Keywords Set Building   In order to extract the keywords from the natural-language description, we first need to segment the text. Fortunately, word segmentation is a basic NLP task, and as such many efficient tools for word segmentation for different natural languages have been implemented [42]. Similar to the procedure we introduced in the Sect. 10.2, we adopted the Language Technology Platform (LTP) to process the Chinese text descriptions. In this procedure, LTP used the Conditional Random Fields (CRF) model to segment Chinese words and adopted the Support Vector Machine (SVM) approach for tagging the POS. After we compute the segmentation results with the POS tags, we filter out relatively meaningless words that could negatively impact the distance calculation and extract only the nouns and verbs to build the keywords sets.

Distance Calculation Our method focuses on processing mobile test reports. Compared with the test reports of desktop or web applications, one characteristic of typical mobile test reports, and based on our experience, is that their text descriptions are shorter and contain more screenshots. As such, we treat all of the words in the text description equally, and we adopted the Jaccard Distance to measure the difference between the text descriptions T_i in the test-report set $R(r)$. The definition of Jaccard Distance used in our technique is presented in the following equation, in which, K_i denotes the *keyword set* of test report T_i, and $DT(r_i, r_j)$ denotes the distance between the text portion of the test reports r_i and report r_j.

$$DT(r_i, r_j) = 1 - \frac{|K_i \cap K_j|}{|K_i \cup K_j|} \tag{10.2}$$

10.3.2.2   Screenshot Processing

Compared with NLP techniques, image understanding techniques are relatively less studied and used in the software-engineering domain. One of our motivations of conducting this research is to propose a method to extract the information from images to assist software-engineering tasks. The workflow of processing screenshots S is presented in the top branch of Fig. 10.3. The process is composed of three key steps to build up the distance between screenshot sets: (1) building feature histograms, (2) calculating distance between individual screenshots, and (3) computing the distance between screenshot sets.

Feature Histogram Building In order to compute the difference between the screenshots, we convert the screenshots into feature vectors. Bug screenshots provide not only views of buggy symptoms, but also app-specific visual appearances. We hope to automatically identify application behaviors based on their visual appearance in the screenshots. However, the screenshots often have variable resolution and complex backgrounds. Therefore, modeling the similarity between the screenshots merely based on RGB is not an approach that is well suited for our task. To address the challenges, we apply the Spatial Pyramid Matching (SPM) [45] to build a global representation of screenshots. Since the details of SPM are beyond our topic, we only briefly introduce it here.

Given an image, SPM partitions it into sub-regions in a pyramid fashion. At each pyramid level, it computes an orderless histogram of low-level features in each sub-region. After decomposition, it concatenates statistics of local features over sub-regions from all levels. After building the "Spatial Pyramid" representation, we apply kernel-based pyramid matching scheme to compute feature correspondence in two images.

(a)   (b)   (c)   (d)

Fig. 10.4 Four example screenshots from the test reports of the CloudMusic application. (**a**) and (**b**) are screenshots of the playing view, and (**c**) and (**d**) are screenshots of the lyrics view of two different songs. (**a**) Playing-1. (**b**) Playing-2. (**c**) Lyrics-1. (**d**) Lyrics-2

Figure 10.4 presents four original and actual screenshots from four test reports of a popular Chinese music-playing app, CloudMusic. Figure 10.4a and b show the music-playing view of the application, and Fig. 10.4c and d show the lyrics view. Note that in each screenshot, the details of the view differ: e.g., different music is playing, different background images appear, different lyrics are shown, and even the screen size is different for the last image. The layout of screenshots and background colors differ and provide challenges for correct matching: although Fig. 10.4a and b have the same view layout, Fig. 10.4b and d share a similar background color. If we were to directly calculate distance based on the RGB histograms, we would incorrectly get a closer distance between Fig. 10.4b and d. Nevertheless, the image-understanding technique should be able to capture the similarities of the similar views. Intuitively, Fig. 10.4a and b should be identified as similar views, and Fig. 10.4c and d should be identified as similar views.

Based on the four images, SPM first builds the histograms of features for each of image. The resulting histograms for these images are shown in Fig. 10.5.

Screenshot Distance Calculation Using the screenshot feature histograms, a distance is computed for each pair of images. To compute such distances between feature histograms, we adopt the chi-square distance metric [78]. The chi-square metric is generally used to compute the distance between two normalized histogram vectors, i.e., their elements sum to 1. Also, both of the pairwise histograms being compared should contain the same number of bins (i.e., the vectors should have the same number of dimensions).

We use $H_i(x_1, x_2, \ldots, x_n)$ to denote the feature histogram of screenshot s_i, and $H_i(x_k)$ to denote the value of kth feature of s_i. The formula used to calculate

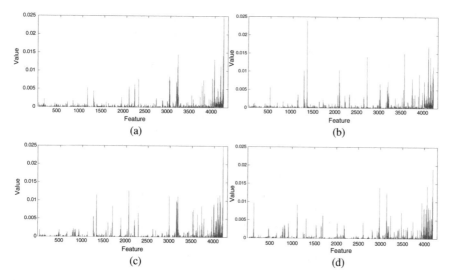

Fig. 10.5 The corresponding feature histograms of the screenshots in Fig. 10.4. (**a**) Playing-1. (**b**) Playing-2. (**c**) Lyrics-1. (**d**) Lyrics-2

Table 10.9 Distance between screenshots of Fig. 10.4

	Playing-1	Playing-2	Lyrics-1	Lyrics-2
Playing-1	0	**0.38957**	0.40255	0.45109
Playing-2	**0.38957**	0	0.51161	0.51873
Lyrics-1	0.40255	0.51161	0	**0.32029**
Lyrics-2	0.45109	0.51873	**0.32029**	0

chi-square distance $Ds(s_i, s_j)$ between screenshot s_i and s_j is defined as follows:

$$Ds(s_i, s_j) = \chi^2(H_i, H_j)$$

$$= \frac{1}{2} \sum_{k=1}^{d} \frac{(H_i(x_k) - H_j(x_k))^2}{H_i(x_k) + H_j(x_k)} \qquad (10.3)$$

Based on Eq. 10.3, we obtain the distance matrix shown in Table 10.9 from the feature histograms of Fig. 10.5.

These results show that the calculated distance between the same views (Playing-1 and Playing-2, and Lyrics-1 and Lyrics-2) have relatively shorter (i.e., smaller) distances (0.389 between playing screenshots and 0.320 between lyrics screenshots) than the across-view distances.

Screenshot Sets Distance Calculation The previous step uses the chi-square distance metric to compute distances between pairs of screenshots. However, in practice, each test report may contain more than one screenshot. So, in this step, we compute the distance between screenshot sets. To account for the diversity of display resolutions of mobile devices and user content (e.g., songs, backgrounds), we set a threshold γ to assess screenshots that match. The γ threshold is first used to find representative members from within the same screenshot set (i.e., from the same test report). Screenshot subsets whose histograms produce chi-square distances that are below the distance threshold (i.e., assessed as representing the same situation) are first represented as an aggregated, summary histogram which is computed as the mean of the feature histograms from the constituent members.

Once the representative set of screenshots are selected from each test report, the chi-squared metric with the γ metric is again used to compute the across-test-report screenshot similarity between the representative screenshots. Again, for screenshots (i.e., their representative histograms) whose distance is less than γ, they are assessed as representing the same view, and as such, the similar and non-similar screenshots from each test report can be used to calculate the inter-test-report screenshot set distance for a pair of reports. For this calculation, we use the Jaccard distance metric. For the test reports r_i and r_j and their respective screenshot sets S_i and S_j, the distance metric is defined as:

$$DS(r_i, r_j) = 1 - \frac{|S_i \cap S_j|}{|S_i \cup S_j|} \tag{10.4}$$

Note that in the special case where both S_i and S_j are the empty set (i.e., no screenshots were included for either test report), we assess DS to be zero.

10.3.2.3 Balanced Formula

Based on above distance computations for both the textual descriptions and the screenshot sets, we combine these distances to produce a hybrid distance. We present Eq. 10.5 to combine these differing distance values. Equation 10.5 is a stepwise formula, where the first condition holds for when the textual descriptions are assessed to be identical by way of the text distance formula DT. In this case, we assess the balanced distance metric to be similarly identical. In the next step, where $DS = 0$, where typically no screenshots were included for either test report, the textual difference is used and scaled to make them more similar, and thus less diverse. This diversity adjustment will make these less descriptive test reports less likely to be highly prioritized in the next prioritization step. In the final step, which holds in all other cases, the harmonic mean is calculated between the textual distance DT and screenshot set distance DS. The resulting balanced distance BD is used to represent the pairwise distance of the corresponding test reports.

$$BD(r_i, r_j) = \begin{cases} 0, & \text{if } DT(r_i, r_j) = 0 \\ \alpha \times DT(r_i, r_j), & \text{if } DS(r_i, r_j) = 0 \\ (1 + \beta^2)\frac{DS(r_i,r_j) \times DT(r_i,r_j)}{\beta^2 DS(r_i,r_j) + DT(r_i,r_j)}, & \text{otherwise} \end{cases} \tag{10.5}$$

10.3.2.4 Diversity-Based Prioritization

Using the computed balanced distance measures for all test reports, we can prioritize the test reports for inspection by developers. The guiding principle of our prioritization approach is to promote diversity of test reports that get inspected. In other words, when a developer inspects one test report, the next test reports that she inspects should be as different as possible to allow her to witness as many diverse behaviors (and bugs) as possible in the shortest order. This diversity-based prioritization strategy has been used by other software-engineering researchers for test prioritization. The goal is for software engineers to find as many bugs as possible in a limited time budget.

Given Q denotes the result queue, the distance between a test report r and Q, denoted by $\mathcal{D}(r, Q)$, is defined by the minimal distance between r and each r_i in Q, i.e., $\mathcal{D}(r, Q) = Min_{r_i \in Q}\{\mathcal{D}(r, r_i)\}$. The algorithm of **BDDiv** is shown in Algorithm 5. In the beginning, Q is empty, we first initialize the algorithm by randomly choosing one report from R and append it to Q. The second step is to calculate the distance between each test report $r_i \in R$ and Q. As soon as we get the distance values, we choose the largest one to append to Q. The whole procedure completes when $|R| = 0$.

Algorithm 5 BDDiv(BD, R)

1: $Q = \varnothing$
2: Randomly choose a test report r_k from R, append r_c to Q
3: $R := R - \{r_k\}$
4: **while** $|R| \neq 0$ **do**
5:      $maxDis := -1, r_c = NULL$
6:      **for all** $r_i \in R$ **do**
7:          $minDis := 2$
8:          **for all** $r_j \in Q$ **do**
9:              **if** $BD(r_i, r_j) < minDis$ **then**
10:                 $minDis = BD(r_i, r_j)$
11:             **end if**
12:         **end for**
13:         **if** $minDis > maxDis$ **then**
14:             $maxDis = minDis$
15:             $r_c = r_i$
16:         **end if**
17:     **end for**
18:     Append r_c to Q
19:     $R := R - \{r_c\}$
20: **end while**
21: **return** Q

Table 10.10 Experimental software subjects

Name	Version	$\lvert R \rvert$	$\lvert F \rvert$	$\lvert S \rvert$	$\lvert R_s \rvert$	$\lvert R_f \rvert$
SE-1800	2.5.1	192	7	856	164	99
CloudMusic	2.5.1	96	16	272	70	40
Ubook	2.1.0	99	22	719	90	99
iShopping	1.3.0	209	73	581	160	130
JustForFun	1.8.5	90	9	109	69	90
Totals	**0.8**	686	127	2537	553	458

10.3.3   Experiment

10.3.3.1   Experimental Design

(1) Experimental Dataset

We collect the crowdsourced testing results of five applications as shown below:

- **JustForFun:** A picture editing and sharing application, produced by Dynamic Digit.
- **iShopping:** A shopping application for Taobao, produced by Alibaba.[8]
- **CloudMusic:** An application for free-sharing music as well as a music player, produced by NetEase.[9]
- **SE-1800:** A monitoring application for a power supply company, produced by Panneng.
- **Ubook:** An application for online education, produced by New Oriental.[10]

The detailed information of the applications is shown in Table 10.10, in which, the $\lvert R \rvert$ denotes the number of reports, $\lvert F \rvert$ denotes the number of faults revealed in the test reports, $\lvert S \rvert$ denotes the number of screenshots contained in the test reports, $\lvert R_s \rvert$ denotes the number of test reports containing at least one screenshot, and $\lvert R_f \rvert$ denotes the number of test reports that revealed faults.

(2) Prioritization Strategies

Technique 1: Ideal   The best result in theory to inspect test reports in such a way as to demonstrate the most unique bugs as early as possible. Represented as IDEAL.

Technique 2: TextDiv   The prioritization strategy based only on the distance between test reports' text descriptions, i.e., in this strategy DT will replace BD as the first parameter of Algorithm 5. Represented as TEXTDIV.

Technique 3: ImageDiv   The prioritization strategy based only on the distance between test reports' screenshots, i.e., in this strategy DS will replace BD as the first parameter of Algorithm 5. Represented as IMAGEDIV.

---

[8] https://guang.taobao.com.

[9] http://music.163.com.

[10] http://www.pgyer.com/y44v.

Technique 4: Random   The random prioritization strategy, which is used to simulate the situation without any prioritization technique. Represented as RANDOM.

Technique 5: Text&ImageDiv   Our prioritization strategy that balances the distance of screenshot sets and text descriptions. Represented as TEXT&IMAGEDIV.

(3) Evaluation Metrics

Considering the goal of this approach is similar to the approach we introduced in the Sect. 10.2.2, we employed the APFD (Average Percentage of Fault Detected) metric and linear interpolation, which are discussed in the Sect. 10.2.3.1, to evaluate the effectiveness of our techniques.

In our experiment, a higher APFD value implies a better prioritization result. That is, it can reveal more faults earlier than the other methods do.

Although the APFD values reflect the global performance of prioritization techniques, in practice developers often cannot inspect all reports in a limited time budget. Thus, we also provide a metric to reveal the percentage of bugs that would be found at certain milestones of inspection. For this, we use linear interpolation to evaluate the partial performance of each prioritization technique. In our experiment, we set the $p \in \{25\%, 50\%, 75\%, 100\%\}$.

(4) Experimental Setup

In order to ensure the correctness of the implementation of SPM, we directly used the MATLAB code provided by the inventors of SPM. There are some key parameters affecting the performance of SPM, which are the size of the descriptor dictionary $DictSize$, number of levels of the pyramid L, and number of images to be used to create the histogram bins $HistBin$. In our experiment, as the recommended values of the SPM inventor, we set $DictSize = 200$, $L = 3$, and $HistBin = 100$. For the NLP technique, because all of test reports in our experiment are in Chinese, we employed the LTP platform to assist the text description analysis.

Moreover, the size of screenshots (i.e., image resolution) submitted by the crowd workers was not fixed; in fact, they varied widely. In order to apply the SPM technique, we resize all screenshots to 480×480 pixels. Given the way that the SPM technique focuses on detecting features within images, resizing the images should not produce a substantial impact to the distance calculation.

In this experiment, we implemented all of the strategies. Particularly for the TEXT&IMAGEDIV strategy, we set the threshold of determining the identity of screenshots γ to 0.1, the factor α that is used to weaken the weight of test reports without any screenshots to 0.75, and the parameter β used to balance the text-based distance and screenshot-set distance to 1, which means, we weigh the two kinds of distance equally.

10.3.3.2 Results and Analysis

RQ1: Can Test-Report Prioritization Substantially Improve Test Report Inspection to Find More Unique Buggy Reports Earlier?
If the software engineers have no test report prioritization technique, they may randomly inspect test reports, in a non-systematic order. $RQ1$ is designed to inform whether prioritization of test reports is, in fact, advantageous. To address the $RQ1$, we conduct the experiment to evaluate the effectiveness of our prioritization techniques alongside a RANDOM-based strategy.

In order to reduce the bias that was introduced by the random initialization of the algorithm and the tie-breaking, we conducted the experiment 30 times and present the result in Fig. 10.6. Figure 10.6a, c, e, g, and i show the boxplots of the APFD results for the five projects, respectively, each aggregated over the 30 experimental runs. Figure 10.6b, d, f, h, and j show the average fault detection rate curves. The exact mean value of APFD is shown in Table 10.11, which also includes the result of one-way ANOVA tests of all strategies: the improved extent over RANDOM, and the gap between our strategies and IDEAL. Furthermore, we present the mean linear interpolation value over the 30 experiment runs in Table 10.12 to demonstrate the performance of our techniques in limited time budgets.

Based on the results shown in Fig. 10.6a, c, e, g, i and in the third column of Table 10.11, we find, to different extents, all of the three diversity-based prioritization strategies outperform RANDOM. Furthermore, in Table 10.11, all F-values are relatively large and the p-values ≤ 0.001, which means the APFD values of the four strategies are significantly different. Compared with the RANDOM strategy, the percentage of improvement of TEXT&IMAGEDIV ranges 9.93%–24.95%.

Summary All of the diversity-based prioritization methods can improve the effectiveness of test report inspection over RANDOM, and thus test-report prioritization can substantially, and significantly, find more unique buggy reports earlier in the prioritized order.

RQ2: To What Extent Can the Image-Based Approaches Improve the Effectiveness of the Text-Only-Based Approach?
$RQ2$ is designed to investigate whether image-understanding techniques can assist the inspection procedure compared with the text-only-based technique. Figure 10.6 reveals that, except on the "JustForFun" project, the TEXT&IMAGEDIV outperforms the TEXTDIV, IMAGEDIV and RANDOM strategies, which means, the image-understanding technique improves the performance of the text-only-based technique. We did a deeper investigation on this problem and found what we speculate to be the reason for the different result for the "JustForFun" project. JustForFun is an image editing and sharing application, and as such, the inherent functionality is to process various user-provided photos. The screenshots for this app largely consist of user content, with relatively few app-specific features in those screenshot images. Thus, the various screenshots of "JustForFun" make the screenshot sets

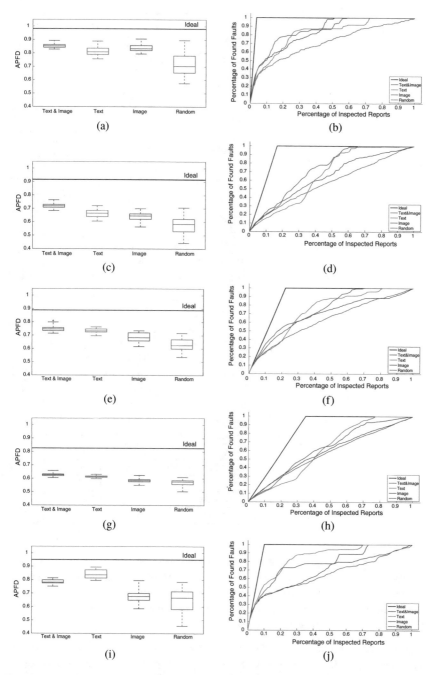

Fig. 10.6 Experiment Results (averaged over 30 runs). (**a**) APFD on SE-1800. (**b**) Average Fault Detection Rates on SE-1800. (**c**) APFD on CloudMusic. (**d**) Average Fault Detection Rates on CloudMusic. (**e**) APFD on Ubook. (**f**) Average Fault Detection Rates on Ubook. (**g**) APFD on iShopping. (**h**) Average Fault Detection Rates on iShopping. (**i**) APFD on JustForFun. (**j**) Average Fault Detection Rates on JustForFun

Table 10.11 One-way ANOVA Tests

Method	APFD Means	Improvement $\frac{X - Random}{Random}$	Gap $\frac{Best - X}{X}$
SE-1800: $F(3, 119) = 54.966$, *p-value* ≤ 0.001			
IDEAL	0.982	37.47%	–
TEXT&IMAGEDIV	0.852	19.32%	15.21%
TEXTDIV	0.817	14.46%	20.10%
IMAGEDIV	0.836	17.04%	17.45%
RANDOM	0.714	–	37.47%
CloudMusic: $F(3, 119) = 73.170$, *p-value* ≤ 0.001			
IDEAL	0.917	58.65%	–
TEXT&IMAGEDIV	0.722	24.95%	26.97%
TEXTDIV	0.664	14.98%	37.98%
IMAGEDIV	0.641	10.99%	42.94%
RANDOM	0.578	–	58.65%
Ubook: $F(3, 119) = 84.167$, *p-value* ≤ 0.001			
IDEAL	0.889	40.92%	–
TEXT&IMAGEDIV	0.750	18.95%	18.47%
TEXTDIV	0.735	16.57%	20.88%
IMAGEDIV	0.686	8.69%	29.65%
RANDOM	0.631	–	40.92%
iShopping: $F(3, 119) = 73.178$, *p-value* ≤ 0.001			
IDEAL	0.825	45.08%	–
TEXT&IMAGEDIV	0.625	9.93%	31.98%
TEXTDIV	0.614	7.88%	34.48%
IMAGEDIV	0.586	2.98%	40.89%
RANDOM	0.569	–	45.08%
JustForFun: $F(3, 119) = 94.482$, *p-value* ≤ 0.001			
IDEAL	0.950	45.89%	–
TEXT&IMAGEDIV	0.784	20.41%	21.16%
TEXTDIV	0.842	29.28%	12.85%
IMAGEDIV	0.681	4.54%	39.55%
RANDOM	0.651	–	45.89%

distance calculating procedure generate large distances, even between the same activity views, which leads to a negative impact on the image-based strategies. In contrast, based on Table 10.12, TEXT&IMAGEDIV outperformed the single text-based prioritization techniques on inspecting different percentage of test report of "SE-1800", "CloudMusic" and "Ubook."

Summary Generally, compared with the text-only-based prioritization strategy, the image-understanding technique is able to improve the performance of prioritizing test reports, both globally (i.e., APFD) and partially (i.e., linear interpolation at many level). However, we found that some classes of apps are naturally less suited

Table 10.12 Linear Interpolation (average number of inspected test reports)

Program	Strategy	25%	50%	75%	100%
SE-1800	IDEAL	1.75	3.50	5.25	7.00
	TEXT&IMAGE	**3.51**	**12.32**	**31.30**	91.70
	TEXTDIV	6.98	23.27	43.27	112.67
	IMAGEDIV	4.21	16.38	50.38	**86.47**
	RANDOM	4.79	31.05	79.36	145.57
CloudMusic	IDEAL	4.00	8.00	12.00	16.00
	TEXT&IMAGE	13.10	**24.30**	**39.33**	62.00
	TEXTDIV	16.10	34.57	44.57	**59.00**
	IMAGEDIV	**11.07**	26.53	49.77	85.83
	RANDOM	14.10	33.97	59.20	88.83
Ubook	IDEAL	5.50	11.00	16.50	22.00
	TEXT&IMAGE	**7.33**	**18.67**	44.17	**64.43**
	TEXTDIV	10.52	23.67	**35.17**	78.03
	IMAGEDIV	8.05	20.20	50.73	95.40
	RANDOM	9.35	29.03	57.82	93.13
iShopping	IDEAL	18.25	36.50	54.75	73.00
	TEXT&IMAGE	37.16	**66.42**	119.27	201.23
	TEXTDIV	52.89	82.82	**111.30**	**160.07**
	IMAGEDIV	**32.60**	75.88	134.59	206.30
	RANDOM	37.20	83.72	144.13	207.13
JustForFun	IDEAL	2.25	4.50	6.75	9.00
	TEXT&IMAGE	2.94	9.32	18.13	64.83
	TEXTDIV	**2.88**	**8.07**	**17.28**	**45.23**
	IMAGEDIV	3.16	18.12	39.01	79.47
	RANDOM	**2.88**	22.25	49.88	80.17

for image-understanding techniques—namely apps where the bulk of the views are composed of user context.

RQ3: How Much Improvement Is Further Possible, Compared to a Best-Case Ideal Prioritization?

$RQ3$ is designed to investigate the gap between the performance of our techniques and the theoretical IDEAL prioritization technique, which could be helpful to engineers in selecting proper techniques in practice and inform the future research in this field. The fourth column of Table 10.11 shows the gap between our strategies and the theoretical IDEAL. We found the gap between TEXT&IMAGEDIV and IDEAL vary from 15.21% to 31.98%. For more details, we can observe the growth curves in Table 10.12. The curve of IDEAL grows at a fast rate. The best situation reached top while the TEXT&IMAGEDIV only stayed around 35%.

Summary We find that our prioritization methods can provide a reasonable small gaps for the theoretical IDEAL result, particularly for some subjects. However, there is room for future work to continue to improve the prioritization ordering of test reports.

10.3.4 Discussion

10.3.4.1 Method Selection

Reflecting on all of our experimental results, we find that image-understanding techniques can provide benefits to test-report prioritization, and that the area of such hybrid text-and-image approaches demonstrates promise. That said, we also observed that different techniques may be more or less applicable for different types of applications. Specifically, we observed that the image editor app produced the worst results for the image-based and hybrid techniques, compared to text-only. In such cases, where the screenshots mainly represent user content, image-based techniques may be less applicable. However, in applications in which little user or external content is displayed, image-based or hybrid techniques may be more applicable.

One noteworthy point is that both the TEXTDIV and TEXT&IMAGEDIV are full-automated, which we believe are more applicable in practice than the semi-automated DivRisk and Risk techniques (introduced in the Sect. 10.2) that require the users to input the inspection result to prioritize the crowdsourced test reports dynamically.

10.3.4.2 Mobile Application Testing

All of our experimentation was conducted on mobile applications, and thus we cannot state with certainty that such results would hold for other types of GUI software, such as desktop or web applications. However, we speculate that while there will likely be new and unique challenges in these domains, the basic concepts would likely hold, at least for the class of applications with relatively less user content. Desktop and web applications have the potential for even more differing screen and window sizes, as well as multiple windows and pop-up dialog windows, and each of these unique aspects would likely need to be addressed. Overall, we speculate that the success of such image-understanding-assisted test-report prioritization techniques would likely depend on the visual complexity of the application views.

Chapter 11
Summarization of Crowdsourced Testing Reports

11.1 Introduction

As we introduced in the Chap. 9, duplicate detection techniques can assist developers in identifying duplicate submissions from the large test report pool, and thus improve the efficiency of test report processing. Prior research primarily focuses on two kinds of information: text descriptions [87, 88] and execution traces [100] to reach this goal. Conventional and widely used issue-tracking systems, such as Bugzilla, Jira, and Mantis, have provided keyword-search-based features for reporters to query similar reports to reduce duplicates. Also, Rastkar et al. presented a test-report summarization technique to assist developers to identify key sentences from test reports to reduce inspection efforts [72].

However, while all of these techniques are built on the assumption that duplicate reports are harmful to software maintenance and aim at filtering out this information, Zimmermann et al. and Bettenburg et al. empirically found that duplicate reports are helpful for report comprehension and debugging [124].

Inspired by this, in this chapter, we introduce a test report summarization technique, which is designed for improving the efficiency of dealing with the set of test reports revealing the same bug. Test report summarization techniques are capable of identifying the critical information, including both the description text and screenshots, from the massive reports, and also extract the information that can be the supplementaries to enrich the bug description.

Different from the conventional bug/test-report-processing techniques, instead of discouraging developers from submitting duplicates and filtering them out, our technique aims at leveraging the additional information provided by them, and summarizing both the *textual and image information* from the grouped duplicates to a comprehensive and comprehensible report.

The proposed CTRAS automatically detects and aggregates the duplicate reports by measuring the similarity of both the text description and screenshots. Based on the aggregation results, for each duplicate report cluster, it identifies the most informative report, which we call the *master report*, and summarizes the supplementary text and screenshots. These supplementaries are sorted by their weight, and CTRAS generates the final summarized report by combining the master report and supplementaries to provide the developer with a comprehensible overview of each test-report duplicate group.

11.2 Crowdsourced Test Report Aggregation and Summarization

11.2.1 Motivation

The high duplicate ratio of crowdsourced testing reports, and their short text descriptions and rich screenshots motivate us to propose an approach to leveraging both the text and image information from duplicate reports to enhance developers' understanding of bugs.

Moreover, a common and conventional belief in software-development practice is that the reporting of duplicate test reports is a bad practice and therefore considered harmful. The long and frequent arguments against duplicates are that they strain issue-tracking systems and waste efforts of software maintainers. Thus, based on this argument, prior researchers have proposed many techniques to assist developers in avoiding wasting time on duplicates. However, there are also arguments to the contrary. Zimmerman et al. [124] claim that the missing information, such as reproduction steps and environment settings, is one of the most serious problems of test reports of open-source projects. They find that developers often need to spend extra time to interact with reporters to identify the missing information and gain enough understanding of the bug. Bettenburg et al. [5] present empirical evidence to show that duplicates provide additional information for describing bugs and this information is helpful for fault localization and fixing. These findings fit the situation of mobile crowdsourced testing, which has been widely adopted in the quality assurance of modern mobile applications.

11.2.2 Approach

We first highlight our main goals and provide definitions and notations that will be used subsequently. Our overall goal is to aggregate duplicate test reports and provide a comprehensible overview of the group. Specifically for mobile software, we seek to provide a technique that is robust and effective in clustering test reports that may contain short text descriptions, but may include screenshots that exhibit failure symptoms.

For a software project with submitted crowdsourced test reports $\mathcal{R}(r) = \{r(S_i, T_i) | i = 0 \ldots n\}$, in which, S denotes the screenshots (i.e., images) containing the views that may capture symptoms of the bug being reported, and T denotes the text describing the buggy behavior. Note that each text description consists of multiple sentences, thus we have $T_i = \{t_{ij} | j = 0 \ldots m\}$, in which, t_{ij} denotes the jth sentence in the test report r_i. Similarly, we employ s_{ij} to denote the jth screenshot in the test report r_i.

Summary The goal of CTRAS is to cluster duplicate reports into groups, each group of duplicate reports is a subset of $\mathcal{R}$, and then to generate a summary $\mathcal{S}$ for each group in $\mathcal{G}$. In our formulation, we define a *summary* for a group of duplicate test reports as a *master report* and a list of *supplementaries*.

Master Report In contrast to traditional testing, crowd workers are often inexperienced and unfamiliar with software testing. They may describe a bug from different aspects and in various ways. This fact leads the quality, writing style, and content of these reports to varying widely [21]. Hence, we seek to find one report that provides a relatively comprehensive description of the issue for the group of duplicates. A *master report* is defined as an individual test report $r^\star \in \mathcal{G}$ that is identified as providing the most information.

Supplementaries Even though presenting the most informative one or its summary is helpful for developers to build a high-level understanding of the bug, the supplementary information, such as different software and hardware settings, diverse inputs, and various triggers, is critical for developers to gain enough knowledge of debugging and fixing. These supplementary details from other test reports in the duplicate group can provide additional insights to developers in understanding the varying conditions that lead to the issue. Hence, we seek to identify the useful information from the redundant information and summarize them into the comprehensible supplementaries. A *supplementary* is defined as the representative information item, i.e., either text or screenshot, which is taken from $(\mathcal{G} - \{r^\star\})$.

Figure 11.1 presents the overview of CTRAS. CTRAS is composed of two main components: *aggregator* and *summarizer*. The *aggregator* is designed for computing the distance between test reports and aggregating the duplicates into group $\mathcal{G}$. We use hierarchical clustering to accomplish this task. To assist developers understanding the content of the duplicate groups quickly, the *summarizer* first picks a single test report that best exemplifies the group of aggregated test reports, then it supplements the information by gradually extracting *supplementary* information, which contains topics or features uncovered by the *master report*.

11.2.2.1 Aggregator

The *aggregator* first computes the distance of test reports and outputs the distance matrix. In the distance computation, we adopt the hybrid strategy, proposed in Chap. 10, to measure the distance between test reports by combining both the image similarity and text similarity. For the textual descriptions, Natural Language Process

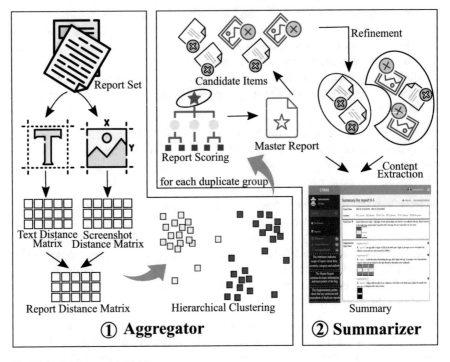

Fig. 11.1 Overview of CTRAS

(NLP) techniques, including tokenization, synonym identification, and keyword vector building, are applied to calculate the text similarity. For the screenshots, the Spatial Pyramid Matching (SPM) [45] technique is adopted to extract the image features and calculate screenshot similarity. The hybrid distance matrix among all reports is built upon the weighted harmonic mean of these two similarities. Applying the SPM algorithm to extract features from one screenshot typically only costs 1-2 s, and computing the distance between two screenshots costs milliseconds.

Based on the distance matrix, the *aggregator* is capable of measuring the similarity between test reports and further grouping the duplicates. Considering that in practice the number of groups cannot be predicted, we adopt Hierarchical Agglomerative Clustering (HAC), which can determine the number of groups based on a threshold distance value, to group the duplicates.

11.2.2.2 Summarizer

The *summarizer* is the core component of CTRAS. For each duplicate test-report group G, it performs the following three steps to generate a summary to assist developers in forming a comprehensive understanding over all reports in G: (1) identifying the master report $r^\star$, (2) generating supplementaries, and (3) forming and generating final summaries.

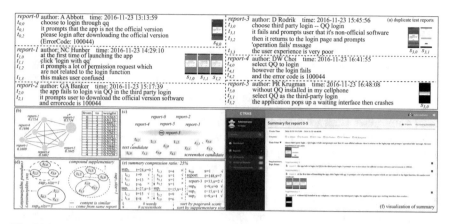

Fig. 11.2 A running example of CTRAS

To ease explanation, we take a real group containing six test reports in our empirical study as an example, and we illustrate each substep in Fig. 11.2. We list the six similar reports in the exemplary group in Fig. 11.2a. Note that all of these reports describe the same bug that involves a problem logging into the app via a third-party tool. Each report of this group consists of its basic attributes, such as report names, creation time, as well as its textual description and several screenshots.

(1) Master Report Identification

To help the developers concisely understand the topic of the test reports within the group, we identify the *master report* $r^\star$ in the first step. We abstract each test-report group into a graph, within which each node represents an individual report. The weight of edges between two nodes indicates the similarity between these two reports. Thus, we can apply the PageRank algorithm, which can compute a numerical rank score and measure the importance for each node within a weighted graph, on each test-report group. CTRAS identifies the test report having the greatest page rank score as the master report for the group.

Example The graph representing the exemplary group is illustrated in Fig 11.2b, and the table shows the hybrid similarity between each pair of these reports. We compute the weight of each node by applying the PageRank algorithm. We find that *report-3* has the highest weight, and thus it is selected as the master report (labeled with $r^\star$) of these six reports. Through reading the contents of *report-3*, developers can reach a high-level understanding of the whole test report group, i.e.,, there is a bug that users can't login the App through QQ social login service as it fails the authentication and is regarded as non-official software.

(2) Supplementary Generation

Even though we have identified the *master report* $r^\star$ and helped the developer get the most informative report within the group G, describing the same bug from other perspectives and providing supplementary materials is critical for developers in fixing the bug properly.

Thus, we further analyze the other reports and identify the content that is shared among them as the supplementary points. In this procedure, we perform two substeps for identifying the supplementaries: (1) identifying candidate items from $(G - \{r^{\star}\})$; (2) grouping the candidate items to form a *supplementary*.

(2.1) Candidate Item Identification Because the sentence is considered to be the immediate integral unit in linguistic theory, a number of prior research efforts that aimed at analyzing test/bug reports to assist developers in understanding the bug descriptions have selected the sentence as the basic unit.

We thus also do so accordingly and measure the similarity between two sentences by computing the Jaccard Distance between their keyword vectors. Jaccard Distance is a useful metric to compare the similarity and diversity of two sets, which is shown in Eq. 11.1. In this equation, t and t' denote the keyword sets of two sentences, $|t \cap t'|$ denotes the number of words in the intersection of both sets, and $|t \cup t'|$ denotes the number of words in the union of both sets. Regarding the screenshot, we adopt the method in Chap. 10 and corresponding parameters to identify different screenshots.

Given a test-report group G and its *master report* $r^{\star}$, to generate supplementaries for $r^{\star}$, the first step is to identify candidate items, i.e., sentences and screenshots, which are NOT included in $r^{\star}$ from $(G - \{r^{\star}\})$. From the set $(G - \{r^{\star}\})$, we extract all singleton items, i.e., individual sentences and screenshots, to get the set of sentences $T = \{t_{ij}\}$ and the set of screenshots $S = \{s_{ij}\}$ of $(G - \{r^{\star}\})$. Similarly, we can get the set of sentences and set of screenshots from $r^{\star}$, and we denote them $T^{\star} = \{t_j^{\star}\}$ and $S^{\star} = \{s_j^{\star}\}$ respectively.

For each sentence whose keyword set is $\{t\}$ in T, if not existing any element in $S^{\star}$ having the $J(t, t^{\star})$ is smaller than the predefined threshold value, we consider it is a candidate sentence for $r^{\star}$. Similarly, given S and $S^{\star}$, we can identify the candidate screenshot for $r^{\star}$.

$$J(t, t') = 1 - |t \cap t'|/|t \cup t'| \tag{11.1}$$

Example As shown in Fig. 11.2c, we label the text items with rectangles and the screenshot items with diamonds. CTRAS identified eight candidate sentences and four candidate screenshots from the exemplary group. For example, $t_{0,2}$ is a candidate sentence as it supplements the "expected result" information (i.e., "ErrorCode: 100044") for $r^{\star}$(i.e., *report-3*); $t_{5,0}$ expresses a special case that "without QQ installed" and $s_{5,0}$ is a candidate screenshot for this case.

(2.2) Candidate Item Refinement Through candidate item identification, all candidate items, which are not similar to any item in the master report, are identified. However, some of these items may be too brief to understand, or they are similar with each other. Therefore, we refine them into concise and representative *supplementaries*.

The refinement process of CTRAS consists of three sub-steps: Step 1 clusters similar candidate items; Step 2 provides an additional clustering of the candidate clusters; and Step 3 weights the candidates within the clusters to identify the most representative among them. In Step 1, we group similar candidate items to remove redundancy and improve the conciseness of the supplementary. In this step, we apply hierarchical agglomerative clustering on the set of candidate sentences to form some candidate sentence clusters. Similarly, we can apply the same strategy on the candidate screenshot set and get the candidate screenshot clusters, using approach Spatial Pyramid Matching described in Sect. 11.2.2.1. Moreover, we record the origin information for each candidate, so that we can map candidates to reports and vice versa. This information is not only useful for further aggregating candidate sentence clusters in the next sub-step but also helpful for developers to track back original reports in practice.

In Step 2, we further group the candidate clusters from Step 1. The purpose of this step is to restore context. This extra level of grouping is useful particularly for singleton clusters (clusters containing only a single candidate item due to the fact it contains distinct information). We merge the clusters based on the origin information: clusters that contain candidates originating from much of the same test reports are clustered.

We define the distance between two candidate item clusters t and s as Eq. 11.2, in which, each cluster can be either candidate sentence cluster or candidate screen cluster and the $\Phi(t)$ represents the set of test reports that contributed to the candidate item cluster t. Based on the Eq. 11.2, candidate item clusters are aggregated into *supplementaries* when the distance between them is smaller than the threshold value θ. *Raw supplementaries* should not be presented to the end-user because they contain too much redundancy.

$$D(t, s) = 1 - |\Phi(t) \cap \Phi(s)| / |\Phi(t) \cup \Phi(s)| \qquad (11.2)$$

In Step 3, we identify the most representative candidate items in each supplementary cluster. Based on our definition of sentence similarity and screenshot similarity, we abstract all sentences and screenshots within a supplementary into a weighted graph respectively and employ the similarity value as the weight of edges. Given these two weighted graphs, we apply the PageRank algorithm and obtain the PageRank score for each of the node, i.e., sentences and screenshots. These weights will be used within the next phase of content extraction to highlight the most relevant and representative information for each supplementary.

Example Figure 11.2d displays the refinement result of all *candidate items*: three *candidate sentences* (i.e.,$t_{0,2}$, $t_{2,1}$ and $t_{4,2}$) are grouped together because they contain "100044 error code"; *candidate clusters* $\{t_{5,0}\}$, $\{t_{5,2}\}$ and $\{s_{5,0}\}$ are grouped because they belong to *report-5*. Particularly, the size of *supplementary-0* is 3 as its content comes from three reports.

(3) Content Extractor
Based on *master report* and *supplementaries*, we can further refine them and generate a concise final summary.

In many textual summarization techniques (e.g., [50, 71, 72]), the compression ratio K controls the conciseness of the final summary.

In previous works, compression ratio is computed as the ratio of the number of selected keywords to the number of total keyword within the original document. However, because CTRAS aims at generating summary over both text and screenshots, we extend the classic definition. For the text, we define the compression ratio as the ratio of the number of unique selected word to the total number of unique word within the supplementary. Similarly, for the screenshot, the compression ratio is the ratio of the number of selected screenshots to the total number of screenshots within the supplementary. We weight text and screenshot equally and thus utilize the mean value of these two compression ratios as the compression ratio for the whole summary.

To generate the final summary, we first include the master report, and then list all *supplementaries* sorted by the number of test reports that contributed to them in descending order. For each *supplementary*, we iteratively select the sentence or screenshot based on the weights (computed in Step 3 of the candidate refinement phase) and include them into the summary, until reaching the summary compression ratio set by the user.

Example The detail summarizing process is shown in Fig. 11.2e. We take the *supplementary-0* as sample. It contains 28 keywords and 0 screenshots. At the beginning of summarization, the sentence $T_{0,2}$ is selected as it has the highest PageRank score, then the summary contains 9 keywords and the compression ratio has reached the limit (i.e., the compression ratio is $9/28 > 0.25$), the summarization process ends.

11.2.2.3 Implementation

We have implemented a web-based test-report-management tool, which not only provides test-report summarization but also extends a number of classic test-report-management functions, such as automatic duplicate detection, a project-report dashboard, keyword searching, bug triaging, and best fixer recommendation.

We present the screenshot of its summary visualization page in Fig. 11.2f, which shows the visualization result of the final summary from the exemplary duplicate group. At the top of this page, we present attribute information about the aggregate report (such as the set of all crowd testers who submitted reports in this set, bug category, severity). And then, we show information from the master report, which aims at assisting users to get an overview understanding of all duplicates. Below the master-report pane, topics of supplementary are listed. We highlight the representative sentences, phrases, and screenshots of each supplementary, which enables end users to understand the main topic of this supplementary at a glance. Further, end users can view the details, including all sentences, screenshots and original reports contributed the supplementary, by clicking these supplementary topics. Using this tool, we conducted comprehensive studies to validate our approach, described in the next section.

11.2.3   Experiment

11.2.3.1   Experiment Design

(1) Research Questions

To assess the performance of CTRAS in achieving its goals, i.e., to assist developers in (1) processing test reports, (2) providing comprehensive and comprehensible summaries, and (3) saving efforts, we conduct mixed evaluations to answer the following three research questions:

RQ1. Effectiveness of Duplicate Aggregator.   Can the *aggregator* accurately group duplicates? To what extent do the screenshots improve the accuracy of detecting and aggregating duplicate reports?

RQ2. Effectiveness of Summarizer.   To what extent can the *summarizer* refine the informative and non-redundant content from the duplicates?

RQ3. Effectiveness of CTRAS.   Can CTRAS help developers save time costs in inspecting mobile crowdsourced test reports without loss of accuracy?

Both RQ1 and RQ2 are designed to evaluate the effectiveness of the *Aggregator* and *Summarizer* components of CTRAS. Because identifying and aggregating duplicate reports are foundational steps of correctly leveraging the information from test reports, RQ1 aims at evaluating the accuracy of CTRAS in detecting duplicates and revealing the effectiveness of employing the screenshot information to aggregate the duplicates. Also, identifying the critical, complementary, and non-redundant information from the large volume of information plays an important role in helping developers to understand and fix the bugs. Thus, RQ2 aims at evaluating the effectiveness of the *summarizer* regarding the metrics of information theory. Further, although RQ1 and RQ2 present quantitative and theoretical evaluations, understanding the practical performance of CTRAS is critical. Thus, we design RQ3, which is a task-based user study, to investigate the efficiency improvement as well as reporting any accuracy loss.

As discussed in Sect. 11.2.2, several fundamental parameters may influence the performance of CTRAS. We set $\beta = 5$ to weight textual descriptions more. There are two fundamental parameters of the HAC algorithm: the linkage type, which defines the method of calculating the distance between clusters, and the threshold γ for terminating the clustering. We choose the single-linkage type because it makes the HAC to solely focus on the area where the two clusters come closest to each other and ignore distant parts [82], which fits the goal of CTRAS well. We set the γ to 0.5 that is the medium value of the scale of the distance between test reports. Further, we apply strict combination strategy by setting $\theta = 0.2$ that we defined in Sect. 11.2.2.2 to group candidate item clusters. In the study of RQ1 and RQ3, we

Table 11.1 Statistical information of testing applications

	Name	Version	Category	$|R|$	$|S|$	$|R_s|$	$|D|$
$p1$	CloudMusic	2.5.1	Music	157	259	62	45
$p2$	Game-2048	3.14	Games	210	219	164	96
$p3$	HW Health	2.0.1	Health	262	327	201	109
$p4$	HJ Normandy	2.12.0	Education	269	436	241	123
$p5$	MyListening	1.6.2	Education	473	418	306	128
$p6$	iShopping	1.3.0	Shopping	290	508	150	83
$p7$	JayMe	2.1.2	Social	1400	1997	1168	678
$p8$	JustForFun	1.8.5	Photo	267	112	76	141
$p9$	Kimiss	2.7.1	Beauty	79	58	48	31
$p10$	Slife	2.0.3	Health	1346	2238	1124	885
$p11$	Tuniu	9.0.0	Travel	531	640	418	236
$p12$	Ubook	2.1.0	Books	329	710	88	108
Total				5613	7922	4046	2663

set the compression ratio $K = 0.25$, which is considered to be a proper value in the paper [71, 72].

(2) Experimental Dataset

To produce the dataset for our evaluation, we utilized the results of the national software-testing contest,[1] which simulated crowdsourced testing of several popular mobile applications across multiple domains (including games, education, social media, and so on).

The contestants of the contest were required to test the applications and report bugs in 4 h. They could write descriptions and take screenshots to document their testing procedures and the unexpected behavior of applications. This contest attracted 4000 participants and generated over 5000 test reports. More than 10 professional testers and members of the organizational committee manually labeled and evaluated the quality of these reports. The detailed information of the dataset is shown in Table 11.1, in which, $|R|$ denotes the number of reports, $|S|$ denotes the number of screenshots, $|R_s|$ denotes the number of reports that contain at least one screenshot and $|D|$ denotes the number of duplicates.

(3) Experimental Design for RQ1: Effectiveness of Duplicate Aggregator

Methods While a number of classic duplicate test-report-detection methods only focus on the textual description to measure the similarity between reports [87, 88], CTRAS employs both textual description as well as screenshots to assist detecting duplicates. Thus, to answer the RQ1, we have the following three methods:

---

[1] http://www.mooctest.org/cst2016/index_en.html.

- **CTRAS.** Our duplicate detection method which employs both textual information and screenshots. In this method, the distance between two reports is calculated based on the balanced distance equation.
- **CTRAS-TXT.** The duplicate detection method employs only textual information. In this method, the distance is calculated based on only textual distance.
- **CTRAS-IMG.** The duplicate detection method employs only screenshot information. In this method, the distance is calculated based on only screenshot distance.

Evaluation Metrics To measure the performance of these three methods, we employ three classic metrics for evaluating clustering: Homogeneity, Completeness, V-Measure [76]. Taking the classes set C and clusters set K as reference, we define the contingency table $\mathcal{A} = \{a_{ij} | i = 1, \ldots, n; j = 1, \ldots, m\}$, where a_{ij} denotes the number of test reports that belongs to both c_i and k_j.

Homogeneity reflects the extent to which each cluster contains only members of a single class. It can be calculated via $h = 1 - H(C|K)/H(C)$, where

$$H(C|K) = -\sum_{j=1}^{|K|} \sum_{i=1}^{|C|} \frac{a_{ij}}{N} \cdot \log \frac{a_{ij}}{\sum_{k=1}^{|C|} a_{kj}} \tag{11.3}$$

$$H(C) = -\sum_{i=1}^{|C|} \frac{\sum_{j=1}^{|K|} a_{ij}}{n} \cdot \log \frac{\sum_{j=1}^{|K|} a_{ij}}{n} \tag{11.4}$$

Completeness is a symmetrical criterion of homogeneity, which measures the extent to which all members of a given class are assigned to the same cluster. It can be calculated via $c = 1 - H(K|C)/H(K)$, where

$$H(K|C) = -\sum_{i=1}^{|C|} \sum_{j=1}^{|K|} \frac{a_{ij}}{N} \cdot \log \frac{a_{ij}}{\sum_{k=1}^{|K|} a_{ik}} \tag{11.5}$$

$$H(K) = -\sum_{j=1}^{|K|} \frac{\sum_{i=1}^{|C|} a_{ij}}{n} \cdot \log \frac{\sum_{i=1}^{|C|} a_{ij}}{n} \tag{11.6}$$

V-measure is the harmonic mean of homogeneity and completeness. It is widely used as the measure of the distance from a perfect clustering. In this chapter, a higher V-Measure score indicates a better duplicate detection and aggregation result, which is calculated by the Eq. 11.7.

$$v = 2 \cdot (h \cdot c)/(h + c) \tag{11.7}$$

(4) Experimental Design for RQ2: Effectiveness of Summarizer

Methods To investigate the theoretical effectiveness of the summarizer of CTRAS, we compared its performance with two classic summarization methods: Max-Coverage-based (MCB) [23, 89] and Maximal Marginal Relevance (MMR) [10].

- **CTRAS.** Our summarization method that generates the summarized report under ratio K.
- **MCB.** The Max-Coverage-based method is a greedy algorithm. *MCB* iteratively selects the test report with maximal coverage score and inserts it into the summarization until K is met. The original definition of coverage score in paper [23, 89] refers the ratio of the number of selected conceptual units to the total number. In this experiment, we have two kinds of conceptual units, i.e., keywords and screenshots. Thus, we define the coverage score as the mean value of the keyword coverage score and screenshot coverage score.
- **MMR.** The MMR method is a typical method for summarizing multiple topically related documents, which employs keywords that have the highest frequency to build a query. This query is used to select the document from a set based on the maximum-marginal-relevance strategy, which selects the one having the largest distance from the selected set while being relevant to query in each step. In our implementation, we adopt the same idea and construct the query with keyword and screenshot having the highest frequency. We employ the distance between test reports, which we defined in Sect. 11.2.2.1, as the distance measurement to implement the maximum-marginal-relevance strategy.

Note that we define the compression ratio of the final summary as the mean value of the text compression ratio and screenshot compression ratio (see Sect. 11.2.2.2)—this strategy is also applied in this experiment.

Evaluation Metrics We adopt a fully automatic evaluation method for content selection: the ***Jensen Shannon divergence*** (JS divergence), which has been shown to be highly correlated with manual evaluations and sometimes even outperforms standard Recall-Oriented Understudy for Gisting Evaluation (ROUGE) scores.

JS divergence employs the probability distribution of words to measure the distance between documents. A good summary is expected to have low divergence with the original document. In this chapter, we calculate the JS divergence of textual information and screenshots respectively.

The JS divergence is represented in Eq. 11.8, in which, P and Q denote the probability distributions of word G and summary S, respectively. We entirely adopt the recommended parameter settings in [51], i.e.,, $A = (P + Q)/2$ denotes the mean distribution of P and Q, C denotes the frequency of keyword ω, N is the sum of frequencies of all keywords, $B = 1.5|V|$ where V denotes the text corpus, and δ is assigned to 0.0005 to perform a small smoothing. JS_S is defined in a similar manner.

$$JS_T(P||Q) = (D(P||A) + D(Q||A))/2 \tag{11.8}$$

where

$$D(P||Q) = \sum_{\omega} p_P(\omega) log_2 \frac{p_P(\omega)}{p_Q(\omega)}$$

$$p(\omega) = (C + \delta)/(N + \delta * B)$$

After JS_T and JS_S are calculated, we utilize their harmonic mean as the measure of these summarization methods.

(5) Experimental Design for RQ3: Effectiveness of CTRAS

Although RQ2 evaluates the theoretical performance of CTRAS, we also seek to understand its practical performance for real users. In [72], Rastkar et al. designed a task-based user study to investigate whether the generated summaries can help developers in processing test reports. In their study, participants were asked to read a new test report and a list of potential duplicated reports, which were presented under their *original* or *summary* format, and then determine for each whether it was duplicated with the new test report or not. Considering both Rastkar et al.'s work and ours share the same goal, we adopt the task-based user study to answer the RQ3. However, because their work is designed to produce a summary for a single test report while CTRAS generates a summary for multiple test reports, we adjust the duplicate test-report-detection task into duplicate test-report clusterization tasks in our study.

For our study, we utilized a modified version of the web-based CTRAS tool to assist participants to cluster test reports. Our participants are given a set of test reports, and optionally a set of summaries, and asked to group duplicate test reports (i.e., test reports describing the same bugs). Our hypothesis is that CTRAS can help developers reach a multi-perspective understanding of the bug and thus identify the duplicates more efficiently without loss of accuracy. The rationale of this study design is straightforward: if the summary generated by CTRAS failed to provide *sufficient* and *correct* knowledge for participants to understand the bug, it cannot help participants and further improve their efficiency in grouping the duplicates that are describing the same bug.

Study Setting   We recruited 30 second-year master students majoring in computer science or software engineering as participants of this study. All of these 30 participants have at least 5 years programming experience but have no experience using any of these experimental applications.

We select 5 applications, i.e., *MyListening (p5)*, *iShopping (p6)*, *Kimiss (p9)*, *Tuniu (p11)*, *Ubook (p12)* as subject programs. The categories of these applications are diverse and the number of reports varies from 79 to 531, thus we believe these applications are representative.

We randomly divide the 30 participants into 3 groups. In the study, these three groups are provided with different reference materials:

- **Group A (Control Group):** The participants of this group are only provided with the original test report. There are no supportive materials for the participants of this group.
- **Group B (CTRAS):** The participants of group B are provided with the original test report and the summary that is generated by CTRAS. Note that, for this group, the summarizer works on the fully-automated aggregator, which groups the test reports based on both image and text similarity.
- **Group C (Golden):** The participants of group C are provided with the original test report and summaries that are generated by the summarizer of CTRAS working on the ground-truth clustering results (as manually determined by the professional developers). Because the quality of summaries is influenced not only by the summarization algorithm but also by the duplicate aggregation algorithm, we set up this group to evaluate the gap between the performance of CTRAS and the perfect situation.

Within each group (10 participants, each), every subject application (5 software applications) is assigned to two participants. Participants are required to manually cluster these original test reports independently—without any collaboration. The modified version of CTRAS shows summaries without showing any information that reveal test report identities—simply showing the summarized sentences and screenshots that describe bugs. This version of CTRAS also provides keyword search and keyword filtering.

We employ CTRAS to generate summaries under the predefined condition of group B and C, and then provide these summaries to the participant of corresponding groups as reference material.

Table 11.2 illustrates summarization results. For each subject application and group (B & C), we show the number of summaries and their mean number of sentences and screenshots.

Evaluation Metrics We evaluate CTRAS based on three aspects: efficiency, accuracy, and satisfaction.

Table 11.2 Details of the summarization result in RQ3

		p5		p6		p9		p11		p12	
		B	C	B	C	B	C	B	C	B	C
#summary		98	97	35	63	15	25	145	182	64	96
#sentences	mean	3.12	4.13	2.33	3.15	2.25	6.00	4.51	4.80	3.85	5.00
	std	1.95	3.77	2.01	1.96	1.85	2.10	3.46	2.63	3.37	7.93
#screenshots	mean	1.73	2.35	3.38	4.05	1.25	4.40	3.51	3.69	7.60	9.42
	std	1.84	2.73	5.38	3.11	1.09	3.38	3.80	3.30	10.69	21.92

Table 11.3 Interview questions in RQ3

1. On a scale of 1–5 with 5 being the most positive, how would you describe the overall performance of the summary in assisting your clusterization task?
2. Does the master report reflect the topic of the summary; if yes, how does it reflect it?
3. Is there additional information in the supplementaries that helped you cluster test reports? If so, describe it.
4. Which type of information is more important for you in inspecting reports: textual descriptions or screenshots? Why?

- **Efficiency.** We adopt the average completion time for each report as the evaluation metric of efficiency.
- **Accuracy.** Using the ground truth data, we determined the accuracy of the participant's inspection by utilizing V-measure metric.
- **Satisfaction.** The satisfaction of summary is measured upon the qualitative feedback from the questionnaire, which is shown in Table 11.3. Particularly, we present the questionnaire only to participants of group B and C.

11.2.3.2 Results and Analysis

In this section, we present the experimental results to answer the three research questions.

(1) Answering RQ1: Effectiveness of the Duplicate Aggregator

We present the homogeneity (H), completeness (C) and V-Measure (V) results of CTRAS and the two baseline techniques in Table 11.4. On average, CTRAS achieves 0.87 V-Measure score, while these two baseline techniques, i.e., CTRAS-TXT and CTRAS-IMG, obtain 0.81 and 0.60 respectively. We use bold values to indicate the best performance per metric and project.

Further, CTRAS outperforms these two baseline techniques over all subject projects except the *"Slife"(p10)*. We investigated the content of test reports of subject projects. We found the application *Slife* is a daily activity tracker, which is designed for tracking the health data of users' daily activity. Even though its operation is simple, the testing procedure, which requires a number of activities beyond the regular operations, becomes relatively difficult. Given the fact that our test reports come from the contest which requires participants to finish the tasks in a short time (4 h), we speculate that the test reports of *Slife* could only reveal simple bugs, and as such and their text descriptions were accurate. Thus, CTRAS-TXT obtains the highest homogeneity score, which results in the relatively higher V-Measure score in comparison with CTRAS.

Summary The high V-Measure score indicates that the *duplicate aggregator* is capable of accurately detecting and aggregating duplicate reports. In comparison with the classic text-only-based strategies, the screenshot information is able

Table 11.4 Evaluation results for the duplicate aggregator: RQ1

		p1	p2	p3	p4	p5	p6	p7
H	CTRAS	**0.967**	**0.991**	**0.990**	**0.991**	0.957	0.948	0.958
	TXT	0.679	0.818	0.918	0.93	0.874	0.857	0.931
	IMG	0.444	0.416	0.724	0.789	0.49	0.507	0.722
C	CTRAS	**0.778**	**0.782**	**0.876**	0.855	**0.925**	**0.904**	**0.851**
	TXT	0.66	0.755	0.872	0.856	0.909	0.903	0.839
	IMG	0.748	0.682	0.863	**0.863**	0.883	0.874	0.821
V	CTRAS	**0.862**	**0.874**	**0.929**	0.918	**0.941**	**0.926**	**0.901**
	TXT	0.67	0.785	0.894	0.891	0.891	0.879	0.883
	IMG	0.557	0.517	0.788	0.824	0.63	0.642	0.768

		p8	p9	p10	p11	p12	Avg
H	CTRAS	0.865	**0.995**	0.862	**0.994**	**0.967**	**0.957**
	TXT	**0.878**	0.9	**0.932**	0.932	0.698	0.862
	IMG	0.222	0.386	0.65	0.703	0.212	0.522
C	CTRAS	**0.493**	**0.845**	**0.657**	0.877	**0.774**	**0.801**
	TXT	0.426	0.834	0.628	**0.880**	0.713	0.773
	IMG	0.318	0.693	0.602	0.864	0.525	0.728
V	CTRAS	**0.628**	**0.914**	0.745	**0.932**	**0.860**	**0.869**
	TXT	0.574	0.866	**0.750**	0.905	0.705	0.808
	IMG	0.262	0.496	0.625	0.775	0.303	0.599

to improve the performance of detecting duplicates (in 11 out of 12 subject applications).

(2) Answering RQ2: Effectiveness of the Summarizer

The results of RQ2 are shown in Fig. 11.3, for all subject application with varying compression ratios. We note that regardless of the compression ratio, CTRAS generally outperforms MCB and MMR methods in all projects except "JustForFun."

Through further investigation, we found that "JustForFun" is an image editing and sharing application. Thus, the screenshots are largely composed of user content (i.e., their photos) instead of more standardized activity views, so most screenshots have a large distance from each other, which causes them to be categorized as independent supplementaries. This causes a decrease in JS divergence. In addition, as the summarization ratio increases, the score of the JS divergence decreases except for the CTRAS result on project "Game-2048," which is caused by the fact that there is only one gaming interface. That is to say the overwhelming majority of screenshots are similar. Few screenshots can represent the whole corpus, thus the JS divergence is smaller under lower summarization ratio.

Summary For most projects, CTRAS is more effective than classic summarization methods: MCB and MMR.

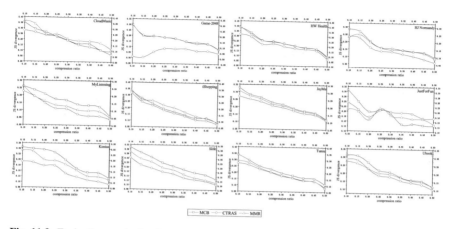

Fig. 11.3 Evaluation results for the summarizer: RQ2 (lower is better)

Table 11.5 Task evaluation results: RQ3

	A	B	C
Completion time (s)	27.6293	19.3179 (30.0%)	20.5754 (25.5%)
v-measure	0.9071	0.9316 (2.7%)	0.94 (3.6%)

(3) Answering RQ3: Effectiveness of CTRAS

Efficiency and Accuracy Table 11.5 shows the average test report inspection time cost, per test report, for group A (i.e., control group), B (i.e., CTRAS) and C (i.e., golden). According to Table 11.5, the average completion time cost of each report are 19.32 and 20.58 s, respectively for group B and C, which saves 30.0% and 25.5% compared with group A (27.63 s); and the average V-measure scores of group A, B, and C are 0.9071, 0.9316, and 0.9400 respectively, which shows that group B and group C improve 2.7% and 3.6% accuracy compared with group A. This result indicates that with the help of summarization, people can substantially save their time in duplicate test report clustering work not only without loss of accuracy, but even with slight improvement.

In addition, surprisingly, group B cost less time than group C on average. We investigated the details of the summarization result that is presented in Table. We find that that CTRAS performs a more strict duplicate aggregation than the professional developers, which leads the number of clusters for group B to be smaller than group C. As such, participants of group B generally have fewer summaries to reference in the inspection procedure. Thus, in comparison with group C, group B can save some time-cost at the expense of loss of accuracy.

Satisfaction The participants' satisfaction rating on average was high: 4.1 on a 1–5-point scale. More subjectively, the semi-structured interviews produced qualitative results. All participants thought that the *master report* can reflect the topic of summary, and it "*helps them get a general idea of the summary*", "*instructs* *the granularity of clustering*", 18 participants (90%) mentioned supplementaries contained additional information which "*is clear and coherent*", "*can be used as valuable reference when it comes to uncertain condition*" and "*provides detailed operation steps.*"

Many participants mentioned text was more useful, which supports our strategy of setting distance calculation parameters. Some participants stated that screenshots "*are open to various interpretations*" and "*can't tell where's the problem.*" Moreover, some suggestions for improvement were proposed, such as "*the description is not well structured,*" and "*highlighting important parts of screenshots.*"

Chapter 12
Quality Assessment of Crowdsourced Testing Cases

12.1 Introduction

While the crowdsourced testing often calls for a large number of end-users, who may have no knowledge on programming, to conduct the black-box testing tasks. It can also gathers a group of professional testers to write test code for white-box testing. To efficiently process the crowdsourced testing reports that consist of textual descriptions and screenshots, we have discussed various crowdsourced test report processing techniques in the previous chapters. However, it is difficult to apply these techniques on test cases which are often implemented in various coding styles.

In crowdsourced testing, the large workforce can naturally generate plenty of test cases. Therefore, on the upside, the likelihood of obtaining high-quality test cases is boosted by crowdsourcing. On the downside, crowdsourcing development generates many low-quality test cases. As executing all test cases is resource-intensive and may introduce security risks, distinguishing the high-quality test cases from the low-quality ones is desired but challenging task. Manually reviewing all test cases is extremely labor-intensive, but is more effective than conventional source-code analysis techniques, which struggle to distinguish the short and similar test cases harvested through crowdsourcing. Meanwhile, static software metrics may provide no useful insights, because the coverage metrics and are often weakly correlated with the quality of a test case [32]. An alternative technique is, mutation testing, which exhaustively executes all artificial buggy versions (mutants), and determines whether the test cases detect these bugs. However, mutation testing requires large time and computational resources [119]. Therefore, to assess the test cases generated by crowdsourcing, we need innovative techniques requiring minimal information.

In practice, software crowdsourcing is often performed on cloud-based platforms [95] which offer an integrated development environment (IDE) for code writing. Cloud-based platforms are an ideal infrastructure solution for software crowdsourcing [95]; in particular, they capture the fine-grained activities of the crowd workers [68, 95]. Using the Hypertext Transfer Protocol (HTTP) communications between

© The Author(s), under exclusive license to Springer Nature Singapore Pte Ltd. 2022   217
Q. Wang et al., *Intelligent Crowdsourced Testing*,
https://doi.org/10.1007/978-981-16-9643-5_12

the browser and the remote server, one can reconstruct the fine-grained dynamic history of the code development,[1] which is represented by the file-size changes of the source-code. The code history provides rich information on the whole problem-solving process of a given code [44]. Moreover, from the fine-grained dynamic code history, we can estimate the quality of the crowdsourced test cases harvested from cloud-based source-code-editing platforms [68, 101].

In this chapter, we present an automated quality assessment technique, called TCQA, for test cases harvested from professional testers in the crowdsourced testing. TCQA assesses the quality of test cases through three steps: (1) modeling the code history to a time series, (2) extracting multiple relevant features from the time series, and (3) building a model to classify test cases into different quality categories using feature-based machine-learning techniques. By leveraging the onsite coding history, TCQA can assess test-case quality without performing expensive source-code analysis nor executing these test cases. Using the data from nine test-development tasks with more than 400 participants, we evaluate TCQA from multiple perspectives. The results demonstrate that TCQA is capable of assessing the quality of test cases with high precision and at fast speed with relatively small overhead, compared with conventional test-case quality-assessment techniques. Moreover, our evaluation indicates that TCQA can yield real-time insights on test-case quality even before they are finished.

12.2   Assessing the Quality of Crowdsourced Test Cases Based on Fine-Grained Code Change History

12.2.1 Motivation

Among the various software development tasks, test-case development is particularly suitable for crowdsourcing. However, the effectiveness and efficiency of any unit testing depends on the quality of the test cases [115, 123]. Whereas writing a good test case can be difficult and tedious, automatic test-case-generation techniques (e.g., [75]) are beset by the external-method-call problem, the object-creation problem, and other problems [106]. Moreover, even when artificial faults are accurately detected, automatically generated unit tests may not detect real faults in practice, for several reasons [2, 83]. Hence, we posit that human intelligence and efforts are often beneficial (and even necessary) for producing high-quality tests [53]. These demands are fully satisfied by crowdsourced test-case development.

---

[1] In this chapter, the word *fine-grained* means that the time unit of the operation history is finer than a revision history that can be captured by a traditional version-control systems (VCS), and which has been sufficiently well studied e.g.,[64] that every character-level source-code change (insertion and deletion) can be traced.

Although crowdsourced test-case development can naturally harvest test cases through human intelligence, assessing the quality of numerous crowdsourced test cases is a challenging task. Processing a large number of test cases by traditional techniques is time- and resource-intensive, but the native features of cloud-based platforms provide new opportunities.

As mentioned above, cloud-based platforms introduce transparency to the entire software crowdsourcing process. Such transparency provides the fine-grained (character-level) history of the source code throughout the crowdsourced test-case development. This history contains rich information of the entire problem-solving process, which is erased in the final source code [113]. Hence, it can be exploited in analytics of wide-ranging concerns in software development, such as developers' subjective experience [101], behavioral characteristics [102], expertise evaluation [68], and, of course, the quality of crowdsourced test cases.

Cloud-based platforms provide support for highly effective and efficient crowdsourced test-case development processes. The cloud-based platforms capture the fine-grained source code history while a crowd worker develops a piece of code. Once the test cases are submitted (or even before submission), their quality can be automatically assessed. Because the fine-grained source code history requires no mutation testing, the time and computational cost of evaluating its quality is minimal. The requester can then decide whether to include or exclude a worker's submission.

12.2.2 Approach

Figure 12.1 describes the whole process of applying TCQA to assess the quality of test cases written by crowd workers. It contains three major steps: from dynamic code history to time-series, extracting time-series features, and predicting the quality of crowdsourced tests.

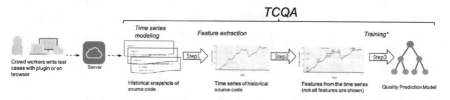

Fig. 12.1 Overview of the process of applying TCQA to assess a test case's quality using dynamic code history

12.2.2.1   From Dynamic Code History to Time-Series

In this work, we follow the insights provided in [101, 102] to focus on the change of the size of source code induced by a crowd worker's activities. For instance, in a crowd worker's *"deletion"* action, we do not care *what* she deletes, but we do care *how much* she deletes. Hence, the first step is straightforward: TCQA simply records the size of the source code (measured as the number of characters) at the corresponding time point and organizes them into a sequence. Suppose there are n periods in total, after this step, a test case's dynamic code history could be represented by the following n-period time series:

$$< t_1, s_1 >, < t_2, s_2 >, \ldots, < t_i, s_i >, \ldots, < t_n, s_n >$$

where t_i is a time and s_i is the size of the test code. Note that TCQA does not require every time series' length is equal because the classifications (Step 3) is based on extracted features (Step 2)—not the raw time series. However, TCQA allows the data prepossessing to generate equal-length time series. This consideration allows TCQA's future extensions of using distance-based classification techniques such as Dynamic Time Wrapping (DTW).

12.2.2.2   Extracting Time-Series Features

Since the prior step creates the time series representing test code histories, TCQA then extracts features from these time series. Given the dynamic nature of time series, there are potentially a large number of features that can be extracted. For example, let's consider a statistical feature: autocorrelation, which is the correlation between the elements of a time series and others from the same time series separated from them by a given interval. Here, by defining different time intervals, it may produce hundreds of features.

To solve this problem, we use the off-the-shelf library *TSFRESH* [96] to extract relevant features from time-series data. *TSFRESH* is a Python package that takes three steps to extract features and evaluate the relevance of the extracted features. It first characterizes time series with comprehensive and well-established feature mappings and considers additional features describing meta-information. Then, each feature vector is individually and independently evaluated with respect to its significance for predicting the target under investigation. Hence, this step generates a vector of multiple *p-values*. In the last step, *TSFRESH* evaluates the vector of *p-values* on the basis of the Benjamini-Yekutieli procedure in order to decide which features to keep.

In total, *TSFRESH* extracts 87 relevant features. These features are in three broad categories: simple metrics (e.g., *maximum*), statistical metrics (e.g., *agg_linear_trend*), and frequency-based metrics (e.g., *fft_coefficient*). Frequency-based metrics are produced by transforming a time series from the *time* domain to the *frequency* domain using the Fast Fourier Transform (FFT) algorithm. We list a

Table 12.1 Extracted features and their meanings

Categories	Features	Meanings
Simple metrics	*maximum*	The highest (normalized) value of the time series.
	mean	The mean of the time series.
	sum_of_reoccurring_values	The sum of reoccurring values in the time series.
Statistical metrics	c3*	The non-linearity of the time series, see [81] for more details.
	abs_energy	The absolute energy of the time series which is the sum over the squared values.
	*agg_linear_trend**	A linear least-squares regression for values of the time series.
Frequency-based metrics	*fft_coefficient**	The Fourier coefficients of the one-dimensional discrete Fast Fourier Transform for real parameters.
	spkt_welch_density	The cross power spectral density of the time series at different frequencies.

* This type of feature may lead to multiple features resulting from different input parameters.

subset of the extracted features and their meanings in Table 12.1. Please note that, due to limited space, we do not exhaustively list all features. Instead, we present several examples for each category of the features to help readers understand the main concepts of the features.

12.2.2.3   Predicting the Quality of Crowdsourced Tests

Machine learning is proposed to learn some predictive models from training data and then make predictions and has been widely used in solving software-engineering problems. Considering the goal of TCQA is to evaluate the quality of a large number of test cases, machine-learning classification is a natural fit, as it can learn a classification model from some instances and then classify new instances into different categories.

Training We seek to automatically classify many crowdsourced test cases into quality categories using limited computational resources. To do so, we first need a method for evaluating the quality of the test cases for the training set of test cases. A number of metrics may be used (and we experiment with some of them, described in Sect. 12.2.3.1), such as mutation score and code coverage metrics. Although these training test cases may need to be executed to evaluate their quality and thus label them according to their relative degree of quality, the machine-learning model can be trained to classify future test cases without the need for such expensive execution or analysis.

Algorithms There are many classification algorithms, e.g., *naive bayes*, *decision tree classifiers*, *neural networks*, *support vector machines (SVM)*, and so on. TCQA uses *Random Forest* as the default classification algorithm. As an ensemble learning method, *Random Forest* [6] improves the robustness of classification models by maintaining the power, flexibility, and interpretability of tree-based classifiers. This decision was made through extensive empirical comparisons with multiple algorithms using our own empirical data. Our results show that *Random Forest*-based models consistently yield the best performances regarding the most important model comparison metrics: *F-measure*. Besides, *Random Forest* can handle imbalanced data [43], which is prevalent for data collected from real-world practices.

Please note that although we use Random Forest as the default algorithm in this work, TCQA is not specific to *Random Forest*. Other algorithms such as *Naive Bayers*, *J48*, *SVM* can be easily implemented in TCQA with only minimal effort. Even non-feature-based time-series-classification algorithms such as DTW [69] also can be easily implemented in TCQA's framework.

12.2.3   Experiment

12.2.3.1   Experiment Design

(1) Experimental Dataset

To produce the dataset for our evaluation, we utilized the results of the International Conference on Software Quality, Reliability, and Security (QRS) software-testing contest,[2] which simulated crowdsourced testing. We implemented a cloud-based programming platform–MoocTest–on which participants can write test cases with any standard web browser. The source-code snapshots will be periodically sent to the server through the http PUT method. All participants were allowed to spend 2 h to write test cases in MoocTest. In total, we collected data from 6 subject programs, each of which is a separate subject task in our evaluation, and obtained 2193 test cases. The quality of the submitted test case was evaluated according to the two classic criteria: coverage score and mutation score [33]. Coverage score is one of the most widely-used criteria used to evaluate the degree to which the source code of a program is executed. A program with a high test coverage score is considered to have a lower chance of containing undetected software bugs in comparison to a program with a lower test coverage score. The mutation score is another popular, yet classic, criteria for evaluating the effectiveness of test suites [38]. Mutation score is computed based on the mutation testing, which involves a number of programs with a small modification. Each modified version is called a mutant. If test suites detect the modification, we call this test case is capable of killing the mutant. Mutation score is the ratio of the number of killed mutants over the total number of mutants.

---

[2] http://paris.utdallas.edu/qrs17/contest.html.

Table 12.2 Statistic information of subjected tasks

Tasks	No. tests	LOC	No. classes
CMD	134	566	1
Datalog	649	589	9
ITClocks	134	1071	13
JMerkle	370	774	5
LunarCalendar	561	1170	8
QuadTree	345	644	6

We employed Jacoco [36] to evaluate the branch coverage of each test case. We computed the coverage score as the percent of covered branches to total branches. We employed the mutation testing tool–PIT [94]–to calculate the mutation score for each test case. The final score of each test case is the average of coverage score and mutation score. These scores were used to provide labels to the training test cases for the machine-learning classifier.

Table 12.2 summarizes some basic information of the six subject programs in the experiment.

In typical crowdsourced software development, a requester may be only interested in a few number of best cases. However, a sustainable crowdsourcing practice should offer opportunities for workers to develop their skills, particularly those who have middle-level skills. Hence, we do not restrict our focus on top test cases. Instead, we categorize these crowdsourced test cases into three levels, i.e., low, medium, and high quality. We sort the final scores of these test cases, and label the top 25% as the "high-quality", the bottom 25% as the "low-quality", and label the rest in the middle as "medium-quality." Note that this method enables us to recognize the middle-level workers and provide them with good test case examples, which could be helpful for improving their software testing skills.

(2) Research Questions

If TCQA is an attractive approach, it should be able to identify the quality of test cases with high accuracy with the minimal time cost. To evaluate the performance of TCQA, we formulated the following three research questions (RQ):

RQ_1: How accurate is TCQA in assessing the quality of crowdsourced test cases using their dynamic code histories? This research question is to evaluate TCQA in terms of effectiveness.

RQ_2: How efficient is TCQA in assessing the quality of crowdsourced test cases compared to the traditional test-case quality-assessment techniques? This research question is to evaluate TCQA in terms of efficiency.

RQ_3: Can TCQA yield real-time insights about the quality of the crowdsourced test cases before they are submitted? This research question is to investigate if a partial dynamic code history is sufficient for TCQA to determine the quality of a crowdsourced test case.

(3) Implementation and Environments

The cloud-based crowdsourcing platform–MoocTest–enables its users to edit their source code in its integrated web IDE. The web IDE is a fully functional IDE in which a user can edit code in the browser and run it on MoocTest's cloud servers. The crowd worker's source code is automatically saved and sent to the cloud server periodically through the PUT method. By specifying the auto-save time intervals, the dynamic code history can be retrieved at varying granularities. In our experiment, we use the default auto-save time interval.

As described above, TCQA creates time series for all test cases in the dataset and extracts features using *TSFRESH*. We build the *Random Forest* classifiers using the scikit-learn library for Python. In the model training phase, we adopt the default parameter settings of scikit-learn library, i.e., the number of trees in the forest is set to 10, the maximum depth of these trees is set to 10, and the minimum number of samples required to split an internal node is set to 2. All experiments were performed on a platform with a 3800MHz CPU of 8 cores, on 64-bit Ubuntu 14.04, and 12 GB of RAM.

(4) Experimental Setup

We designed three independent experiments to address the three research questions respectively. In this section, we overview the high-level experimental design.

Experiment I (RQ_1) Given the nature of the data (6 independent tasks), whether a model built with data from multiple tasks can be applied to an instance from a specific target task requires a comprehensive evaluation. This inherits the problem of transfer learning [66, 67]. Hence, we need to evaluate the performance of TCQA in multiple scenarios. We define three scenarios as follows:

- **Within-task scenario**: Using the same task's data to train the model and evaluate the performance.
- **Whole-sample scenario**: Using any 5 tasks' data to train the model and evaluate the performance with the rest task's data.
- **Cross-task scenario**: Using a task's data to train the model and evaluate the performance with each of the remaining 5 tasks' data.

There are some special considerations in performing experiments with these three scenarios, and we will introduce them along with the results for readers' convenience.

Experiment II (RQ_2) The second experiment is to compare the efficiency of TCQA with traditional techniques. We include two traditional techniques for comparison. The first is coverage metrics; the second is mutation testing. Although we are confident that TCQA uses much less time to evaluate a test than mutation testing, we want to have a precise measure because this helps get precise performance estimation when deploying TCQA in real-world cloud-based crowdsourcing platforms. TCQA's performance will be compared with the method used for evaluating the MoocTest's submissions.

Experiment III (RQ_3) Since RQ_3 is about TCQA's ability to generate real-time insights about the test cases' quality, we need to simulate experimental conditions which only parts of the whole time series is available. In this experiment, we create 9 experimental conditions: 10%, 20%, 30%, 40%, 50%, 60%, 70%, 80%, 90% and 100% (the whole time series) as the baseline condition. In each experimental condition of $x\%$, we only use the first $x\%$ of each time series to make prediction and evaluate the model performance. For example, in 50% condition, we only use the first 50% of whole time series for making prediction. If the results of any $x\%$ condition are comparable to those of the baseline condition (100%), we can conclude that TCQA only relies on the part of a time series to assess the quality of a test case. Hence, TCQA can provide real-time insights even before the submission of a crowdsourced test case.

(5) Evaluation Metrics

Following the conventions of evaluating machine-learning models, we consider the following common metrics. Note that *TP*, *FP*, *FN*, and *TN* denote true positive, false positive, false negative, and true negative, respectively. Given the nature of the multi-class classification and the imbalance data, based on the suggestions of machine learning literatures, we use weighted metrics [86].

Precision The fraction of true positive instances in the instances that are predicted to be positive. For a class c, its precision P_c is given by $\frac{TP_c}{TP_c+FP_c}$. Let's suppose there are k_c instances in class c, and C represents the collection of all classes, the overall weighted precision is shown in Eq. 12.1. The higher it is, the less prediction errors are.

Recall The fraction of true positive instances in the instances that are actual positive. For a class c, its recall R_c is $\frac{TP_c}{TP_c+FN_c}$. Similar to what we do for precision, the overall weighted recall is shown in Eq. 12.2.

$$Precision = \frac{1}{\sum_{c\in C} k_c} \sum_{c\in C} k_c P_c \qquad Recall = \frac{1}{\sum_{c\in C} k_c} \sum_{c\in C} k_c R_c \qquad (12.2)$$

$$(12.1)$$

F-measure The harmonic mean between recall and precision. For a class c: $F_c = 2 \times \frac{P_c \times R_c}{P_c + R_c}$. Similarly, the overall weighted F-measure is shown in Eq. 12.3.

$$F - Measure = \frac{1}{\sum_{c\in C} k_c} \sum_{c\in C} k_c F_c \qquad (12.3)$$

A high F-measure guarantees that both precision and recall are at reasonably high levels. Note that we do not include **AUC**, since TCQA employs a 3-class classifier, it is impossible to calculate AUC.

12.2.3.2 Results and Analysis

This section reports the analysis of the results of the experiments for investigating the three research questions. Please note that we report the results of the models built with *Random Forest*. Because training a *Random Forest* model is inherently non-deterministic [6], the results reported in this section are based on the average of 30 independent training of *Random Forest* models.

RQ_1. **How Accurate Is TCQA in Assessing the Quality of Crowdsourced Test Cases Using Their Dynamic Code Histories?**

Within-Task Results The within-task scenario is "training on one task's data, and testing on itself." Note that in this scenario, we do not separate the training data and the testing data. Instead, we perform 10-fold cross-validation. Table 12.3 presents the results of the within-task scenarios. From the table, we can easily draw a conclusion that TCQA performs reasonably well on the data from each of the six subjected tasks. Almost all of them achieve high precision more than 0.7 (except ITClocks). Four out of six (66.67%) subject tasks' performance are roughly at the 0.8 level.

Whole-Sample Results We use TCQA to build a classification model based on any five tasks to predict the test cases' quality of the remaining subjected task. Please note that when constructing the training data, in case that the data of some tasks with a large number of data instances (e.g., Datalog: 649) may overwhelm those of tasks with much fewer data instances (e.g., CMD: 134) in building the classification model, we assign weights to each instance according to the sizes of projects following the standard way used in machine learning. The results are shown in Table 12.4.

In general, the results of the whole-sample scenario is comparable to those of the within-task scenario, all precision values are ≥ 0.7. This has particular importance when deploying TCQA in production environments. Consider that there may be hundreds of requesters publishing thousands of tasks, we are hereby confident that TCQA should continuously collect data from multiple tasks (i.e., possibly from multiple components or systems being tested) and use this self-growing data to refine machine-learning models. Hence, the models could be highly robust.

Cross-Task Results The third scenario is "*training on one task's data, testing on another task's data.*" The cross-task scenario's results help evaluate how sensitive

Table 12.3 Within-task scenario results

Task	Precision	Recall	F-Measure
CMD	0.77	0.83	0.78
Datalog	0.80	0.82	0.81
ITClocks	0.65	0.75	0.68
JMerkle	0.76	0.79	0.76
LunarCalendar	0.70	0.76	0.71
QuadTree	0.78	0.79	0.78

Table 12.4 Whole-sample scenario results

Testing task	Precision	Recall	F-Measure
CMD	0.71	0.80	0.74
Datalog	0.67	0.66	0.66
ITClocks	0.70	0.74	0.71
JMerkle	0.60	0.84	0.73
LunarCalendar	0.71	0.81	0.74
QuadTree	0.71	0.80	0.72

Table 12.5 The average precision of 30 runs in Cross-task scenarios

Task	Testing task					
	CMD	Datalog	ITClocks	JMerkle	LunarCalendar	QuadTree
CMD	–	0.41	0.34	0.33	0.35	0.52
Datalog	0.62	–	0.61	0.63	0.64	0.60
ITClocks	0.68	0.59	–	0.60	0.65	0.59
JMerkle	0.57	0.57	0.55	–	0.57	0.60
LunarCalendar	0.60	0.58	0.62	0.62	–	0.60
QuadTree	0.58	0.57	0.56	0.60	0.59	–

the models are regarding the different training and testing data. We report the results in Table 12.5. In this table, each row represents a subjected task's data as the training dataset, and each column represents the testing dataset. For example, a cell [Datalog, CMD] shows the classifier's performance with task Datalog's data as the training data, and task CMD's data as the testing data.

In general, the performances in the cross-task scenarios are lower than what TCQA achieves in another two scenarios. It suggests that we should be cautious when using TCQA in cross-task scenarios.

Based on the results of above three experimental scenarios, we can summarize the **answer to** RQ_1:

> TCQA *is able to predict the quality of crowdsourced test cases. It incurs only a small accuracy error for most of the tasks.* TCQA*'s performances in within-task and whole-sample scenarios are slightly better than the cross-task scenario. Particularly, the high accuracy in whole-sample enhances our confidence in using multiple tasks' data to train models and then apply them for predictions of a specific task.*

RQ_2. **How Efficient Is TCQA in Assessing the Quality of Crowdsourced Test Cases Compared to the Traditional Test-Case Quality-Assessment Techniques?**
Table 12.6 presents the time cost of TCQA, and the comparisons with traditional test quality assessment techniques (e.g., mutation testing and execution coverage). It shows that the feature-extraction procedure is the most time-consuming step of TCQA, which ranges from 29s to 103s and accounts for > 99% of TCQA's

Table 12.6 The comparison of efficiency on coverage metrics and mutation testing (in seconds)

Task	Traditional Scoring	TCQA Feature Extraction	Training	Prediction	TCQA in Production Environment (Feature Extraction + Prediction)
CMD	763.29	29.79	0.02	0.02	$29.81(25.60x)$
Datalog	1987.59	103.60	0.04	0.01	$103.61(19.18x)$
ITClocks	448.57	26.77	0.02	0.01	$26.78(16.75x)$
JMerkle	859.68	46.85	0.03	0.01	$46.86(18.35x)$
LunarCalendar	5035.04	89.88	0.04	0.02	$89.90(56.00x)$
QuadTree	982.64	46.62	0.02	0.01	$46.63(21.07x)$

total time cost. We also add column 6, which simulates the situation of deploying TCQA in production environments. Since TCQA uses an offline learning strategy, the predictive models can be built off-line, ahead of assessment. Thus, the computation time cost of TCQA in predicting a new upcoming submission contains two parts: feature-extraction time and prediction time. No time is required for training the models when a new test case arrives for evaluation. According to Table 12.6, TCQA outperforms the traditional test-case quality-assessment techniques on efficiency. The last column shows the speed up TCQA achieves compared with traditional methods. There is the order of magnitude speed up from $16.75x$ to $56.00x$.

In fact, our efficiency evaluation is very conservative. First, the performance of traditional method is based on only 10 mutants. In mutation-testing practice, a 1 KLoC program is often tested with over 100 mutants. Second, all the 6 subject tasks are not complex programs, hence executing them does not cost too much time. When the target program becomes complex, the time cost will increase dramatically. However, TCQA does not require any execution of the target program in the prediction phase. Its most time-consuming part (feature extraction) only depends on a test case's time series of development, so its performance is more stable.

Hence, we have **answers to** RQ_2:

> *Compared with traditional quality-assessment techniques,* TCQA *cost much less time. More specifically, it achieves 16.75x–56.00x speedup for the six subjected tasks.*

RQ_3. **Can TCQA Yield Real-Time Insights About the Quality of the Crowdsourced Test Cases Before They Are Submitted?**
Figure 12.2 describes the changes of classification precision values on the different amount of data for six tasks. Let's take Fig. 12.2b as an example. Figure 12.2b describes the change of precision values on different amounts of data used by TCQA

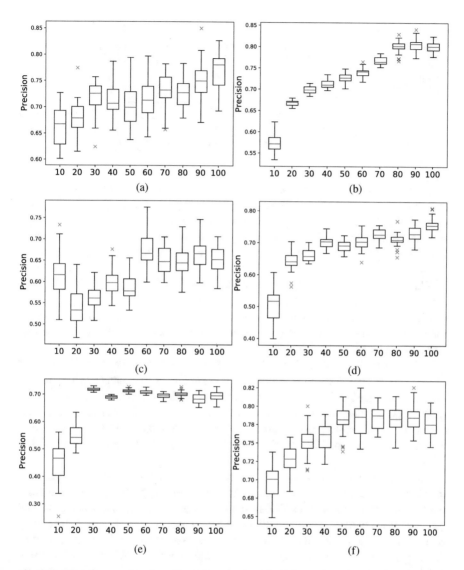

Fig. 12.2 The change of each task's performance on precision with different amount of data (within-task scenarios). (**a**) CMD. (**b**) Datalog. (**c**) ITClocks. (**d**) JMerkle. (**e**) LunarCalendar. (**f**) QuadTree

in prediction. The first box shows the precision values using the only first 10% of the whole time series to make prediction. The second is the case of using 20% of the whole time series. The remaining 8 boxes are the cases of 30%–100% with 10% as an interval, respectively.

Table 12.7 The average precision value of 30 runs with the feature from last X percent time series

Task	100%	90%	80%	70%	60%	50%
CMD	0.77	0.75	0.73	0.73	0.72	0.70
Datalog	0.80	0.81	0.80	0.77	0.74	0.73
ITClocks	0.65	0.66	0.65	0.65	0.67	0.59
JMerkle	0.76	0.73	0.71	0.73	0.70	0.69
LunarCalendar	0.70	0.68	0.70	0.70	0.71	0.71
QuadTree	0.78	0.78	0.78	0.78	0.78	0.78

For a time series, the more percentage of it used for predicting the quality of the test case it represented, the more accurate TCQA's prediction is. However, we also observe that TCQA's highest performance is often not achieved when the whole time series is included. For example, on average, the best prediction happens when using 90% of the data in Fig. 12.2b while using 80% of the data is not apparently worse.

This may not be surprising. The end part of a time series is often *flat*. A crowd worker often stops editing but reads her code before submitting it. For crowd workers' behavior (e.g., checking the code before submission) may be almost identical no matter whether their test cases are high quality or not, including that parts do not help classify the test cases.

Indeed, for all six subjected tasks, the results become stable when the amount of the data reaches 50%–60%. Table 12.7 clearly shows this pattern. These results provide evidence for TCQA's ability to make real-time estimations of a test case's quality. TCQA does not need to wait for a crowd worker to submit her test case to make a reasonable prediction on her test case's quality. TCQA can provide a reasonably good prediction when she is still halfway to the finishing of her work.

Such early prediction is a very attractive feature for crowdsourcing test-case development. A requester can use it to do real-time planning for microwork publishing. If a requester uses TCQA and finds that a test case that is being worked on by a crowd worker is not very likely to have good quality, she can immediately republish the microwork to have another worker working on it. This saves a lot of waiting time for a requester and makes the whole crowdsourcing workflow more efficient. Moreover, this process can be easily automated to optimize the process further.

Based on above results, we have **answers to** RQ_3:

> TCQA *is able to provide real-time insights of test cases' quality even before crowd workers submit them. Such early prediction may help optimize the process of crowdsourced test case development.*

12.2.4 Discussion

12.2.4.1 Characteristics of Quality Test Cases

To further gain some intuitive insights into what may characterize high-, medium-, and low-quality test cases, we looked further into the data by averaging the time-series data of all test-case-growth and visualizing the results. Figure 12.3 shows representative time-series graphs, where the x-axis represents the percentage of the time used for development, and the y-axis represents the size growth of the test-case code.

From these representative time series, we observed that low-quality-classified test cases (e.g., Fig. 12.3a) often contained patterns of growth with multiple sudden and large drops in the size of the test code. We speculate that these deletions of code may characterize uncertainty or mistakes made during the coding of the test cases. In contrast, many of the high-quality-classified test cases (e.g., Fig. 12.3c) showed more smoothly increasing test code size. Moreover, in Fig. 12.3c, we observe that at the beginning of performing this task, the crowd worker did not edit the code—we ascribe this behavior to a period of assessment and thinking before approaching the solution. Wang et al. [102] have previously found that the "*think first, code second*" pattern is often associated with more qualified developers. Figure 12.3b demonstrates an example medium-quality test case's time series, which shows some of the characteristics (e.g., smoothness of growth and drops in size) of the other two, but to a smaller degree. These intuitive patterns suggest local shape features of time series (shapelets, see [112]) may be helpful to provide better quality prediction, and we will explore this possibility in future work.

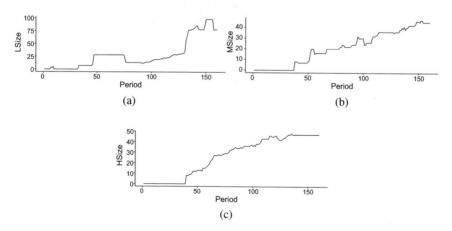

Fig. 12.3 Representative dynamic code histories for different levels of quality. (**a**) Low quality tests. (**b**) Medium quality tests. (**c**) High quality tests

12.2.4.2   Implications to Research and Practice

Our work has significant implications for both research and practice. From the perspective of research, our work rediscovers the importance and value of fine-grained dynamic code history. As shown in our work, with proper modeling and analyzing techniques, fine-grained dynamic source code history can help generate useful insights of test cases' quality without time-consuming mutation testing. While the source code represents the final product of the problem-solving process of programming, code history reflects the entire problem-solving process. Hence, they are complementary to each other. Combining them may enable us to gain a more holistic picture of the programming activity, enrich our knowledge, and ultimately help us design innovative techniques and software engineering tools. We hope more SE researchers, including ourselves, to continue working in this direction.

From the perspective of practice, TCQA will be a part MoocTest's production environment and support future crowdsourced test-case harvesting activities. Compared with the mainstream industrial solutions, it has several advantages. First, it does not require any specific techniques of testing frameworks (e.g., JUnit) to execute test cases, hence is able to support development in multiple languages and platforms. Although the test cases are written in Java in our experiment, there is no difference for any other languages such as Python, Ruby, or C#. While this guarantees high scalability, the maintenance cost is also minimal. Because the training and predicting phases in TCQA only require small amount of computing resources, it saves a large amount of hardware investments. Even using TCQA only as an auxiliary method to the traditional techniques (e.g., mutation testing), the benefits can still be substantial, for it excludes a large number of test cases before applying the traditional techniques. Moreover, the ability of generating real-time insights fits the context of cloud-based crowdsourcing well, and can be used to optimize the process of crowdsourced test-case development.

Part V
Conclusions and Future Perspectives

Chapter 13
Conclusions

Software testing is an important, yet often overlooked, part of the software development lifecycle. Traditionally, software testing was conducted by dedicated quality assurance teams with formally trained testers. Although these quality assurance teams are reliable, the high cost and delayed responses made them hard to scale and non-flexible for rapid update needs for the software industry today. Automated testing could be one solution, but the inability to create realistic user behavior test cases makes them hard to rely on given the variations in software products. Crowdsourced testing is an emerging practice that enables testing with more flexibility and scalability than quality assurance teams.

Despite of the advantages of crowdsourced testing, it is a new testing schema with unmatured operational strategies, and underdeveloped supporting technologies. Benefit from the rapid development of artificial intelligence, this book employs the intelligent algorithms to facilitate various activities in crowdsourced testing. It provides supporting technologies in terms of the crowdsourced testing task, the crowd workers, and the testing results, which can increase the bug detection efficiency, reduce the manual effort, and potentially attract more crowd workers to promote the prosperity of a platform.

This book begins with the introduction of crowdsourced testing, and related preliminaries in Part I.

In Part II, we have introduced the supporting technologies from the viewpoints of crowd workers. We first presented a worker characterization model in Chap. 4, where a crowd worker is depicted with the activeness, preference, expertise, and device, automatically extracted from the historical repositories of a crowdsourced testing platform. Armed with the worker characterization model, we introduced the task recommendation approach in Chap. 5, which can recommend suitable testing tasks for a crowd worker, so as to maximize their winning chances in taking a task and potentially minimize the wasteful effort.

In Part III, we presented the supporting technologies from the viewpoints of testing tasks. Again with the worker characterization model introduced in Part II,

© The Author(s), under exclusive license to Springer Nature Singapore Pte Ltd. 2022
Q. Wang et al., *Intelligent Crowdsourced Testing*,
https://doi.org/10.1007/978-981-16-9643-5_13

we developed the crowd worker recommendation approaches in Chap. 6, which can recommend a set of capable crowd workers for a specific testing task. Two worker recommendation approaches are presented in this chapter, among which one conducts recommendation at the beginning of a crowdsourced testing task, and the other can dynamically recommend workers during the crowdsourced testing process to further improve the bug detection efficiency. We then introduced the crowdsourced testing task management approaches in Chap. 7 aiming at the automated decision support to manage the crowdsourced testing practices more effectively. We presented a task management approach as well as its extension, while the latter can suggest the closing time for testing tasks more accurately.

Part IV introduced the supporting technologies for testing results. First, the report classification and duplication detection approaches are presented respectively in Chaps. 8 and 9, which help classify the testing reports with bugs and duplicate reports involving same bug. Then we introduced the reports prioritization approaches in Chap. 10 to facilitate the inspection of received testing reports so that the unique bug-revealing reports can be inspected earlier. Following that, we presented reports summarization approach which detects and aggregates the duplicate reports, and identifies the most informative report in each duplicate report cluster. Furthermore, we presented the quality assessment of crowdsourced testing cases which is another important testing outcome submitted together with the testing reports. The presented quality assessment approach can help the task requester to decide whether to include or exclude a worker's submission.

Finally, in Part V, we wrap the book with conclusions and future perspectives about this new testing schema.

Chapter 14
Perspectives

14.1 Fairness-Aware Recommendation

The growing ubiquity of data-driven learning models in algorithmic decision-making has recently boosted concerns about the issues of fairness and bias. Friedman defined that a computer system is biased "if it systematically and unfairly discriminates against certain individuals or groups of individuals in favor of others" [24]. For example, job recommenders can target women with lower-paying jobs than equally-qualified men. News recommenders can favor particular political ideologies over others. And even ad recommenders can exhibit racial discrimination. The fairness in data-driven decision-making algorithms (e.g., recommendation systems) requires that similar individuals with similar attributes, e.g., gender, age, race, religion, etc., be treated similarly.

Another type of unfairness in recommendation systems, which is also well studied by researchers [1, 61], is the problem of popularity bias, i.e., popular items are being recommended too frequently while the majority of other items do not get the deserved attention. However, less popular, long-tail items are precisely those that are often desirable recommendations. A market that suffers from popularity bias will lack opportunities to discover more obscure products and will be dominated by a few large brands or well-known artists. Such a market will be more homogeneous and offer fewer opportunities for innovation and creativity.

In crowdsourced testing scenario, we have introduced the crowd worker recommendation and crowdsourced task recommendation approaches. These approaches can also suffer from the popularity bias.

Take the crowd worker recommendation as an example. With the MOCOM or iRec, some highly experienced crowdworkers could be recommended for almost all the tasks, while some less experienced workers rarely get recommended. Such popularity bias not only leads to recommendation results biased towards experienced workers, but lacks of support for less experienced workers. Existing work showed that in software crowdsourcing market, the majority long-tail workers are less-experienced, learning-oriented workers [111]. In this study, we argue that such less-experienced workers are often desirable recommendations, not only because they are thirsty for recommendation, but the lack of consideration or accommodation in recommendation systems would lead to unfair recommendations, potential discouraging worker motivation, and hindering the prosperous of the platform.

To conduct the fairness-aware recommendation, one can consider the recommendation frequency related indicator, and try to balance the recommendation frequency among the registered crowd workers. This can be done by designing it as one objective and optimize it together with other objectives in the multi-objective optimization approach as MOCOM introduced in this book.

14.2 Guidance in Crowdsourced Testing

Compared with automated GUI testing, human testers in crowdsourced testing are able to discover more diverse and complicated bugs, especially those related to user experience. But there are also several limitations in current crowdsourced testing practice. First, the performance of manual testing is unstable as it highly depends on the testers' capability and experience, and testers may miss some minor functionalities especially for those unfamiliar apps. Second, the human testers may execute repeated actions during the exploration of the app, which is a waste of time. Third, the crowdsourced testing often results in a high degree of test duplication, because crowd workers tend to navigate the same common paths while working in parallel. This duplication of tests can lead to lower test coverage, making testing process less effective or more costly.

We observe the interaction behavior of human testers when conducting app testing. Figure 14.1 presents an example exploration graph of a tester. We can see that some functionalities are rarely explored such as "About" in the Setting page and "change the date" in the Main page. Besides, the tester also repeatedly visit the same page multiple times, e.g., "Account" and "Report" page. What's more, the tester is also trapped into the loop for a long time, or hesitated on one page, without knowing the next step. During our observation, we find the low coverage, duplication, and hesitation phenomena are quite common in manual testing. In addition, some testers freely admit that they visit some pages repeatedly, as they could not remember which page has been visited or which action can trigger a new page.

The above observations motivate the need for tester guidance to potentially avoid missing some functionalities or making repeated exploration steps. This can be done through tracing the testers' testing steps and help navigate or remind testers with unexplored pages. To provide more user-friendly human-computer interaction, augmenting the run-time GUI with visual hit moves is preferred, which is similar to the flashing candies (hint/suggested moves) when a player hesitates to make a move in playing Candy Crush (a popular free-to-play match-three puzzle video game).

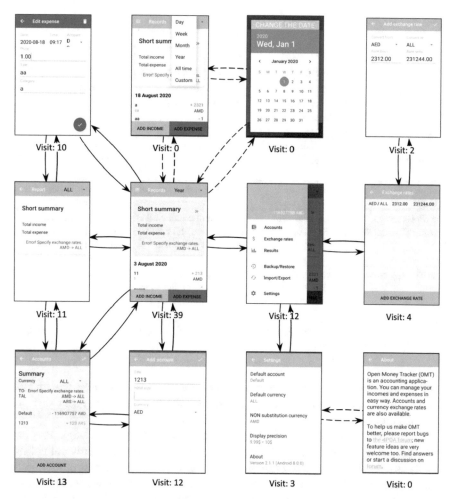

Fig. 14.1 Example of a tester's exploration graph. The solid line represent the explored path while dotted line is the unexplored path. Number below each page is the visit time of the tester

14.3   Data-Enabled Crowdsourced Testing

The crowdtesting platform can accumulate plenty of crowd-contributed data related with the knowledge of mobile application quality. These data can enable the platform to come out with more efficient task design guidelines, testing guidance strategies, and automated testing tools.

Table 14.1 demonstrates the bugs reported across mobile apps. From example 1, we can see that two apps from finance domain, *FinAdvisor* and *JFU wallet*, share the same feature *inspect yield curve*. The bug reports show that both apps encounter the same crash issues associated with this feature. Example 2 shows similar case,

Table 14.1 Observations about bug-prone knowledge across mobile apps

Example 1		Example 2	
A: FinAdvisor (sina.licaishi)	**A:** JFU wallet (bank9f.weilicai)	**A:** PDReader (nd.android.pandareader)	**A:** Buyer (veding.buyer109_3545)
D: Finance	**D:** Finance	**D:** Education	**D:** Lifestyle
B: Crash after inspect yield curve	**B:** Crash when inspect yield curve	**B:** Fail to pay with credit card	**B:** Cannot pay with credit card to order products
R: ...2. Enter inspect yield curve	**R:** 1. Select fund companies	**R:** ...2. Browse books	**R:** 1. Input MILK-TEA and press search
...4. Repeat five times	...4. Select the second last fund	...4. Click the payment reminder	...4. Choose pay with credit card
5. Press return using physical key	5. Enter inspect yield curve	...6. Input credit card information and receive success notification, then return	6. Input credit card information and receive success notification, then return
6. The app crash	6. No chart is displayed and the app crashes	7. There is still a payment reminder even pressing refresh several times	7. No ordering information

Note: **A** - App name; **D** - domain; **B** - bug summary; **R** - excerpted reproducing steps from corresponding bug reports;

where two apps *PDReader* and *Buyer* have the feature *pay with credit card* and the bug reports show there is a common bug among the two apps, i.e., users have not finished the payment yet receive a successful notification.

In practice, the mobile apps usually share similar features, e.g., Google Play has 62 video-related mobile apps with similar features for hosting and sharing of videos. Partly as a result, common bugs are frequently observed across diverse mobile apps, such as crashing after tapping a button, repeated results on the list, etc. There are two possible reasons. One is related to the so-called code reuse myth, due to a plethora of modern frameworks, libraries, and components for building good apps. The second is due to platform-specific challenges, which requires an app must correctly handle all possible system actions.

Therefore, considering similar features might have been uncovered as 'buggy' in a crowd-contributed bug repositories, one can explore whether the crowd-generated bug-prone information of one mobile app can be transferable to other apps, thus learn knowledge of bug-prone feature prediction.

Also note that there are common domain-related bugs, i.e., the apps in the same domain typically correspond with similar features, as well as common bug profiles, as demonstrated in example 1 in Table 14.1. There are also common utility- or platform-related bugs across domains, i.e., the apps from different domains can employ similar platform-based or other utilities, thus possess similar bug-prone features, as demonstrated in example 2 in Table 14.1. This might because utilities such as *payment, registration, photo-taking* are commonly-used to support high-level features and cross cut multiple domains. Hence, learning the potential bug-prone features should consider the crowd-wisdom accumulated in other mobile apps through two perspectives, i.e., within individual domain and across multiple domains.

The predicted bug-prone information for a new app can assist the crowd workers in testing the app more efficiently. For instance, they can allocate more effort in those bug-prone features, or testing these features earlier. Other knowledge can also be learned from the crowd-contributed testing data, and enable various types of software quality assurance activities.

14.4   Screenshots Learning

We have mentioned that when dealing with the crowdsourced testing reports, besides the textual descriptions, often the report is associated with the screenshots of apps. In Sect. 9.2, we have proposed SETU which combines information from the screenshots and textual descriptions to detect duplicate crowdsourced testing reports. Yet, more knowledge can be learned from the associated screenshots of bug reports, so as to facilitate the follow-up testing activities.

We know that, the graphical user interface (GUI) has provides a visual bridge between a software application and end users through which they can interact with each other. Yet more and more fancy visual effects in GUI design such as intensive median embedding, animation, light and shadows post a great challenge for developers in the implementation. And we have observed many display issues, such as *text overlap, missing image, blurred screen*, in the crowdsourced testing reports, as shown in Fig. 14.2.

Although human testers can spot these UI display issues, it requires significant human effort as testers have to manually explore tens of pages by different interactive ways and also need to check the UI display on different OS versions and devices with different resolution or screen size. Hence, we need the automatic testing method for detecting UI display issues from the screenshots of the apps.

Considering the fact that the display bugs can be easily spotted by human eyes, the visual understanding techniques can be used to separate the pages with display issues from normal ones. We can utilize the screenshots with display issues accumulated in the crowdtesting platform to train an effective visual understanding model. Furthermore, the related model can be integrated with such tool as DriodBot which can dynamically explore different pages of the mobile apps, so as to fully automatically collect the screenshots and detect the UI display issues. In this way, the human testers detect UI display issues with the demonstrated screenshots, and facilitate by these screenshots, automatic tools are developed to reduce the human testers' effort in finding such issues.

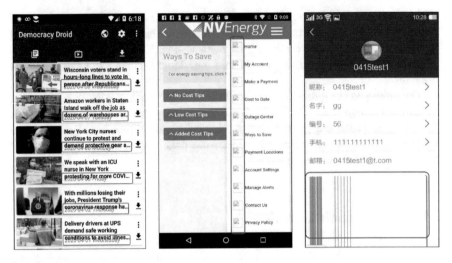

Fig. 14.2 Examples of UI display issues

14.5   Quality Assessment of Crowdsourced Testing

Although the open form of crowdsourced testing provides the flexible acquisitions of large amount of cheap resources, it leads to a high degree of uncertainty associated with the crowd worker, the testing technologies, and the platform. Under such environment, the outcome of crowdsourced testing varies a lot and lacks trustworthiness, which hinds the crowdsourced testing becoming the mainstream testing schema. Providing the quality assessment of crowdsourced testing can increase the confidence for those who are hesitating in stepping into the crowdsourced market.

On the other hand, the data accumulated in crowdsourced testing platform are from diverse workers, target at different aspects, and tend to complement with each other. Hence, benefiting from the diversified data, the quality assessment can be conducted more effectively, compared with traditional testing.

The quality of the testing service for a specific task is the foundation of the quality assessment of crowdsourced testing. Since there are several phases composing a crowdsourced testing task, e.g., task design, task launch, task execution, and result integration, etc., there should be different assessment criteria correspondingly. For task design, the quality assessment should focus on whether a task has good specifications to facilitate the workers in testing, whether a software is decomposed reasonably, and whether a task has detailed illustrations about the required crowd workers. For task publish, the assessment should consider the recruited crowd workers and their qualification status to the task. The task execution assessment can put more attention on the operation steps of each worker, the detected number of bugs, the bug severity and distribution, etc. The result integration aims at generating a summarized version of crowdsourced testing outcomes, thus the assessment should focus on the generated testing materials. All the aforementioned aspects together make up the service quality of a task.

The second dimension is the quality of the contractor who will take the crowdsourced testing task. The contractor can be the single crowd worker, or the testing organization. This book has presented the characterization of crowd worker in Chap. 4, which is mainly used for the crowd worker recommendation and task recommendation. This characterization does not depict whether a crowd worker is qualified for a task, or the credibility of a worker in taking the critical or secret tasks. The quality assessment of crowd worker should also consider the stability of the crowd workers, the completion rate, the response time, the bug detection rate, etc. Besides, the crowdsourced testing platform can provide mechanism to let the task publisher to grade the crowd workers, which can also be treated as indispensable factors when assessing the quality of task contractor. When it comes to the testing organization, apart from the crowd workers belonging to the organization, the testing equipment, including the hardware and software, should also be characterized.

The third dimension is the quality of the product which is under crowdsourced testing. The most important thing a task publisher wants to know is to what degree the software after crowdsourced testing is sufficiently tested. This book has introduced approaches for determining whether a crowdsourced testing task can be closed based on the observed test adequacy criteria in Chap. 7. Yet, the presented approaches are only based on the bug arrival information, and the derived coverage of task descriptions. Besides, they donot use the ground truth software quality to evaluate whether the prediction is correct. In other words, with the proposed approaches, even a crowdsourced testing task is predicted to be close, it can still have bugs. More metrics are needed to be considered to assess the product quality undergone testing. These metrics should include the profiles of crowd workers who participant in the task, the characteristics of the revealed bugs, the distribution of these bugs in the software, etc.

The quality assessment of a crowdsourced testing task can be conducted manually by examining the data generated in a task. Or better yet, it can be done automatically by extracting the multiple viewpoints represented in the data accumulated in the crowdsourced testing platform.

References

1. Abdollahpouri, H., Mansoury, M., Burke, R., Mobasher, B.: The unfairness of popularity bias in recommendation. In: Proceedings of the Workshop on Recommendation in Multi-stakeholder Environments co-located with the 13th ACM Conference on Recommender Systems (RecSys 2019), Copenhagen, Denmark, September 20, 2019 (2019)
2. Almasi, M.M., Hemmati, H., Fraser, G., Arcuri, A., Benefelds, J.: An industrial evaluation of unit test generation: Finding real faults in a financial application. In: Proceedings of the 39th International Conference on Software Engineering: Software Engineering in Practice Track, ICSE-SEIP '17, pp. 263–272. IEEE Press, Piscataway, NJ, USA (2017). https://doi.org/10.1109/ICSE-SEIP.2017.27
3. Awasthi, P., Rao, D., Ravindran, B.: Part of speech tagging and chunking with hmm and crf. Proceedings of NLP Association of India Machine Learning Contest (2006)
4. Badihi, S., Heydarnoori, A.: Crowdsummarizer: Automated generation of code summaries for java programs through crowdsourcing. IEEE Software **34**(2), 71–80 (2017)
5. Bettenburg, N., Premraj, R., Zimmermann, T.: Duplicate bug reports considered harmful ... really? In: IEEE International Conference on Software Maintenance, pp. 337–345 (2008)
6. Breiman, L.: Random forests. Machine learning **45**(1), 5–32 (2001)
7. Brown, P.F., Desouza, P.V., Mercer, R.L., Pietra, V.J.D., Lai, J.C.: Class-based n-gram models of natural language. Computational Linguistics **18**(4), 467–479 (1992)
8. Callison-Burch, C.: Crowd-workers: Aggregating information across turkers to help them find higher paying work. In: Proceedings of the AAAI Conference on Human Computation and Crowdsourcing, HCOMP 2014 (2014)
9. Canfora, G., Di Penta, M., Oliveto, R., Panichella, S.: Who is going to mentor newcomers in open source projects? In: FSE'12, p. 44 (2012)
10. Carbonell, J., Goldstein, J.: The use of mmr, diversity-based reranking for reordering documents and producing summaries. In: Proceedings of the 21st annual international ACM SIGIR conference on Research and development in information retrieval, pp. 335–336. ACM (1998)
11. Chen, F., Kim, S.: Crowd debugging. In: Proceedings of the 2015 10th Joint Meeting on Foundations of Software Engineering, pp. 320–332 (2015)
12. Chen, T.Y., Kuo, F.C., Merkel, R.G., Tse, T.: Adaptive random testing: The art of test case diversity. Journal of Systems and Software **83**(1), 60–66 (2010)
13. Chen, W., Li, Z., Liu, T.: LTP: A Chinese language technology platform. In: Proceedings of the 23rd International Conference on Computational Linguistics: Demonstrations, pp. 13–16. Association for Computational Linguistics (2010)

14. Chouldechova, A., Roth, A.: A snapshot of the frontiers of fairness in machine learning. Commun. ACM **63**(5), 82–89 (2020)
15. Cooper, N., Bernal-Cárdenas, C., Chaparro, O., Moran, K., Poshyvanyk, D.: It takes two to tango: Combining visual and textual information for detecting duplicate video-based bug reports. In: 2021 IEEE/ACM 43rd International Conference on Software Engineering (ICSE), pp. 957–969. IEEE (2021)
16. Cui, Q., Wang, J., Yang, G., Xie, M., Wang, Q., Li, M.: Who should be selected to perform a task in crowdsourced testing? In: COMPSAC'17, pp. 75–84 (2017)
17. Cui, Q., Wang, S., Wang, J., Hu, Y., Wang, Q., Li, M.: Multi-objective crowd worker selection in crowdsourced testing. In: SEKE'17, pp. 218–223 (2017)
18. Dang, Y., Wu, R., Zhang, H., Zhang, D., Nobel, P.: Rebucket: a method for clustering duplicate crash reports based on call stack similarity. In: Proceedings of the 34th International Conference on Software Engineering, pp. 1084–1093. IEEE Press (2012)
19. Deb, K., Agrawal, S., Pratap, A., Meyarivan, T.: A fast elitist non-dominated sorting genetic algorithm for multi-objective optimization: Nsga-II. In: International Conference on Parallel Problem Solving From Nature, pp. 849–858. Springer (2000)
20. Fang, C., Chen, Z., Wu, K., Zhao, Z.: Similarity-based test case prioritization using ordered sequences of program entities. Software Quality Journal **22**(2), 335–361 (2014)
21. Feng, Y., Chen, Z., Jones, J.A., Fang, C., Xu, B.: Test report prioritization to assist crowdsourced testing. In: Joint Meeting, pp. 225–236 (2015)
22. Feng, Y., Jones, J.A., Chen, Z., Fang, C.: Multi-objective test report prioritization using image understanding. In: 2016 31st IEEE/ACM International Conference on Automated Software Engineering (ASE), pp. 202–213. IEEE (2016)
23. Filatova, E., Hatzivassiloglou, V.: A formal model for information selection in multi-sentence text extraction. In: Proceedings of the 20th international conference on Computational Linguistics, p. 397. Association for Computational Linguistics (2004)
24. Friedman, B., Nissenbaum, H.: Bias in computer systems. ACM Trans. Inf. Syst. **14**(3), 330–347 (1996)
25. Guo, C., He, T., Yuan, W., Guo, Y., Hao, R.: Crowdsourced requirements generation for automatic testing via knowledge graph. In: Proceedings of the 29th ACM SIGSOFT International Symposium on Software Testing and Analysis, pp. 545–548 (2020)
26. Hanrahan, B.V., Willamowski, J.K., Swaminathan, S., Martin, D.B.: Turkbench: Rendering the market for turkers. In: Proceedings of the 33rd Annual ACM Conference on Human Factors in Computing Systems, CHI '15, p. 1613–1616 (2015)
27. Hao, R., Feng, Y., Jones, J.A., Li, Y., Chen, Z.: Ctras: Crowdsourced test report aggregation and summarization. In: 2019 IEEE/ACM 41st International Conference on Software Engineering (ICSE), pp. 900–911. IEEE (2019)
28. Harman, M., Mansouri, S.A., Zhang, Y.: Search-based software engineering: Trends, techniques and applications. ACM Computing Surveys (CSUR) **45**(1), 11 (2012)
29. Hosseini, M., Phalp, K., Taylor, J., Ali, R.: The four pillars of crowdsourcing: A reference model. In: Research Challenges in Information Science (RCIS), 2014 IEEE Eighth International Conference on, pp. 1–12. IEEE (2014)
30. Howe, J., et al.: The rise of crowdsourcing. Wired magazine **14**(6), 1–4 (2006)
31. Huang, S., Jin, R., Zhou, Z.: Active learning by querying informative and representative examples. IEEE Trans. Pattern Anal. Mach. Intell. **36**(10), 1936–1949 (2014)
32. Inozemtseva, L., Holmes, R.: Coverage is not strongly correlated with test suite effectiveness. In: Proceedings of the 36th International Conference on Software Engineering, ICSE 2014, pp. 435–445. ACM, New York, NY, USA (2014). https://doi.acm.org/10.1145/2568225.2568271
33. Inozemtseva, L., Holmes, R.: Coverage is not strongly correlated with test suite effectiveness. In: Proceedings of the 36th International Conference on Software Engineering, pp. 435–445. ACM (2014)

34. Irani, L.C., Silberman, M.S.: Turkopticon: Interrupting worker invisibility in amazon mechanical turk. In: Proceedings of the SIGCHI Conference on Human Factors in Computing Systems, CHI '13, p. 611–620 (2013)
35. Irani, L.C., Silberman, M.S.: Stories we tell about labor: Turkopticon and the trouble with "design". In: Proceedings of the 2016 CHI Conference on Human Factors in Computing Systems, CHI '16, p. 4573–4586 (2016)
36. Jacoco: http://www.eclemma.org/jacoco/ (2020). [Online; accessed 11-Jan-2020]
37. Jeong, G., Kim, S., Zimmermann, T.: Improving bug triage with bug tossing graphs. In: FSE'09, pp. 111–120 (2009)
38. Jia, Y., Harman, M.: An analysis and survey of the development of mutation testing. IEEE transactions on software engineering 37(5), 649–678 (2010)
39. Jiang, B., Zhang, Z., Chan, W.K., Tse, T.: Adaptive random test case prioritization. In: Proceedings of the 24th IEEE/ACM International Conference on Automated Software Engineering, pp. 233–244. IEEE (2009)
40. Jurafsky, D., James, H.: Speech and language processing an introduction to natural language processing, computational linguistics, and speech. Pearson Education (2000)
41. Kan, S.H.: Metrics and models in software quality engineering. Addison-Wesley Longman Publishing Co., Inc. (2002)
42. Kao, A., Poteet, S.R.: Natural language processing and text mining. Springer (2007)
43. Khoshgoftaar, T.M., Golawala, M., Van Hulse, J.: An empirical study of learning from imbalanced data using random forest. In: Tools with Artificial Intelligence, 2007. ICTAI 2007. 19th IEEE international conference on, vol. 2, pp. 310–317. IEEE (2007)
44. LaToza, T.D., Myers, B.A.: Hard-to-answer questions about code. In: Evaluation and Usability of Programming Languages and Tools, PLATEAU '10, pp. 8:1–8:6. ACM, New York, NY, USA (2010). https://doi.acm.org/10.1145/1937117.1937125
45. Lazebnik, S., Schmid, C., Ponce, J.: Beyond bags of features: Spatial pyramid matching for recognizing natural scene categories. In: Computer Vision and Pattern Recognition, 2006 IEEE Computer Society Conference on, vol. 2, pp. 2169–2178. IEEE (2006)
46. Ledru, Y., Petrenko, A., Boroday, S.: Using string distances for test case prioritisation. In: Proceedings of the 24th IEEE/ACM International Conference on Automated Software Engineering, pp. 510–514. IEEE (2009)
47. Ledru, Y., Petrenko, A., Boroday, S., Mandran, N.: Prioritizing test cases with string distances. Automated Software Engineering 19(1), 65–95 (2012)
48. Liu, D., Feng, Y., Zhang, X., Jones, J., Chen, Z.: Clustering crowdsourced test reports of mobile applications using image understanding. IEEE Transactions on Software Engineering (2020)
49. Liu, D., Zhang, X., Feng, Y., Jones, J.A.: Generating descriptions for screenshots to assist crowdsourced testing. In: 2018 IEEE 25th International Conference on Software Analysis, Evolution and Reengineering (SANER), pp. 492–496. IEEE (2018)
50. Lotufo, R., Malik, Z., Czarnecki, K.: Modelling the hurried bug report reading process to summarize bug reports. Empirical Software Engineering 20(2), 516–548 (2015)
51. Louis, A., Nenkova, A.: Automatically evaluating content selection in summarization without human models. In: Proceedings of the 2009 Conference on Empirical Methods in Natural Language Processing: Volume 1-Volume 1, pp. 306–314. Association for Computational Linguistics (2009)
52. Ma, D., Schuler, D., Zimmermann, T., Sillito, J.: Expert recommendation with usage expertise. In: ICSM'09, pp. 535–538 (2009)
53. Mao, K., Capra, L., Harman, M., Jia, Y.: A survey of the use of crowdsourcing in software engineering. Journal of Systems and Software 126, 57–84 (2017)
54. Mao, K., Yang, Y., Wang, Q., Jia, Y., Harman, M.: Developer recommendation for crowdsourced software development tasks. In: SOSE'15, pp. 347–356 (2015)
55. Martin, D., Hanrahan, B.V., O'Neill, J., Gupta, N.: Being a turker. In: Proceedings of the 17th ACM Conference on Computer Supported Cooperative Work & Social Computing, CSCW '14, p. 224–235 (2014)

56. McInnis, B., Cosley, D., Nam, C., Leshed, G.: Taking a hit: Designing around rejection, mistrust, risk, and workers' experiences in Amazon Mechanical Turk. Conference on Human Factors in Computing Systems—Proceedings pp. 2271–2282 (2016)
57. Miller, G.A.: Wordnet: a lexical database for english. Communications of the ACM **38**(11), 39–41 (1995)
58. Mondal, D., Hemmati, H., Durocher, S.: Exploring test suite diversification and code coverage in multi-objective test case selection. In: Software Testing, Verification and Validation (ICST), 2015 IEEE 8th International Conference on, pp. 1–10. IEEE (2015)
59. Monperrus, M., Maia, A.: Debugging with the crowd: a debug recommendation system based on stackoverflow. Ph.D. thesis, Université Lille 1-Sciences et Technologies (2014)
60. Moran, K., Linares-Vásquez, M., Bernal-Cárdenas, C., Vendome, C., Poshyvanyk, D.: Crash-scope: A practical tool for automated testing of android applications. In: 2017 IEEE/ACM 39th International Conference on Software Engineering Companion (ICSE-C), pp. 15–18. IEEE (2017)
61. Morik, M., Singh, A., Hong, J., Joachims, T.: Controlling fairness and bias in dynamic learning-to-rank. In: Proceedings of the 43rd International ACM SIGIR conference on research and development in Information Retrieval, SIGIR 2020, Virtual Event, China, July 25–30, 2020, pp. 429–438 (2020)
62. Nam, J., Pan, S.J., Kim, S.: Transfer defect learning. In: ICSE '13, pp. 382–391 (2013)
63. Nazar, N., Jiang, H., Gao, G., Zhang, T., Li, X., Ren, Z.: Source code fragment summarization with small-scale crowdsourcing based features. Frontiers of Computer Science **10**(3), 504–517 (2016)
64. Negara, S., Vakilian, M., Chen, N., Johnson, R.E., Dig, D.: Is it dangerous to use version control histories to study source code evolution? In: European Conference on Object-Oriented Programming, ECOOP '12, pp. 79–103. Springer (2012)
65. Nguyen, A.T., Nguyen, T.T., Nguyen, T.N., Lo, D., Sun, C.: Duplicate bug report detection with a combination of information retrieval and topic modeling. In: ASE'12, pp. 70–79 (2012)
66. Pan, S.J., Tsang, I.W., Kwok, J.T., Yang, Q.: Domain adaptation via transfer component analysis. Trans. Neur. Netw. **22**(2), 199–210 (2011). https://doi.org/10.1109/TNN.2010.2091281
67. Pan, S.J., Yang, Q.: A survey on transfer learning. IEEE Trans. on Knowl. and Data Eng. **22**(10), 1345–1359 (2010). https://doi.org/10.1109/TKDE.2009.191
68. Park, J., Park, Y.H., Kim, S., Oh, A.: Eliph: Effective visualization of code history for peer assessment in programming education. In: Proceedings of the 2017 ACM Conference on Computer Supported Cooperative Work and Social Computing, CSCW '17, pp. 458–467. ACM, New York, NY, USA (2017). https://doi.acm.org/10.1145/2998181.2998285
69. Petitjean, F., Forestier, G., Webb, G.I., Nicholson, A.E., Chen, Y., Keogh, E.: Faster and more accurate classification of time series by exploiting a novel dynamic time warping averaging algorithm. Knowl. Inf. Syst. **47**(1), 1–26 (2016). https://doi.org/10.1007/s10115-015-0878-8
70. Podgurski, A., Leon, D., Francis, P., Masri, W., Minch, M., Sun, J., Wang, B.: Automated support for classifying software failure reports. In: Proceedings of the 25th International Conference on Software Engineering, pp. 465–475. IEEE (2003)
71. Rastkar, S., Murphy, G.C., Murray, G.: Summarizing software artifacts: a case study of bug reports. In: Proceedings of the 32nd ACM/IEEE International Conference on Software Engineering-Volume 1, pp. 505–514. ACM (2010)
72. Rastkar, S., Murphy, G.C., Murray, G.: Automatic summarization of bug reports. IEEE Transactions on Software Engineering **40**(4), 366–380 (2014)
73. Ren, X., Xing, Z., Xia, X., Li, G., Sun, J.: Discovering, explaining and summarizing controversial discussions in community q&a sites. In: 2019 34th IEEE/ACM International Conference on Automated Software Engineering (ASE), pp. 151–162. IEEE (2019)
74. Rocha, H., Valente, M.T., Marques-Neto, H., Murphy, G.C.: An empirical study on recommendations of similar bugs. In: SANER'16, pp. 46–56 (2016)

75. Rojas, J.M., Fraser, G., Arcuri, A.: Automated unit test generation during software development: A controlled experiment and think-aloud observations. In: Proceedings of the 2015 International Symposium on Software Testing and Analysis, ISSTA 2015, pp. 338–349. ACM, New York, NY, USA (2015). https://doi.acm.org/10.1145/2771783.2771801

76. Rosenberg, A., Hirschberg, J.: V-measure: A conditional entropy-based external cluster evaluation measure. In: Proceedings of the 2007 joint conference on empirical methods in natural language processing and computational natural language learning (EMNLP-CoNLL) (2007)

77. Rothermel, G., Untch, R., Chu, C., Harrold, M.: Test case prioritization: an empirical study. In: Proceedings of the International Conference on Software Maintenance, pp. 179–188 (1999)

78. Rubner, Y., Tomasi, C., Guibas, L.J.: The earth mover's distance as a metric for image retrieval. International journal of computer vision 40(2), 99–121 (2000)

79. Runeson, P., Alexandersson, M., Nyholm, O.: Detection of duplicate defect reports using natural language processing. In: Proceedings of the 29th International Conference on Software Engineering, pp. 499–510. IEEE (2007)

80. Saito, S., Chiang, C., Savage, S., Nakano, T., Kobayashi, T., Bigham, J.P.: Turkscanner: Predicting the hourly wage of microtasks. In: The World Wide Web Conference, WWW 2019, pp. 3187–3193 (2019)

81. Schreiber, T., Schmitz, A.: Discrimination power of measures for nonlinearity in a time series. Physical Review E 55(5), 5443 (1997)

82. Schütze, H., Manning, C.D., Raghavan, P.: Introduction to information retrieval, vol. 39. Cambridge University Press (2008)

83. Shamshiri, S., Just, R., Rojas, J.M., Fraser, G., McMinn, P., Arcuri, A.: Do automatically generated unit tests find real faults? an empirical study of effectiveness and challenges (t). In: Proceedings of the 2015 30th IEEE/ACM International Conference on Automated Software Engineering (ASE), ASE '15, pp. 201–211. IEEE Computer Society, Washington, DC, USA (2015). https://doi.org/10.1109/ASE.2015.86

84. Shapiro, S.C.: Encyclopedia of artificial intelligence second edition. John (1992)

85. Silva, R.F., Roy, C.K., Rahman, M.M., Schneider, K.A., Paixao, K., de Almeida Maia, M.: Recommending comprehensive solutions for programming tasks by mining crowd knowledge. In: 2019 IEEE/ACM 27th International Conference on Program Comprehension (ICPC), pp. 358–368. IEEE (2019)

86. Sokolova, M., Lapalme, G.: A systematic analysis of performance measures for classification tasks. Information Processing & Management 45(4), 427–437 (2009)

87. Sun, C., Lo, D., Khoo, S.C., Jiang, J.: Towards more accurate retrieval of duplicate bug reports. In: Proceedings of the 2011 26th IEEE/ACM International Conference on Automated Software Engineering, pp. 253–262. IEEE Computer Society (2011)

88. Sun, C., Lo, D., Wang, X., Jiang, J., Khoo, S.C.: A discriminative model approach for accurate duplicate bug report retrieval. In: Proceedings of the 32nd ACM/IEEE International Conference on Software Engineering-Volume 1, pp. 45–54. ACM (2010)

89. Takamura, H., Okumura, M.: Text summarization model based on maximum coverage problem and its variant. In: Proceedings of the 12th Conference of the European Chapter of the Association for Computational Linguistics, pp. 781–789. Association for Computational Linguistics (2009)

90. Tamrawi, A., Nguyen, T.T., Al-Kofahi, J.M., Nguyen, T.N.: Fuzzy set and cache-based approach for bug triaging. In: FSE'11, pp. 365–375 (2011)

91. Tantithamthavorn, C., McIntosh, S., Hassan, A., Matsumoto, K.: An empirical comparison of model validation techniques for defect prediction models. TSE'16 43, 1–18 (2016)

92. Thomas, S.W., Hemmati, H., Hassan, A.E., Blostein, D.: Static test case prioritization using topic models. Empirical Software Engineering 19(1), 182–212 (2014)

93. Tian, Y., Sun, C., Lo, D.: Improved duplicate bug report identification. In: Software Maintenance and Reengineering (CSMR), 2012 16th European Conference on, pp. 385–390. IEEE (2012)

94. mutation test tool, P.: http://pitest.org/ (2020). [Online; accessed 11-Jan-2020]
95. Tsai, W.T., Wu, W., Huhns, M.N.: Cloud-based software crowdsourcing. IEEE Internet Computing **18**(3), 78–83 (2014). https://doi.org/10.1109/MIC.2014.46
96. TSFRESH: http://tsfresh.readthedocs.io/en/latest/ (2020). [Online; accessed 11-Jan-2020]
97. Wang, J., Cui, Q., Wang, Q., Wang, S.: Towards effectively test report classification to assist crowdsourced testing. In: ESEM '16, pp. 6:1–6:10 (2016)
98. Wang, J., Wang, S., Cui, Q., Wang, Q.: Local-based active classification of test report to assist crowdsourced testing. In: Proceedings of the 31st IEEE/ACM International Conference on Automated Software Engineering, pp. 190–201 (2016)
99. Wang, S., Ali, S., Yue, T., Li, Y., Liaaen, M.: A practical guide to select quality indicators for assessing pareto-based search algorithms in search-based software engineering. In: ICSE'16, pp. 631–642 (2016)
100. Wang, X., Zhang, L., Xie, T., Anvik, J., Sun, J.: An approach to detecting duplicate bug reports using natural language and execution information. In: Proceedings of the 30th international conference on Software engineering, pp. 461–470. ACM (2008)
101. Wang, Y.: Characterizing developer behavior in cloud based ides. In: Proceedings of the 2017 ACM/IEEE International Symposium on Empirical Software Engineering and Measurement (ESEM), pp. 48–57 (2017). https://doi.org/10.1109/ESEM.2017.27
102. Wang, Y., Wagstrom, P., Duesterwald, E., Redmiles, D.: New opportunities for extracting insights from cloud based ides. In: Proceedings of the 36th International Conference on Software Engineering, ICSE Companion 2014, pp. 408–411. ACM, New York, NY, USA (2014). https://doi.acm.org/10.1145/2591062.2591105
103. Wei, L., Liu, Y., Cheung, S.: Pivot: learning api-device correlations to facilitate android compatibility issue detection. In: Proceedings of the 41st International Conference on Software Engineering, ICSE 2019, Montreal, QC, Canada, May 25–31, 2019, pp. 878–888 (2019)
104. Wong, W., Horgan, J., London, S., Agrawal, H.: A study of effective regression testing in practice. In: Proceedings of the International Symposium on Software Reliability Engineering, pp. 264–274 (1997)
105. Xia, X., Feng, Y., Lo, D., Chen, Z., Wang, X.: Towards more accurate multi-label software behavior learning. In: Software Maintenance, Reengineering and Reverse Engineering (CSMR-WCRE), 2014 Software Evolution Week-IEEE Conference on, pp. 134–143. IEEE (2014)
106. Xiao, X., Xie, T., Tillmann, N., de Halleux, J.: Precise identification of problems for structural test generation. In: Proceedings of the 33rd International Conference on Software Engineering, ICSE '11, pp. 611–620. ACM, New York, NY, USA (2011). https://doi.acm.org/10.1145/1985793.1985876
107. Xie, M., Wang, Q., Yang, G., Li, M.: Cocoon: Crowdsourced testing quality maximization under context coverage constraint. In: ISSRE'17, pp. 316–327 (2017)
108. Xu, B., Xing, Z., Xia, X., Lo, D.: Answerbot: Automated generation of answer summary to developers' technical questions. In: 2017 32nd IEEE/ACM International Conference on Automated Software Engineering (ASE), pp. 706–716. IEEE (2017)
109. Xu, J., Yao, Y., Tong, H., Tao, X., Lu, J.: Ice-breaking: Mitigating cold-start recommendation problem by rating comparison. In: Proceedings of the Twenty-Fourth International Joint Conference on Artificial Intelligence, IJCAI 2015, pp. 3981–3987 (2015)
110. Yang, X., Lo, D., Xia, X., Bao, L., Sun, J.: Combining word embedding with information retrieval to recommend similar bug reports. In: ISSRE'16, pp. 127–137 (2016)
111. Yang, Y., Karim, M.R., Saremi, R., Ruhe, G.: Who should take this task?: Dynamic decision support for crowd workers. In: ESEM'16, p. 8 (2016)
112. Ye, L., Keogh, E.: Time series shapelets: A new primitive for data mining. In: Proceedings of the 15th ACM SIGKDD International Conference on Knowledge Discovery and Data Mining, KDD '09, pp. 947–956. ACM, New York, NY, USA (2009). https://doi.acm.org/10.1145/1557019.1557122

113. Ying, A.T., Murphy, G.C., Ng, R., Chu-Carroll, M.C.: Predicting source code changes by mining change history. IEEE transactions on Software Engineering **30**(9), 574–586 (2004)
114. Yoo, S., Harman, M., Tonella, P., Susi, A.: Clustering test cases to achieve effective and scalable prioritisation incorporating expert knowledge. In: Proceedings of the eighteenth international symposium on Software testing and analysis, pp. 201–212. ACM (2009)
115. Young, M.: Software testing and analysis: process, principles, and techniques. John Wiley & Sons (2008)
116. Yu, S., Fang, C., Cao, Z., Wang, X., Li, T., Chen, Z.: Prioritize crowdsourced test reports via deep screenshot understanding. In: 2021 IEEE/ACM 43rd International Conference on Software Engineering (ICSE), pp. 946–956. IEEE (2021)
117. Yu, S., Fang, C., Li, T., Du, M., Li, X., Zhang, J., Yun, Y., Wang, X., Chen, Z.: Automated mobile app test script intent generation via image and code understanding. arXiv preprint arXiv:2107.05165 (2021)
118. Yu, S., Fang, C., Yun, Y., Feng, Y.: Layout and image recognition driving cross-platform automated mobile testing. In: 2021 IEEE/ACM 43rd International Conference on Software Engineering (ICSE), pp. 1561–1571. IEEE (2021)
119. Zhang, J., Wang, Z., Zhang, L., Hao, D., Zang, L., Cheng, S., Zhang, L.: Predictive mutation testing. In: Proceedings of the 25th International Symposium on Software Testing and Analysis, ISSTA 2016, pp. 342–353. ACM, New York, NY, USA (2016). https://doi.acm.org/10.1145/2931037.2931038
120. Zhao, G., da Costa, D.A., Zou, Y.: Improving the pull requests review process using learning-to-rank algorithms. Empirical Software Engineering **24**(4), 2140–2170 (2019)
121. Zhou, M., Mockus, A.: What make long term contributors: Willingness and opportunity in OSS community. In: ICSE'12, pp. 518–528 (2012)
122. Zhou, M., Mockus, A.: Who will stay in the floss community? modeling participant's initial behavior. IEEE Transactions on Software Engineering **41**(1), 82–99 (2015)
123. Zhu, H., Hall, P.A.V., May, J.H.R.: Software unit test coverage and adequacy. ACM Comput. Surv. **29**(4), 366–427 (1997). https://doi.acm.org/10.1145/267580.267590
124. Zimmermann, T., Premraj, R., Bettenburg, N., Just, S., Schröter, A., Weiss, C.: What makes a good bug report? Software Engineering, IEEE Transactions on **36**(5), 618–643 (2010)

Printed in the United States
by Baker & Taylor Publisher Services